First World War
and Army of Occupation
War Diary
France, Belgium and Germany

29 DIVISION
87 Infantry Brigade
Royal Inniskilling Fusiliers
1st Battalion
1 March 1916 - 31 January 1918

WO95/2305/2

The Naval & Military Press Ltd
www.nmarchive.com
Published in association with The National Archives

Published by

The Naval & Military Press Ltd

Unit 10 Ridgewood Industrial Park,

Uckfield, East Sussex,

TN22 5QE England

Tel: +44 (0) 1825 749494

www.naval-military-press.com

www.nmarchive.com

Contents

Document type	Place/Title	Date From	Date To
Heading	WO95/2305-2 1 Battalion Royal Iniskilling Fusiliers Mar 16-Jan 18		
Heading	29th Division 87th Infy Bde 1st Bn Innis. Fus. Mar 1916-Jan 1918 To 36 Div 109 Bde		
Heading	29th Division. 87th Infantry Brigade. Arrived Marseilles from Egypt 18.3.16 1st Battalion Inniskilling Fusiliers March 1916		
Heading	R. Innisk Fus Vol I B.E.F. From M.E.F		
War Diary	Suez	01/03/1916	09/03/1916
War Diary	At Sea	10/03/1916	26/03/1916
War Diary	Ergmes	27/03/1916	30/03/1916
War Diary	Amplier	31/03/1916	31/03/1916
Heading	29th Division. 87th Infantry Brigade. 1st Battalion Inniskilling Fusiliers April 1916		
War Diary	Amplier	01/04/1916	04/04/1916
War Diary	Mailly-Maillet	05/04/1916	07/04/1916
War Diary	Trenches	08/04/1916	13/04/1916
War Diary	Acheux	14/04/1916	28/04/1916
War Diary	Mailly Mailley	29/04/1916	30/04/1916
Heading	29th Division 87th Infantry Brigade. 1st Battalion Royal Inniskilling Fusiliers May 1916		
War Diary	Mailly-Mailley	01/05/1916	02/05/1916
War Diary	Trenches	03/05/1916	13/05/1916
War Diary	Engletelmes.	14/05/1916	18/05/1916
War Diary	Louvencourt	19/05/1916	27/05/1916
War Diary	Trenches	28/05/1916	31/05/1916
Operation(al) Order(s)	87th Brigade Operation Order No. 22. by Brigade General C.H. Tindall Lucas. Commanding 87th Infantry Brigade.	01/05/1916	01/05/1916
Operation(al) Order(s)	Operation Order No 23 By Brigade General C.H. Tindall Lucas. Commanding 87th. Infantry Brigade.	16/05/1916	16/05/1916
Heading	29th Division. 87th Infantry Brigade. 1st Battalion Royal Inniskilling Fusiliers June 1916		
War Diary	Trenches	01/06/1916	07/06/1916
War Diary	Engelbelmer	08/06/1916	15/06/1916
War Diary	Louvencourt	16/06/1916	22/06/1916
War Diary	Firing Line	23/06/1916	30/06/1916
Miscellaneous	O.C. 1st. R1. Innis. Fus.	29/06/1916	29/06/1916
Heading	29th Division. 87th Infantry Brigade. 1st Battalion Royal Inniskilling Fusiliers July 1916		
War Diary	Firing Line	01/07/1916	01/07/1916
War Diary	St Johns. Road	02/07/1916	02/07/1916
War Diary	Hamel	03/07/1916	08/07/1916
War Diary	Achieu	09/07/1916	09/07/1916
War Diary	Acheux	10/07/1916	16/07/1916
War Diary	Mailly-Maillet	17/07/1916	21/07/1916
War Diary	Firing Line	22/07/1916	24/07/1916
War Diary	Bus	25/07/1916	25/07/1916
War Diary	Amplier	26/07/1916	27/07/1916
War Diary	L Camp W Of Poperinghe	28/07/1916	31/07/1916

Heading	29th Division. 87th Infantry Brigade. 1st Battalion Royal Inniskilling Fusiliers August 1916 Battalion Operation Orders Attached.		
Heading	1st Royal Inniskilling Fusiliers War Diary From 1-8-16 To 31-8-16 Volume 17		
Miscellaneous	The Staff Captain 87th Inf. Bde	01/09/1916	01/09/1916
War Diary	Poperinghe 'L' Camp	01/08/1916	01/08/1916
War Diary	Ypres	02/08/1916	06/08/1916
War Diary	Firing Line	07/08/1916	09/08/1916
War Diary	Brandhoek Camp "C"	10/08/1916	18/08/1916
War Diary	Ypres	19/08/1916	28/08/1916
War Diary	Firing Line	29/08/1916	31/08/1916
Operation(al) Order(s)	87th Infantry Brigade Operation Order No. 38	05/08/1916	05/08/1916
Miscellaneous	Operation Order. No. 5 by Major J. Hardress-Lloyd. Commanding 1st Battalion The Royal Inniskilling Fusiliers.	06/08/1916	06/08/1916
Miscellaneous	1st Battalion The Royal Inniskilling Fusiliers	09/08/1916	09/08/1916
Operation(al) Order(s)	Operation Order No. 6. by Major J. Hardress-Lloyd Commanding 1st Battalion The Royal Inniskilling Fusiliers.	19/08/1916	19/08/1916
Operation(al) Order(s)	Operation Order No. 6. By Major J. Hardress-Lloyd. Commanding 1st Battalion The Royal Inniskilling Fusiliers.	29/08/1916	29/08/1916
Heading	29th Division. 87th Infantry Brigade 1st Battalion Royal Inniskilling Fusiliers September 1916 Battalion Operation Orders Attached.		
War Diary	Firing Line	01/09/1916	09/09/1916
War Diary	Brandhoek "C" Camp	10/09/1916	17/09/1916
War Diary	Elverdinghe	18/09/1916	19/09/1916
War Diary	Ypres	20/09/1916	24/09/1916
War Diary	Firing Line	25/09/1916	29/09/1916
War Diary	Ypres	30/09/1916	30/09/1916
Miscellaneous	Orders For Relief By Major J. Hardress-Lloyd Commanding 1st Battalion The Royal Inniskilling Fusiliers.	08/09/1916	08/09/1916
Miscellaneous	Operation Orders By Major J. Hardress-Lloyd Commanding 1st Battalion The Royal Inniskilling Fusiliers.	19/09/1916	19/09/1916
Miscellaneous	Operation Order No.6. By Major J. Hardress-Lloyd Commanding 1st Battalion The Royal Inniskilling Fusiliers.	24/09/1916	24/09/1916
Miscellaneous	Operation Orders By Major J. Hardress-Lloyd Commanding 1st Battalion The Royal Inniskilling Fusiliers.	29/09/1916	29/09/1916
Heading	29th Division. 87th Infantry Brigade. 1st Battalion Royal Inniskilling Fusiliers October 1916 Operation Orders Etc Attached.		
Heading	War Diary 1st Royal Inniskilling Fusiliers 1st October To 31st October 1916 Volume XX		
War Diary	Ypres	01/10/1916	03/10/1916
War Diary	Poperinghe "K" Camp	04/10/1916	07/10/1916
War Diary	Allochville	08/10/1916	10/10/1916
War Diary	Buire	11/10/1916	13/10/1916
War Diary	Fricourt Camp	14/10/1916	19/10/1916
War Diary	Gueudecourt	20/10/1916	23/10/1916
War Diary	Switch Trench	24/10/1916	25/10/1916

War Diary	Gueudecourt	26/10/1916	28/10/1916
War Diary	Bull Trench	29/10/1916	30/10/1916
War Diary	Fricourt	31/10/1916	31/10/1916
Miscellaneous	Operation Order By Lieut-Colonel J. Hardress-Lloyd Commanding 1st Battalion The Royal Inniskilling Fusiliers.	10/10/1916	10/10/1916
Miscellaneous	Operation Order by Lieut-Colonel J. Hardress-Lloyd.	10/10/1916	10/10/1916
Miscellaneous	The Officer Commanding , 2nd South Wales Borderers.	18/10/1916	18/10/1916
Miscellaneous	Officer Commanding, 2nd South Wales Borderers.	18/10/1916	18/10/1916
Miscellaneous	R.S.M. Framingham		
Miscellaneous	Fourth Army.	20/10/1916	20/10/1916
Miscellaneous			
Miscellaneous	Officer Commanding 1st Royal Inniskilling Fusiliers.	27/10/1916	27/10/1916
Miscellaneous	Operation Order by Major C.G. Lendrum 1st Batt. The Royal Inniskilling Fusiliers	06/10/1916	06/10/1916
Heading	29th Division. 87th Infantry Brigade. 1st Battalion Royal Inniskilling Fusiliers November 1916 Battalion Operation Orders Attached.		
War Diary	Fricourt Camp	01/11/1916	03/11/1916
War Diary	Behencourt	04/11/1916	13/11/1916
War Diary	Citadel Camp	14/11/1916	14/11/1916
War Diary	Carnoy	15/11/1916	16/11/1916
War Diary	Guillemont	17/11/1916	23/11/1916
War Diary	Carnoy	24/11/1916	30/11/1916
Miscellaneous	Realm Orders No. 3		
Operation(al) Order(s)	Operation Order No. 4 by Lt. Colonel G. Hardress-Lloyd Commdg REALM	22/11/1916	22/11/1916
Miscellaneous	Operation Order by Lieut-Col. G. Hardress. Lloyd. Commdg 1st Royal Inniskilling Fusiliers.	15/11/1916	15/11/1916
Heading	29th Division. 87th Infantry Brigade. 1st Battalion Royal Inniskilling Fusiliers December 1916		
Heading	War Diary of 1st Bn The Royal Inniskilling Fusiliers From 1/12/16 To 31/12/1916. Volume No 21		
War Diary	Ox Trench	01/12/1916	01/12/1916
War Diary	Carnoy	02/12/1916	04/12/1916
War Diary	Guillimont	05/12/1916	08/12/1916
War Diary	Carnoy	09/12/1916	09/12/1916
War Diary	Mirecourt	10/12/1916	12/12/1916
War Diary	Picquigny	13/12/1916	31/12/1916
Operation(al) Order(s)	Realm Operation Orders No. 9	07/12/1916	07/12/1916
Heading	War Diary of 1st Bn, The Royal Inniskilling Fusiliers. From 1st Jany, 1917 To 31st Jany, 1917 Volume I		
War Diary	Picquigny	01/01/1917	12/01/1917
War Diary	Bresle	13/01/1917	14/01/1917
War Diary	Carnoy	15/01/1917	15/01/1917
War Diary	Guillemont	16/01/1917	19/01/1917
War Diary	Carnoy	20/01/1917	31/01/1917
Miscellaneous	Realm Advance Orders.	20/01/1917	20/01/1917
Operation(al) Order(s)	Realm Orders No. 3	21/01/1917	21/01/1917
Operation(al) Order(s)	Realm Order No. 4	22/01/1917	22/01/1917
Miscellaneous	Report On Action of 27.1.17 Opposite Le Transloy.	27/01/1917	27/01/1917
Operation(al) Order(s)	Realm Order No. 5	25/01/1917	25/01/1917
Operation(al) Order(s)	Realm Orders No. 9	31/01/1917	31/01/1917
War Diary	Carnoy	01/02/1917	09/02/1917
War Diary	Meault	10/02/1917	18/02/1917
War Diary	Bronfay	19/02/1917	28/02/1917

Operation(al) Order(s)	Realm Order No. 11	19/02/1917	19/02/1917
Operation(al) Order(s)	Realm Order No. 12	21/02/1917	21/02/1917
Operation(al) Order(s)	Realm Order No. 13	21/02/1917	21/02/1917
Operation(al) Order(s)	Realm Order No. 14	22/02/1917	22/02/1917
Operation(al) Order(s)	Realm Order No. 15	24/02/1917	24/02/1917
Operation(al) Order(s)	Realm Order No. 16	27/02/1917	27/02/1917
Heading	War Diary of 1st Bn, The Royal Inniskilling Fusiliers From 1st March 1917 To 31st March 1917, Vol 13		
War Diary	Frigicourt	01/03/1917	02/03/1917
War Diary	Ville	03/03/1917	03/03/1917
War Diary	Laneuville	04/03/1917	19/03/1917
War Diary	Airainnes	20/03/1917	31/03/1917
Heading	War Diary of 1st Bn, The Royal Inniskilling Fusiliers From 1st April 1917 To 30th April, 1917 Volume 25		
War Diary	Bonneville	01/04/1917	08/04/1917
War Diary	Monchiet	09/04/1917	12/04/1917
War Diary	Feuchy	13/04/1917	19/04/1917
War Diary	Arras	20/04/1917	27/04/1917
War Diary	Saulty	28/04/1917	30/04/1917
Operation(al) Order(s)	Battalion Order No. 6	05/04/1917	05/04/1917
Operation(al) Order(s)	Battalion Order No. 7	06/04/1917	06/04/1917
Operation(al) Order(s)	Battalion Order No. 12	30/04/1917	30/04/1917
Operation(al) Order(s)	87th Infantry Brigade Order No. 10	30/04/1917	30/04/1917
Heading	War Diary of 1st. Battn. R. Inniskilling Fusrs. From 1st May 1917 To 31st May 1917 Volume 27		
War Diary	Saulty	01/05/1917	01/05/1917
War Diary	Wanquentin	02/05/1917	02/05/1917
War Diary	Arras	03/05/1917	07/05/1917
War Diary	Duisans	08/05/1917	13/05/1917
War Diary	Arras	14/05/1917	14/05/1917
War Diary	In Trenches	15/05/1917	19/05/1917
War Diary	Arras	20/05/1917	30/05/1917
War Diary	Brown Line	31/05/1917	31/05/1917
Operation(al) Order(s)	Battalion Order No. 13	02/05/1917	02/05/1917
Operation(al) Order(s)	Realm Order No. 8	05/02/1917	05/02/1917
Operation(al) Order(s)	Battalion Order No. 14	06/05/1917	06/05/1917
Operation(al) Order(s)	87th Infantry Brigade Order No 14	06/05/1917	06/05/1917
Operation(al) Order(s)	Battalion Order No. 15	13/05/1917	13/05/1917
Operation(al) Order(s)	Battalion Order No. 16	14/05/1917	14/05/1917
Operation(al) Order(s)	87th Infantry Brigade Order No. 16	14/05/1917	14/05/1917
Diagram etc			
Miscellaneous			
Map			
Miscellaneous	Realm.	15/05/1917	15/05/1917
Map	Eterpigny		
Operation(al) Order(s)	87th Infantry Brigade Order No. 19	17/05/1917	17/05/1917
Miscellaneous	The Officer Commanding, 2nd South Wales Borderers.	18/05/1917	18/05/1917
Map	Barrage Map Top Section 29th Div.		
Operation(al) Order(s)	Battalion Order No 17	19/05/1917	19/05/1917
Operation(al) Order(s)	87th Infantry Brigade Order No. 20	20/05/1917	20/05/1917
Operation(al) Order(s)	Battalion Order No. 18	26/05/1917	26/05/1917
Operation(al) Order(s)	87th Infantry Brigade Order No. 21	28/05/1917	28/05/1917
Operation(al) Order(s)	1st. Royal Inniskilling Order No. 19	30/05/1917	30/05/1917
Operation(al) Order(s)	87th Infantry Brigade Order No. 22	31/05/1917	31/05/1917
Miscellaneous	29th Division Administrative Orders No. 14	30/05/1917	30/05/1917
Operation(al) Order(s)	Appendix to 29th Division Order No. 121		

Miscellaneous	March Table.		
Heading	War Diary of 1st Battalion R. Inniskilling Fusiliers 1st-30 June 1917 Volume XXVIII		
War Diary	Brown Line	01/06/1917	05/06/1917
War Diary	Fienvillers	06/06/1917	30/06/1917
Operation(al) Order(s)	1/R. Inniskilling Fus Order No 20	01/06/1917	01/06/1917
Operation(al) Order(s)	87th Infantry Brigade Order No. 23	01/06/1917	01/06/1917
Operation(al) Order(s)	29th Division Administrative Orders No. 14 Appendix II	03/06/1917	03/06/1917
Miscellaneous	87th Brigade Administrative Order.	02/06/1917	02/06/1917
Operation(al) Order(s)	87th Infantry Brigade Order No. 24	02/06/1917	02/06/1917
Operation(al) Order(s)	1st. Royal Inniskilling Fusiliers Order No.21	03/06/1917	03/06/1917
Miscellaneous	Movement Table.		
Operation(al) Order(s)	87th Infantry Brigade Order No. 25	25/06/1917	25/06/1917
Miscellaneous	87th Infantry Brigade Administrative Order.	25/06/1917	25/06/1917
Operation(al) Order(s)	1st. Royal Inniskilling Order No. 23	25/06/1917	25/06/1917
Miscellaneous	Movement Table.		
Operation(al) Order(s)	87th Infantry Brigade Order No. 26	26/06/1917	26/06/1917
Miscellaneous	Movement Table.		
Operation(al) Order(s)	1/R. Inniskilling Order No 24	28/06/1917	28/06/1917
Operation(al) Order(s)	1st. Royal Inniskilling Fusiliers Order No. 23		
Miscellaneous	Captain Stokes.	30/06/1917	30/06/1917
Miscellaneous	A Form. Messages And Signals.		
Miscellaneous	Dispositions Front Line "B" Co. (2 Offrs. 100 O.R.)	29/06/1917	29/06/1917
War Diary	Trenches	01/07/1917	19/07/1917
War Diary	P2 Area.	19/07/1917	30/07/1917
War Diary	Trenches	31/07/1917	31/07/1917
Operation(al) Order(s)	1st. Royal Inniskilling Fusiliers Order No. 24	02/07/1917	02/07/1917
Operation(al) Order(s)	87th Infantry Brigade Order No. 27		
Miscellaneous	1st. Royal Inniskilling Fusiliers No. 25	05/07/1917	05/07/1917
Miscellaneous	Movement Table.		
Operation(al) Order(s)	1st. Royal Inniskilling Fusiliers Order No. 26	13/07/1917	13/07/1917
Miscellaneous	Movement Table.		
Miscellaneous	87th. Infantry Brigade Instructions No. 1	14/07/1917	14/07/1917
Operation(al) Order(s)	1st. Royal Inniskilling Fusiliers Order No. 29	19/07/1917	19/07/1917
Miscellaneous	87th. Infantry Brigade Instructions No. 3	12/07/1917	12/07/1917
Operation(al) Order(s)	1st. Royal Inniskilling Fusiliers Order No. 28	30/07/1917	30/07/1917
Operation(al) Order(s)	87th Infantry Brigade Order No. 34		
Miscellaneous	87th Infantry Brigade Administrative Instruction No. 2	30/07/1917	30/07/1917
Miscellaneous	29th. Division No. C.G.S. 73/7		
Miscellaneous	Arrangements For Aeroplane Cont of Patrols Appendix "A"		
Miscellaneous	2 Battalions Left Guards Bde.		
Heading	War Diary Of 1st. Battalion Royal Inniskilling Fusiliers From 1.8.17 To 31.8.17 Volume No. 30		
War Diary	Fred Area	01/08/1917	03/08/1917
War Diary	Proven 2 Area	04/08/1917	07/08/1917
War Diary	Forest Area	08/08/1917	31/08/1917
Heading	War Diary of 1st Bn The Royal Inniskilling Fusiliers From 1st Sept.1917 To 30th Sept 1917 Volume 30		
War Diary	Plurendon Camp	01/09/1917	08/09/1917
War Diary	Herzeele	09/09/1917	12/09/1917
War Diary	Plurendon Camp.	13/09/1917	20/09/1917
War Diary	Caribu	21/09/1917	30/09/1917
Operation(al) Order(s)	1st Bn. The Royal Inniskilling Fusiliers. Order No. 39	07/09/1917	07/09/1917
Operation(al) Order(s)	1st Bn. The Royal Inniskilling Fusiliers. Order No. 41		

Operation(al) Order(s)	87th Infantry Brigade Order No. 45	06/09/1917	06/09/1917
Operation(al) Order(s)	Addenda To 87th Brigade Order No. 45	07/09/1917	07/09/1917
Operation(al) Order(s)	87th Infantry Brigade Order No. 46. (Training.)	08/09/1917	08/09/1917
Miscellaneous	87th Infantry Brigade Instruction No. 1	09/09/1917	09/09/1917
Operation(al) Order(s)	1st. Royal Inniskilling Fusiliers Order No. 1-Training.	09/09/1917	09/09/1917
Operation(al) Order(s)	1st. Royal Inniskilling Fusiliers Order No. 1	10/09/1917	10/09/1917
Operation(al) Order(s)	1st. Bn The Royal Inniskilling Fusiliers Order No. 40	11/09/1917	11/09/1917
Miscellaneous	March Table.		
Operation(al) Order(s)	87th Infantry Brigade Order No. 49	12/09/1917	12/09/1917
Miscellaneous	Movement Table.		
Operation(al) Order(s)	87th Infantry Brigade Order No. 50	28/09/1917	28/09/1917
Miscellaneous	Amendment To 87th Infantry Brigade Order No. 50	27/09/1917	27/09/1917
Miscellaneous	Relief Table.		
Operation(al) Order(s)	1st Battalion The Royal Inniskilling Fusiliers. No. 42	27/09/1917	27/09/1917
Operation(al) Order(s)	1st. Battalion The Royal Inniskilling Fusiliers Order No. 43	28/09/1917	28/09/1917
Map	Training Area Map Top Section 29th Div Scale 1.10,000 4.9.17		
Heading	War Diary of 1st Battalion The Royal Inniskilling Fusiliers From 1st October 1917 To 31st October 1917 Volume 31		
War Diary		01/10/1917	20/10/1917
War Diary	Bailleulval	21/10/1917	31/10/1917
Operation(al) Order(s)	87th Infantry Brigade Order No. 51	01/10/1917	01/10/1917
Operation(al) Order(s)	87th Infantry Brigade Order No. 52	01/10/1917	01/10/1917
Operation(al) Order(s)	87th Infantry Brigade Order No. 53	04/10/1917	04/10/1917
Operation(al) Order(s)	Instruction To Be Attached To 87th Infantry Brigade Order No. 52		
Operation(al) Order(s)	Administrative Order No. 18	04/10/1917	04/10/1917
Miscellaneous	Notice (published With XIV C.R.O. Dated 5/10/17)	05/10/1917	05/10/1917
Operation(al) Order(s)	1st Battalion The Royal Inniskilling Fusiliers Order No. 45	05/10/1917	05/10/1917
Operation(al) Order(s)	87th Infantry Brigade Order No. 54	06/10/1917	06/10/1917
Operation(al) Order(s)	1st Battalion The Royal Inniskilling Fusiliers Order No. 46		
Miscellaneous	March Table		
Operation(al) Order(s)	87th Infantry Brigade Order No. 55	08/10/1917	08/10/1917
Operation(al) Order(s)	1st Battalion The Royal Inniskilling Fusiliers Order No. 47	09/10/1917	09/10/1917
Miscellaneous	The Officer Commanding, 2nd South Wales Borderers.	08/10/1917	08/10/1917
Operation(al) Order(s)	87th Infantry Brigade Order No. 56 (Warning Order)	11/10/1917	11/10/1917
Miscellaneous	29th Division No. 2014/2	13/10/1917	13/10/1917
Operation(al) Order(s)	Administrative Order No. 20	14/10/1917	14/10/1917
Operation(al) Order(s)	87th Infantry Brigade Order No. 56	14/10/1917	14/10/1917
Miscellaneous	1st Battalion The Royal Inniskilling Fusiliers.	14/10/1917	14/10/1917
Miscellaneous	Entrain Peselhoek.		
Miscellaneous	Headquarters, 87th Infantry Brigade	23/12/1917	23/12/1917
War Diary	Bailleulval	01/11/1917	17/11/1917
War Diary	Haut Allaines	18/11/1917	20/11/1917
War Diary	Marcoing	20/11/1917	30/11/1917
Operation(al) Order(s)	1st Bn The Royal Inniskilling Fusrs Order No 49	16/11/1917	16/11/1917
Operation(al) Order(s)	1st Royal Inniskilling Fusrs Order No 50	18/11/1917	18/11/1917
Operation(al) Order(s)	1st Battalion The Royal Inniskilling Fusiliers Order No 51	19/11/1917	19/11/1917
Operation(al) Order(s)	87th. Infantry Brigade Order No. 57		
Operation(al) Order(s)	87th Infantry Brigade Order No. 60	19/11/1917	19/11/1917

Miscellaneous	Officer Commanding. 2nd S.W. Borderers.	19/11/1917	19/11/1917
Operation(al) Order(s)	1st Battn The Royal Inniskilling Fusiliers Administrative Order No 1	19/11/1917	19/11/1917
Operation(al) Order(s)	87th. Infantry Brigade Order No. 62	25/11/1917	25/11/1917
Operation(al) Order(s)	1st Bn Royal Inniskilling Fusiliers Order No. 52		
Operation(al) Order(s)	87th. Infantry Brigade Order No. 64	29/11/1917	29/11/1917
Miscellaneous	1st. Royal Inniskilling Fusiliers Instruction No. 1		
Operation(al) Order(s)	1st. Bn Royal Inniskilling Fusr Order No 52		
Miscellaneous	87th. Infantry Brigade Instruction No. 1		
Miscellaneous	Accomodation In New Area.		
Diagram etc	Haut Allaines		
War Diary	Marcoing-Mearire Line	01/12/1917	02/12/1917
War Diary	Hindenburg Line	03/12/1917	04/12/1917
War Diary	Sorel	05/12/1917	05/12/1917
War Diary	Beaufort	06/12/1917	16/12/1917
War Diary	Bourbers Sur Canche	17/12/1917	17/12/1917
War Diary	Le Parr	18/12/1917	18/12/1917
War Diary	Coupelle-Vieille	19/12/1917	31/12/1917
Operation(al) Order(s)	1st. Battalion The Royal Inniskilling Fusiliers Order No. 54	02/12/1917	02/12/1917
Operation(al) Order(s)	1st. Royal Inniskilling Fusiliers Order No.56	04/12/1917	04/12/1917
Operation(al) Order(s)	87th. Infantry Brigade Order No. 56		
Operation(al) Order(s)	1st Battalion The Royal Inniskilling Fusiliers Administrative Instructions To Accompany Battn. Order No. 57	03/12/1917	03/12/1917
Operation(al) Order(s)	1st Battalion The Royal Inniskilling Fusiliers Order No.57	16/12/1917	16/12/1917
Operation(al) Order(s)	1st Battalion The Royal Inniskilling Fusiliers Order No. 58	17/12/1917	17/12/1917
Operation(al) Order(s)	1st Battalion The Royal Inniskilling Fusiliers Order No 59	18/12/1917	18/12/1917
Operation(al) Order(s)	1st Battalion The Royal Inniskilling Fusiliers Order No.60	29/12/1917	29/12/1917
Operation(al) Order(s)	1st Battalion The Royal Inniskilling Fusiliers Order No 60		
Operation(al) Order(s)	Administrative Order To Accompany Battalion Order No. 60	29/12/1917	29/12/1917
Operation(al) Order(s)	1st Battalion The Royal Inniskilling Fusiliers Order No.61	31/12/1917	31/12/1917
Miscellaneous	1st Border Regiment. 1st Royal Inniskilling Fusiliers.		
Operation(al) Order(s)	87th. Infantry Brigade Administrative Instructions To Accompany Brigade Order No. 63	16/12/1917	16/12/1917
Operation(al) Order(s)	1st Battalion The Royal Inniskilling Fusiliers. Operation Order No. 55		
Operation(al) Order(s)	Appendix to 87th. Infantry Brigade Order No. 67		
Operation(al) Order(s)	87th. Infantry Brigade Order No. 67	16/12/1917	16/12/1917
Operation(al) Order(s)	87th. Infantry Brigade Order No. 68	16/12/1917	16/12/1917
Operation(al) Order(s)	87th. Infantry Brigade Order No. 68	28/12/1917	28/12/1917
War Diary	Waemaers	01/01/1918	01/01/1918
War Diary	Ebblinghem	02/01/1918	02/01/1918
War Diary	Waemaers Capelle Herzeele	03/01/1918	04/01/1918
War Diary	Paddington Camp	05/01/1918	05/01/1918
War Diary	Lower Baboon Camp	06/01/1918	18/01/1918
War Diary	Warrington Camp	19/01/1918	26/01/1918
War Diary	Hasler Camp	27/01/1918	31/01/1918

Operation(al) Order(s)	1st Battalion The Royal Inniskilling Fusiliers Order No. 63	02/01/1918	02/01/1918
Operation(al) Order(s)	1st Battalion The Royal Inniskilling Fusiliers Order No. 64	03/01/1918	03/01/1918
Miscellaneous	Officer Commanding 1st. Royal Inniskilling Fusiliers.	04/01/1918	04/01/1918
Operation(al) Order(s)	Administrative Order To Accompany Battalion Order No. 65	04/01/1918	04/01/1918
Operation(al) Order(s)	1st Battalion The Royal Inniskilling Fusiliers Order No. 65	04/01/1918	04/01/1918
Operation(al) Order(s)	1st Battalion The Royal Inniskilling Fusiliers Order No. 66	15/01/1918	15/01/1918
Operation(al) Order(s)	Administrative Order To Accompany Battalion Order No.66	16/01/1918	16/01/1918

WO/95/2305/2

1 Battalion Royal Inniskillin Fusiliers

Mar '16 – Jan '18

29TH DIVISION
87TH INFY BDE

1ST BN INNIS. FUS.

MAR 1916-JAN 1918

2305

29th Division.

87th Infantry Brigade.

Arrived MARSEILLES from EGYPT 18.3.16.

1st BATTALION

INNISKILLING FUSILIERS

MARCH 1 9 1 6

52

1 R. Inniskg Fus

Vol ~~XX~~
IBEF
from MEF

Army Form C. 2118.

March 1916

WAR DIARY
or
INTELLIGENCE SUMMARY.
(Erase heading not required.) 1/1st Royal Inniskilling Fusiliers No. 1

Instructions regarding War Diaries and Intelligence Summaries are contained in F. S. Regs., Part II. and the Staff Manual respectively. Title pages will be prepared in manuscript.

Place	Date	Hour	Summary of Events and Information	Remarks and references to Appendices
SUEZ	1st March		Camp Routine, C Company Preliminary Musketry	W.A.M.
"	2nd March		Camp Routine. Battalion route march, distance about twelve miles, with manoeuvring en route. Battalion left Camp at 5 a.m. and returned again at 8.45 a.m.	W.A.M.
"	3rd March		Camp Routine, Garrison Duties &c. D Company Preliminary Musketry. 9 Officers of Various Service Units attached to the Battalion for duty. Brigade Machine Gun Section formed. 4 new Lewis Machine guns issued to replace those taken to form Brigade Section.	W.A.M.
"	4th March		Camp Routine & Drill.	W.A.M.
"	5th March		Camp Routine. Divine Service parades.	W.A.M.
"	6th March		Camp Routine. Ceremonial parades & Lectures.	W.A.M.
"	7 March		Camp Routine. Route March. A.B.C. Musketry Instruction Lectures. Capt. J. C. Kent, 2 Officers + 29 men rejoined Battalion. Capt. J. C. Kent takes up appointment of Adjutant.	J.C.K.
"	8 March		Tactical scheme near Oil Wells. Left camp 7.30 am returned 12.30 pm	
	9 March		Ceremonial Parade. Orders received to embark at Suez on S.S. Wandalla on 10th	

1577 Wt. W10791/1773 500,000 1/15 D. D. & L. A.D.S.S./Forms/C. 2118.

Instructions regarding War Diaries and Intelligence Summaries are contained in F. S. Regs., Part II. and the Staff Manual respectively. Title pages will be prepared in manuscript.

WAR DIARY
or
INTELLIGENCE SUMMARY.
(Erase heading not required.)

March 1916. Army Form C. 2118.

1/R. Inniskilling Fus.

No. 2.

Place	Date	Hour	Summary of Events and Information	Remarks and references to Appendices
At sea	10th		Battalion paraded at 11 am for inspection by Colonel-in-Chief, Gen Sir A.J. Murray KCMG, KCB, MVO, DSO, who expressed his great satisfaction of the smart appearance of the battalion & addressed the battalion as follows:- Officers & men, I have not come down here only as C-in-C but as Colonel of my own Regiment to wish you one & all Godspeed & good luck. When one has spent the best years of one's life in a Regiment one can never lose one's love & interest in it. I joined this Regiment as a boy of 18, & spent 23 years in it, & have never [illegible] in any other. I served as adjutant of this battalion & commanded the 2nd battalion, & have seen the fine battalions of the Ulster Division & of the 16th Div, & the two at Salonika, all of whom have done so much to uphold the glorious reputation of this old Inniskilling Regt. Some of you [illegible] with me & there are many I know, who heard me speak to the 2nd Battalion, some months ago near ST OMER. I have the same thing to say here. When times of stress come, as come they must & you feel you have stuck it as long as you can, then you must stick it out doubly. I have no doubt you will do so & maintain the unblemished record of this Regiment as you did in the Dardanelles. St Lucia [illegible] [illegible] are all old honours, but you are now [illegible] to make a new page of history. The climax of the war is approaching & you are going where the fighting is bound to be severe but where the end is not in doubt. We have now got the upper hand & Germany's day is [illegible] [illegible] is [illegible] having the honour of the Regiment in your hands, I am sure you will maintain it. I wish also to welcome those officers now serving with the battalion whom you come from [illegible] Regiments all of which have glorious records also. They are	
			Effective strength 28 officers 758. OR	

1577 Wt. W10791/1773 500,000 1/15 D. D. & L. A.D.S.S./Forms/C. 2118.

Instructions regarding War Diaries and Intelligence Summaries are contained in F. S. Regs., Part II. and the Staff Manual respectively. Title pages will be prepared in manuscript.

WAR DIARY
or
INTELLIGENCE SUMMARY.
(Erase heading not required.)

Army Form C. 2118.

March 1916.

1/R. Innis Fusiliers No 2(a)

Place	Date	Hour	Summary of Events and Information	Remarks and references to Appendices
			are doing in the honour of serving with us & feel that they will be as ready to uphold the good name of this Regiment as they would their own. In conclusion I again wish you individually & collectively the [illegible] of luck & God speed.	[illegible]

1577 Wt. W10791/1773 500,000 1/15 D. D. & L. A.D.S.S./Forms/C. 2118.

Instructions regarding War Diaries and Intelligence Summaries are contained in F. S. Regs., Part II. and the Staff Manual respectively. Title pages will be prepared in manuscript.

WAR DIARY
or
INTELLIGENCE SUMMARY.
(Erase heading not required.)

1/R. Inniskilling Fus. March 1916 No 3.

Army Form C. 2118.

Place	Date	Hour	Summary of Events and Information	Remarks and references to Appendices
At sea	10th		Battalion embark on S.S. WANTILLA at Port Tewfik, Suez at 3 pm 27 Officers 722 O.R. 1st line transport 1 officer 31 O.R. going on another boat. Gen Sir A.J. Murray C in C M.E.F. visits the battalion on board & is given a cheer on departure. Leave at 6 pm. 2 officers, Lts Costello & Moberly, & 26 O.R. transferred to Machine Gun Corps.	JRCD
At sea	11th		Arrive Port Said 7am. Ships routine.	JRCD
"	12th		Ship mounting gun for voyage.	JRCD
"	13th		Sailed at 1130 am. Ships routine, allotment of boat stations etc	JRCD
"	14th		Ships routine. Alarm practice.	JRCD
	15th		Ships routine.	JRCD
	16th		" " Sports	JRCD
	17th		" "	JRCD
	18th		Arrived MARSEILLES 1300, disembarked at 1800, entrained at 2100. Leave MARSEILLES at 2230.	JRCD
	19th		On train	JRCD
	20th		On train	JRCD
	21st		Arrive PONT REMY at 2415 & march to ERNGIES arriving 0530 & detailed to billets.	JRCD
	22nd		Company Route marching & training.	JRCD
	23rd		Company parades & interior economy. Capt Blucorin & Hamilton & 16 O.R. to leave U.K.	JRCD
	24th		Company Route march & training.	JRCD
	25th		Marching order parade at 11 am with transport loaded. Route march ERGNIES – BRUCAMPS – GORENFLOS – ERGNIES.	JRCD
	26th		Church Parades & interior economy. Issue of gas helmets.	JRCD

Army Form C. 2118.

WAR DIARY
or
INTELLIGENCE SUMMARY

(Erase heading not required.)

1/R. Inniskilling Fus. March 1916 No 4.

Instructions regarding War Diaries and Intelligence Summaries are contained in F. S. Regs., Part II. and the Staff Manual respectively. Title pages will be prepared in manuscript.

Place	Date	Hour	Summary of Events and Information	Remarks and references to Appendices
ERGNIES	27th		Brigade route march. ERGNIES – BRUCAMPS – ST OUEN – FLIXECOURT – LAFOLIE – ERGNIES. 0800 – 1330.	JRCD
"	28th		Company route marches & training.	JRCD
"	29th		Company route march & training	JRCD
"	30th		March with Brigade to Reserve area 8th Corps. Leave Ergnies 0645 & meet remainder of Brigade at starting point – clear of East end of DOMART en PONTHIEU at junction of roads from BERNEUIL & B de DOMART. Route DOMART – BERNEUIL – MONTRELET – BONNEVILLE – BEHUVAL – HULEUX – FRESHEVILLERS – AMPLIER. Arrive AMPLIER about 1700 & go into billets.	JRCD
AMPLIER	31st		Interior economy. Effective strength 29 Officers (including MO & Chaplain) & 745 OR	JRCD

R C Pierce Lieut Col:
Cmdg. 1/R Inniskillings

1577 Wt. W10791/1773 500,000 1/15 D. D. & L. A.D.S.S./Forms/C. 2118.

29th Division.
87th Infantry Brigade.

1st BATTALION

INNISKILLING FUSILIERS

APRIL 1 9 1 6

Instructions regarding War Diaries and Intelligence Summaries are contained in F. S. Regs., Part II. and the Staff Manual respectively. Title pages will be prepared in manuscript.

WAR DIARY
or
INTELLIGENCE SUMMARY.
(Erase heading not required.)

Army Form C. 2118.

April 1916

1/R. Inniskilling Fus. No 1

Place	Date	Hour	Summary of Events and Information	Remarks and references to Appendices
AMPLIER	1st		Company parades + Training.	JRCO
	2nd		Remainder of Brigade leave for billets near the firing line.	JRCO
	3rd		Company parades + Training.	JRCO.
	4th		Battalion leave for MAILLY-MAILLET at 2.30 pm. Route SARTON – LOUVENCOURT – BERTRANCOURT – MAILLY-MAILLET, arriving 8.15 pm. March past VIII Corps Commander near MARIEUX. Go into billets.	JRCO.
MAILLY-MAILLET	5th		A Company move up to AUCHONVILLERS at 6.30 pm.	JRCO.
	6th		B company move up to AUCHONVILLERS at 6.30 pm. Bombardment by enemy of E of AUCHONVILLERS, 2100 to 2230 + elsewhere. Energetically replied to.	JRCO
	7th		Work on communication trenches from Auchonvillers to firing line.	
	7th		Repairing of Avenues 1, 2 + 3 + fire trenches Sections B + C. Half a company sent to SWB trench to repair damage done on previous night.	JRCO
TRENCHES.	8th		Start to take over trenches occupied by SWBs at 7.15 pm. Line Q17 c 6.3 to Q10 b 0.2. Three companies in firing line viz A.B.C. + reserve D. Relief complete 9.15 pm. All quiet during night. Battalion dump at ENGELBELMER.	JRCO
	9th		Improvement of trenches + repairing of parapets damaged in bombardment of 6th. Work done. (1) Regent St + Charing Cross Road, deepened etc + generally put in a state of defence. 2. Repair of salient Mary Redoubt 3. Short Strand deepened 4. Shaftesbury Avenue. Top end being straightened + bombing sap started 25x from top 5. Firing line minor improvements. Deepening, clearing debris, etc.	

X 12

1577 Wt. W10791/1773 500,000 1/15 D. D. & L. A.D.S.S./Forms/C. 2118

Instructions regarding War Diaries and Intelligence Summaries are contained in F. S. Regs., Part II. and the Staff Manual respectively. Title pages will be prepared in manuscript.

WAR DIARY
or
INTELLIGENCE SUMMARY.
(Erase heading not required.)

1/R Inniskilling Fus.

Army Form C. 2118.

April 1916

No 2.

Place	Date	Hour	Summary of Events and Information	Remarks and references to Appendices
Trenches	9th		6. Improvements made to Communication trench leading to Piccadilly 7. Latrine built in Mount St. 8. Sap leading from Q16: b 6 4 9. Wire repaired in front of Q16 b. 6.4.	JRCW
	10th		No action by enemy or ourselves. Wire repaired & trenches improved. Support line improved	JRCW
	11th		Wiring party & patrols out at night. No action. Arrival of draft 268 OR.	JRCW
	12th 13th		Improvement of trenches. Relieved by Munster Fus. in the evening & marched into billets (huts) at ACHEUX. via MAILLY-MAILLET — FORCEVILLE. Effective strength 28 offrs 1012 OR. Issue of Divisional scheme of defence attached.	JRCW
ACHEUX	14th to 19th		Company training, training of specialists. Fatigues.	JRCW.
	20th to 25th		Company training, training of specialists. 25th Inspection of those officers & other ranks who landed in Gallipoli a year ago by Lieut Gen Sir Aylmer Hunter-Weston KCB. DSO Commanding 8th Corps. Numbers on parade 20 officers 300 Other Ranks. Effective Strength 22nd 29 officers 1012 OR.	
	26-27th		Training & fatigues.	
	28th 29th		Fatigues. 7 pm. Move to MAILLY-MAILLET in front line, Brigade Reserve. 10.30 pm. New Communication trench 1st Avenue started. Q8d central to Q9d central.	JRCW

1577 Wt. W10791/1773 500,000 1/15 D. D. & L. A.D.S.S./Forms/C. 2118.

Instructions regarding War Diaries and Intelligence Summaries are contained in F. S. Regs., Part II. and the Staff Manual respectively. Title pages will be prepared in manuscript.

WAR DIARY
or
INTELLIGENCE SUMMARY.
(Erase heading not required.)

April 1916. Army Form C. 2118.

1/R Inniskilling Fus. No 3

Place	Date	Hour	Summary of Events and Information	Remarks and references to Appendices
MAILLY MAILLEY.	29th		AUCHONVILLER defence reconnoitred & section allotted, to companies in accordance with Divl defence scheme attached. Work carried on 1st Avenue communication trench by day & night. Effective Strength 28 officers 1004 OR.	JRCD.
	30th		Work on 1st Avenue day & night	JRCD.

J R Devend Capt
O.C. 1/R. Inniskilling Fus.

29th Division

87th Infantry Brigade.

1st BATTALION

ROYAL INNISKILLING FUSILIERS

M A Y 1916

26 2

Army Form C. 2118.

I

Instructions regarding War Diaries and Intelligence Summaries are contained in F. S. Regs., Part II. and the Staff Manual respectively. Title Pages will be prepared in manuscript.

WAR DIARY
or
INTELLIGENCE SUMMARY

(Erase heading not required.) 1st Royl Inniskilling Fus/ May 1916.

Vol 3

Place	Date	Hour	Summary of Events and Information	Remarks and references to Appendices
Mailly-Maillet	1st		Working day & night on New Communication Trench 1st Avenue	
	2nd			
Trenches	3rd		Take over trenches from 2nd Hants. Line same as previous time Q17c 6.3 to Q10b 0.3 Three companies in the firing line viz. A D C from right to left. B Coy in Reserve Battalion Dump at Mailly-Maillet. All quiet during night	
	4th		Enemy put 6 Minenwerfer bombs into REDAN at 0315.	
			Work done: i Deepening CONSTITUTION HILL & REGENT ST BROOK ST deepened & firing step repaired	
			ii Saps 1 & 2 drained & cleaned	
			iii Communication Trench from firing line to PICCADILLY deepened	
			iv Wiring in front of Sap 2.	
	5th		Work done: i Deepening CONSTITUTION HILL & PICCADILLY	
			ii Deepening of Saps leading to New Fire Trench on left of Battalion Line	
			iii Wiring in front of NEW TRENCH	
			iv Revetting & deepening of New Firing Line	
			v Parados of NEW TRENCH raised	
			Patrol of 1 N.C.O. & 3 men examined wire & ground at head of Sap Q17 19 were reported to be in fair condition. Covering party for wiring in front of New Firing Line	
	6th		Work done: i Revetting & deepening of New Firing Line in left sector	
			ii Deepening & traversing of Saps in left sector	
			iii Wiring in front of Q10.4	

Mrs Brown (9)

X.13

2449 Wt. W14957/M90 750,000 1/16 J.B.C. & A. Forms/C.2118/12.

Instructions regarding War Diaries and Intelligence Summaries are contained in F. S. Regs., Part II. and the Staff Manual respectively. Title Pages will be prepared in manuscript.

WAR DIARY
or
INTELLIGENCE SUMMARY

(Erase heading not required.)

Army Form C. 2118.

May 1916

1st Royal Inniskilling Fus/

9

II

Place	Date	Hour	Summary of Events and Information	Remarks and references to Appendices
Trenches	6th		Work done. iv Deepening CONSTITUTION HILL, KNIGHTSBRIDGE & PICCADILLY	[illegible]
			Enemys artillery was active throughout the day	
	7th		Work done i. Work on New Fire Trench continued	
			ii. CONSTITUTION HILL deepened.	
			iii. Repair of trenches damaged by artillery fire	
			iv. Work on Saps & bombing station in left sector continued	
			Enemy shelled our trenches almost continuously from dawn to dusk which interfered with work. About 40 minenwerfer bombs put into REDAN during the day. Our trenches heavily bombarded from 2300 to 23 45 when our artillery bombarded enemy trenches very heavily till [illegible] of the 8th. Our casualties were slight & outside the REDAN little damage was done to our trenches. The REDAN is held very lightly there being only [illegible] during the bombardment	
	8th		Very quiet throughout the day	
			Work done i Repair trenches damaged by artillery	
			ii Wiring continued in front of New Trench	
			iii KNIGHTSBRIDGE and CONSTITUTION HILL deepened	
	9th-12th		Work in trenches continued	
	13th		Relieved by 1st K O S B starting at 1630 Completed 2000. Moved into Billets at Englebelmer	

Instructions regarding War Diaries and Intelligence Summaries are contained in F. S. Regs., Part II. and the Staff Manual respectively. Title Pages will be prepared in manuscript.

WAR DIARY
or
INTELLIGENCE SUMMARY
(Erase heading not required.)

Army Form C. 2118.

III

May 1916

1st R. Inniskilling Fus

Place	Date	Hour	Summary of Events and Information	Remarks and references to Appendices
Englebelmer	14		Inspections etc	
			Work on Gabion Avenue etc Battalion stood to during the night + two companies manned the "GREEN LINE" trenches	
			Work on GABION AVENUE etc continued	
	17		~~C + D~~ Coys continue work on GABION AVENUE, PICADILLY + UXBRIDGE ROAD	[illegible]
	18	[illegible]	C + D Coys continue work on GABION AVENUE	
	~~17~~	21.00	The Battalion leaves ENGLEBELMER for LOUVENCOURT arriving 23.30 + go into Billets	[illegible]
LOUVENCOURT	19	09.00	Coy parade for demonstration "contact patrol aeroplanes"	
	20		Coys on fatigues road making loading + unloading trucks etc remainder Coy training + washing parades at [illegible] Baths LOUVENCOURT	[illegible]
	21		Two companies + part of [illegible] on fatigues, remaining Coy inspections, lectures, instruction in rapid wiring ~~[illegible]~~ bathing	[illegible]
	22	09.40	All available Officers + NCOs attend demonstration by RE in Draining + Revetting	[illegible]
		14.30	" " " " " " Bangalore Torpedo	
	23	17.00	Battalion parade. Officers under instruction in Lewis Gun. Fatigues + Coy training + bathing parades	[illegible]

2449 Wt. W14957/M90 750,000 1/16 J.B.C. & A. Forms/C.2118/12.

Instructions regarding War Diaries and Intelligence Summaries are contained in F. S. Regs., Part II. and the Staff Manual respectively. Title Pages will be prepared in manuscript.

WAR DIARY
or
INTELLIGENCE SUMMARY

(Erase heading not required.)

May 1916. 1/R Innis Fusiliers

Army Form C. 2118.

IV

Place	Date	Hour	Summary of Events and Information	Remarks and references to Appendices
				JRC
				JRC
				JRC
				JRC
Trenches	28	13 30	Marched by half companies at ten minutes interval to the trenches and relieved the HANTS Regt. line taken over from Q 16 6 south to BUCKINGHAM PALACE ROAD. D coy on the left. A coy centre. B coy right and C coy in Reserve. the night was quiet	JRC
"	29			
	30 & 31st		Nothing to report. Effective Strength 37 officers 957 OR.	J R Cowen Capt & Adjt for Lt Col 1/R Innis Fusiliers

2449 Wt. W14957/M90 750,000 1/16 J.B.C. & A. Forms/C.2118/12.

SECRET. Copy No. 5.

87TH BRIGADE OPERATION ORDER NO. 32.
by
BRIGADE GENERAL C.H.TINDALL LUCAS.
COMMANDING 87TH INFANTRY BRIGADE...
=:=:=:=:=:=:=:=:::::=:=:=:=:=:=:=:

In the Field,
1st May 1918.

---

1. The Brigade will be relieved by the 86th Brigade in the left sector of the Divisional Line and take over the right sector at present held by the 88th Brigade on the night of the 3rd/4th May.

Reliefs as under:-

1st Royal Inniskilling Fusiliers relieve 2nd Hampshire Regt. in the front line and extend their line up to junction of Q.10.6 and Q.16.7.

2nd South Wales Borderers. relieve Newfoundland Regt. in front line from junction of Q.10.6 and Q.16.7 to their present left.

On relief 1st Border Regt relieve 1st Essex Regt. in Brigade Reserve in the yellow line and at ENGLEBELMER.

On relief 1st K.O.S.B relieve 4th Worcester Regt. in Divisional Reserve at ENGLEBELMER.

2. Details of reliefs including guides will be arranged between the units concerned. Battalions in the firing line will arrange to relieve their specialists--Lewis Gunners etc., and take over Company and Battalion Trench Stores by day.

3. Battalions will hand over the relieving Battalions-- Cookers- Reserve Ammunition- Bombs- Picks and shovels and take over those of the Battalion they will relieve.

4. The 87th Brigade Machine Gun Coy. will remain in their present positions and come under the orders of the 86th Brigade.

5. Units will report to Brigade Headquarters on completion of relief and render disposition return by [illegible] a.m. the following day.

Signed. J. C. Brand Capt.
Brigade Major 87th Infantry Brigade.

Issued at 1200.

1/3. Office.
4. 2/S.W.B.
5. 1/R.I.F.
6. 1/Border.
7. 1/K.O.S.B.
8. 87/1/3/.T.M.B.
9. 86th Bde.M.G.Co.
10. [illegible]3rd Brigade
11. 88th Brigade.
12. Left Group R.A.

SECRET. Copy No. 6.

OPERATION ORDER NO 23
BY
BRIGADE GENERAL C.H.TINDALL LUCAS.
.COMMANDING 87TH.INFANTRY BRIGADE.
:+++++++++++++:+:+:+:+++++++++++++

IN - THE - FIELD.
MAY 16TH 1916.

1. The brigade will be relieved in the line by the 88th Brigade during the 18/19th May.
On relief the Brigade will move into Corps Reserve.
Reliefs as under :-

The 1st K.O.S.B. will be relieved by 2nd Hampshire Regiment, and on relief will move into billets at MAILLEY WOOD vacated by 4th Worcester Regiment.

The 1st Border Regiment will be relieved by the 1st Newfoundland Regiment and on relief will move into billets at LOUVENCOURT vacated by 1st Newfoundland Regiment.

The 2nd South Wales Borderers and the 1st Rl. Inniskilling Fusiliers will be relieved by the 4th Worcester Regiment and 1st Essex Regiment respectively, and on relief will move into billets at ACHEAUX and LOUVENCOURT vacated by the 1st ESSEX Regiment and 2nd Hampshire Regiment respectively.

The 87/1 Trench Mortar Batteries will be relieved by the 88/1 and 88/2 Trench Mortar Batteries and on relief will move into billets at LOUVENCOURT vacated by the 88/1 and 88/2 Trench Mortar Batteries.

2. Details of relied including guides will be arranged between Units concerned.

3. ~~Details of relief including guides~~. Units will arrange to hand over Cookers, Reserve Small Arms Ammunition, Bombs, and Picks and Shovels to relieving units and to take over those left in the billets to which they are going.

4. Billeting parties will proceed on the morning of relied, to take over billets and will make all arrangements direct with the Town Commandants.

5. The 87th Brigade Machine Gun Company will remain in its present position and will come under the orders of the 88th Brigade.

6. Units will report to the Brigade Headquarters when the relief is completed.

Signed. J. G. Brand Captain.
Brigade Major. 87th Inf. Brigade.

Issued at 0900.
Copies 1-3 Office.
Copy. 4 2nd KOSB.
5 2nd SWB
6 1 R.I.F.
7 1 Borders
8 87th.M.G.Co.
9 87/1 T.M.B.
10 87/2 T.M.B.
11 88th Bde (for information)
12 88th " "
13 Right Group R.A. "
14 108 Bde. "

29th Division.

87th Infantry Brigade.

1st BATTALION

ROYAL INNISKILLING FUSILIERS

JUNE 1916

Instructions regarding War Diaries and Intelligence Summaries are contained in F. S. Regs., Part II. and the Staff Manual respectively. Title Pages will be prepared in manuscript.

WAR DIARY
or
INTELLIGENCE SUMMARY
(Erase heading not required.)

Army Form C. 2118.

87/29

1/R. Inniskilling Fus June 1916

I

Vol 4

Place	Date	Hour	Summary of Events and Information	Remarks and references to Appendices
Trenches	1st		Work on trenches. 2 officers patrols out at night, nothing to report. Two minnenwerfer were fired on Redan at 8 pm.	JRCD.
	2nd		Officers patrol out at night, nothing to report. Enemy shelled Gabion Avenue.	JRCD
	3rd		A few enemy shells on our front, apparently ranging. Three minnenwerfer in the evening on MARY REDAN. Two officers patrols go out during night. Effective strength 38 officers 942 O.R.	JRCD.
	4th		Artillery bombarded enemy's trenches, only slight retaliation. Raid carried out on our left by next brigade. Enemy used a searchlight & did not reply very heavily on us.	JRCD.
	5th		Artillery quiet. Hostile aeroplane flew over our lines at 7.50am at great height but retired on being fired on by A.A. guns.	JRCD.
	6th		Artillery registered over battalion area. Raid on our right at 11pm our artillery assisting. enemy replied on us. 2Lieut Walshe wounded.	JRCD
	7th		Enemy shelled GABION AVENUE with H.E. during the morning apparently searching for batteries just behind our lines. Relieved during the afternoon by KOSBs & go into billets at ENGLEBELMER. See attached order.	JRCD
ENGLEBELMER	8th – 13th		Whole Battalion on working parties day & night. Effective strength. 38 officers 971.	JRCD.
	14th		Working parties.	
	15th		Relieved by 9th [illegible] Rd & whole brigade go into billets at LOUVENCOURT. See orders attached.	JRCD
LOUVENCOURT	16th		Bde: Preliminary orders for attack received. See attached Operation order 28.	JRCD
	17th		Battalion practice attack on German trenches marked out on ground. Parade at 6am. Issue of stores etc to be carried. Operation order 29 received. Draft of 90 OR arrive.	JRCD

X. 14

2449 Wt. W14957/M90 750,000 1/16 J.B.C. & A. Forms/C.2118/12.

Effective Strength

Army Form C. 2118.

WAR DIARY
or
INTELLIGENCE SUMMARY

(Erase heading not required.)

Instructions regarding War Diaries and Intelligence Summaries are contained in F. S. Regs., Part II. and the Staff Manual respectively. Title Pages will be prepared in manuscript.

June 1916

1/R Inniskilling Fus.

No II.

Place	Date	Hour	Summary of Events and Information	Remarks and references to Appendices
	18th		Brigade practice attack on German trenches. Parade 10 am. Issue of stores etc	JRCD
	19th		" " " " " " in accordance with Operation orders. Operation order 30 received	JRCD.
LOUVENCOURT	20th		Brigade practice attack on German trenches. Parade 10 a.m.	W.A.M
— " —	21st		— Ditto —	W.A.M
— " —	22nd		— Ditto —	W.A.M
Firing Line	23rd		Relieved of Hants Regt. in firing line Q.14.12 - Q.16.6.4 Relief completed at 21.00. A B & D Companies in firing line "C" Company in Reserve at ENGLEBELMER all quiet.	W.A.M
Do	24th		U. Day. Steady bombardment started at 5 a.m. on Enemy trenches, very little reply by Enemy. Discharge of gas on Enemy trenches arranged for 22.00. but postponed owing to unfavourable wind.	W.A.M
Do	25th		V. Day. Our Bombardment increased in intensity, mostly centred upon cutting wires in front of enemy trenches, with Heavier Battery firing on enemy back or support trenches. Enemy replying more effectively. Casualties 3. KILLED. 2 WOUNDED. Discharge of gas arranged for 12. MIDNIGHT. O.S. 30. DRESDEN. postponed 12.M.NIGHT. DRESDEN.	W.A.M

2449 Wt. W14957/M90 750,000 1/16 J.B.C. & A. Forms/C.2118/12.

Army Form C. 2118.

WAR DIARY
or
INTELLIGENCE SUMMARY
(Erase heading not required.)

Instructions regarding War Diaries and Intelligence Summaries are contained in F. S. Regs., Part II. and the Staff Manual respectively. Title Pages will be prepared in manuscript.

June '16

1/R. Inniskilling Fusiliers

No III

Place	Date	Hour	Summary of Events and Information	Remarks and references to Appendices
			wire cutting by 36th Battery on our front from Q. 11. c 65.02 to Q. 14. a. 96.80	
Firing line	26th		W. Day. 01.00 FRANKFORT. 05.00 ^ 09.00 DRESDEN. 09.30. BERLIN 10.15. Gas discharged in Left Sub-sector of Right-Sector. Enemy retaliate heavily on our trenches 12.00. Message received 36th DIVISION. DRESDEN at 13.30. 14.30. Gas and smoke were discharged by 31st DIVISION on our Right from THIEPVAL-WOOD and vicinity	W.A.M
– " –	27th		X. Day. Bombardment heavier, wire cutting and heavy guns on Villages. No gas or smoke in our Sector. A Raid by 1st Border Regt from our lines at [illegible] partially unsuccessful. 3 Officers Patrols go out to examine enemy wire. [illegible] Patrol cut wire with Bangalore torpedo, 2nd torpedo fails to explode	W.A.M
– " –	28th		Y. Day. Bombardment continues. Notified that 00.00 is 7.30. a.m. on Z. Day. 4.30 p.m. Z. Day postponed for 48 Hours owing to bad weather 11.30 pm Three officers patrols out to inspect enemy wire. Patrols interrupted by Machine Gun fire from about point 45.	W.A.M
– " –	29th		Y.1. Day. Bombardment continues and very little reply on front line trenches	W.A.M
– " –	30th		Y.2. Day. Raid by 1st Innis. Regt from our lines at 12.30 am on Point 60. entered trenches and killed two Germans. Raid, we B.14 attached, to be carried out by Battalion cancelled. Message received at 2 p.m. that 1st July to be Z. Day and 00.00 to be 7.30 a.m.	W.A.M

2449 Wt. W14957/M90 750,000 1/16 J.B.C. & A. Forms/C.2118/12.

Army Form C. 2118.

June 1916

WAR DIARY
or
INTELLIGENCE SUMMARY

(Erase heading not required.)

Instructions regarding War Diaries and Intelligence Summaries are contained in F. S. Regs., Part II. and the Staff Manual respectively. Title Pages will be prepared in manuscript.

1/1st Royal Inniskilling Fus

No XV

Place	Date	Hour	Summary of Events and Information	Remarks and references to Appendices
Firing Line	30th		Effective Strength:- Officers 43. Other Ranks 1026.	
			Casualties 26th to 30th 5 KILLED 1. MISSING. 16 WOUNDED	
			W. H. Morris Captain	
			for Lieut. Colonel	
			Commdg 1/1st Royal Inniskilling Fusiliers	

2449 Wt. W14957/M90 750,000 1/16 J.B.C. & A. Forms/C.2118/12.

SECRET. B.24.

O.C. Ist.Rl.Innis.Fus.

In the event of active operations being further postponed, theBrigade has been ordered to make a raid on the German Trenches tomorrow night. TheG.O.C. wishes this raid if required, to be carried out by the Battalion under your command

Pleaseconsider point of entry and all details and what artillery you wish .

NOt more than 1 Officer & 20 other ranks should be employed.
It is only required to obtain identification in the shape of one or two prisoners.

All preparations should be made at once as there will be very short notice given if it has to take place.

Please acknowledge.

[illegible] Captain
Brigade Major
[illegible] Brigade

24 6 [illegible]

True Copy

W.A. Morris Captain
1/R. Inniskilling Fus.

29th Division.

87th Infantry Brigade.

1st BATTALION

ROYAL INNISKILLING FUSILIERS

J U L Y 1 9 1 6

Army Form C. 2118.

87/29 July 1916

Vol 5 No I

Instructions regarding War Diaries and Intelligence Summaries are contained in F. S. Regs., Part II. and the Staff Manual respectively. Title Pages will be prepared in manuscript.

WAR DIARY

Brigade Major
8?th Infantry Brigade

Herewith Original "War Diary" of the battalion for the month of July 1916.

Kindly acknowledge receipt

1/8/16

C. J. [illegible] Major
Comdg 1st R. Inniskilling Fus.

Place	Date	Hour	Summary of Events and Information	Remarks and references to Appendices
Firing Line	July 1st		I Day. In ... [illegible] ...ttalion advanced on the objective, wh... [illegible] ... of German trenches. the Batt. ... [illegible] ... single file on the following ... [illegible] ... held in Reserve in the original ... [illegible] ... lines appeared on the parapet ... [illegible] ... cross fire to bear ... [illegible] ... being able to gain further ground ... [illegible] ... circumstances the Batt ... decided ... [illegible] ... as it was also found impossible ... [illegible] ... Battalion on entering the action: ... [illegible] ... Officers LIEUT. BLANNERHASSETT?, PIERCE (Temp) ... [illegible] ... BOARD and 2 LIEUT. PORTER ... [illegible] ... Other Ranks: KILLED 50. KILLED — MISSING 4. WOUNDED ... [illegible] MISSING 225, WOUNDED 265. Remainder of Batt. relieved in our front sector, near St. JOHNS ROAD. —	W.A.M

2449 Wt. W14957/M90 750,000 1/16 J.B.C. & A. Forms/C.2118/12.

Army Form C. 2118.

Instructions regarding War Diaries and Intelligence Summaries are contained in F. S. Regs., Part II. and the Staff Manual respectively. Title Pages will be prepared in manuscript.

WAR DIARY
or
INTELLIGENCE SUMMARY
(Erase heading not required.)

1st R. Inniskilling Fusiliers 87/29 July 1916 Vol 5 No I.

Place	Date	Hour	Summary of Events and Information	Remarks and references to Appendices
Firing Line	July 1st 1916		I Day. In accordance with Orders the Battalion advanced on the objective which consisted of the first three lines of German trenches, the Batt. advancing in lines of Platoons in single file on the following relation B. A. D. Coys. C. Company being held in Reserve in our original first line trench. Immediately our lines appeared on the parapet the enemy brought heavy Machine gun cross fire to bear which heavily diminished the advance, none being able to gain further ground from the enemy's Wire. Under the circumstances the advance failed on the sector allotted to the Batt. as it was also found impossible to bring up Reserves. Strength of Battalion on entering the action:- Officers 36. Other Ranks 916. Casualties: Officers LIEUT. COLONEL PIERCE (Temp) CAPTAIN FRENCH, LIEUT. HARBOARD and 2 LIEUT. PORTER KILLED – MISSING 4. WOUNDED 11. Other Ranks:- KILLED 50. MISSING 225. WOUNDED 265. Remainder of Batt. rallied in our front sector, near St. JOHNS ROAD. –	W.A.M.

2449 Wt. W14957/M90 750,000 1/16 J.B.C. & A. Forms/C.2118/12.

Army Form C. 2118.

Instructions regarding War Diaries and Intelligence Summaries are contained in F. S. Regs., Part II. and the Staff Manual respectively. Title Pages will be prepared in manuscript.

WAR DIARY
or
INTELLIGENCE SUMMARY
(Erase heading not required.)

July 1916

1/ R Inniskilling Fusiliers

No II.

Place	Date	Hour	Summary of Events and Information	Remarks and references to Appendices
ST JOHNS RD	2nd		Under orders received at 10.00 Battalion under the temporary Command of (Capt) Captain NICHOLLS marched to HAMEL and took up their position in Brigade Reserve - Major HARDRESS-LLOYD arriving to take over Command. Captain Nicholls taking up the duties of Acting Adjutant. Casualties NIL	W.A.M
HAMEL	3rd		Batt in Brigade Reserve. Casualties NIL	W.A.M
"	4th		Batt in Brigade Reserve. A Patrol sent out to locate an enemy post in the marsh below THIEPVAL WOOD: Casualties Other Ranks Killed 3. DIED OF WOUNDS. 3, WOUNDED. 3.	W.A.M
"	5th		Batt in Brigade Reserve. Casualties NIL	W.A.M
"	6th		Batt in Brigade Reserve - Casualties, Other Ranks WOUNDED. 1	W.A.M
"	7th		Batt in Brigade Reserve - Reinforcing Draft of 1 Officer + 40 O.Ranks joined from Base. Casualties Other Ranks WOUNDED 3.	W.A.M
"	8th		Batt in Brigade Reserve, relieved at 19.00 by 2/ Royal FUSILIERS and returned to ACHIEU. Casualties - Other Ranks KILLED 2 WOUNDED 3	W.A.M
ACHIEU	9th		Batt with remainder of Brigade at REST Strength. Officers 21 O.Ranks 360	W.A.M

2449 Wt. W14957/M90 750,000 1/16 J.B.C. & A. Forms/C.2118/12.

Instructions regarding War Diaries and Intelligence Summaries are contained in F. S. Regs., Part II. and the Staff Manual respectively. Title Pages will be prepared in manuscript.

WAR DIARY
or
INTELLIGENCE SUMMARY
(Erase heading not required.)

Army Form C. 2118.

July 1916

4th Royal Inniskilling Fusiliers

No. III

Place	Date	Hour	Summary of Events and Information	Remarks and references to Appendices
ACHEUX	10th		Batt. at Rest. Kit inspection, Baths, etc	W.A.M
...	11th		Batt. at Rest Camp. Company parades & training, etc	W.A.M
...	12th		Battalion at Rest Camp. Company parades, training of Specialists etc	C.R
...	13th		Battalion Route March with 1st line Transport via:- BUS-LES-ARTOIS – LOUVENCOURT. Training of Specialists etc in afternoon.	C.R
...	14th		Battalion at Rest Camp. Company parades. Training of Specialists etc.	C.R
...	15th		Battalion at Rest Camp. Company parades. Training of Specialists etc	C.R
...	16th		Battalion at Rest Camp. Church parade. Arrival of draft 136 O.R. Strength 25 officers 584 other ranks.	C.R
MAILLY-MAILLET	17th		Relieved 2/HANTS. Regt in MAILLY WOOD. Relief completed at 1800.	C.R
...	18th		Battalion in Brigade Reserve – Training of Specialists. Found working party of 150 men for work on new advanced line. Casualties. Other ranks: Shell Shock 2. – Taken on Strength of Bn 2 O.R. from 1/R.D.F.	C.R
...	19th		Battalion in Brigade Reserve. 150 men working party on new advanced line. Casualties. Other ranks KILLED 1. WOUNDED 5. Shell Shock 1. MISSING 1. Training of Lewis Gunners & Bombers.	C.R

2449 Wt. W14957/M90 750,000 1/16 J.B.C. & A. Forms/C.2118/12.

Instructions regarding War Diaries and Intelligence Summaries are contained in F. S. Regs., Part II. and the Staff Manual respectively. Title Pages will be prepared in manuscript.

WAR DIARY
or
INTELLIGENCE SUMMARY
(Erase heading not required.) 1/R. Inniskilling Fus^rs

Army Form C. 2118.

July 1916

No. 4

Place	Date	Hour	Summary of Events and Information	Remarks and references to Appendices
MAILLY-MAILLET	20th		Battalion in Brigade Reserve – Training of Bombers & Lewis Gunners – Working party of 150 men to work on new advanced line out of which a party of 20 men & 1 officer for burying purposes. 6 officers joined from the Base & were taken on the strength of the Bn. Casualties – WOUNDED 6 – Shell Shock 8.	C.R.
— " —	21st		Battalion in Brigade Reserve – Training of Lewis Gunners – Working party of 150 men to work on new advanced line – Casualties – WOUNDED 7.	C.R.
Firing line	22nd		Relieved 1/K.O.S.B. in firing line from "B" Street (left), to LONG ACRE (right) exclusive. Relief completed 1900 – "B" "C" & "D" Coys in firing line, "A" Coy in support in UXBRIDGE ROAD & JETHARD S^T. Situation all quiet. Casualties – nil – Strength 31 officers, 557 other ranks.	C.R.
— " —	23rd		Repairing of old firing line, clearing communication trenches, salvage etc – Intermittent shelling by enemy artillery in region of MARY REDAN & SHAFTESBURY AV., portion of trench in REGENT S^T blown in about 2800. Casualties – nil. Draft 68 O.R. joined from Base.	C.R.
— " —	24th		87th B^de relieved by 74th B^de. 2/R. Irish Rifles relieving us in right sub-sector, relief completed 1830. On relief the Battalion marched to Billets at BUS via GABION AV – ROTTEN ROW – BERTRANCOURT. – Work done general cleaning up & salvage of trenches. Burial parties went out between old line & advanced line on night 23/24th. Enemy shelled intermittently MARY REDAN – Casualties – nil – Draft 28 O.R. joined from Base.	C.R.
BUS	25th		The Battalion marched to AMPLIER via AUTHIE – THIEVRES – ORVILLE leaving at 0930 & arriving at 1230 & billeted in huts. 1st line transport accompanied the B^n. 3 officers joined from Base & were taken on the strength of the B^n.	C.R.

2449 Wt. W14957/M90 750,000 1/16 J.B.C. & A. Forms/C.2118/12.

Instructions regarding War Diaries and Intelligence Summaries are contained in F. S. Regs., Part II. and the Staff Manual respectively. Title Pages will be prepared in manuscript.

WAR DIARY
or
INTELLIGENCE SUMMARY
(Erase heading not required.) 1/R. Inniskilling Fus:

Army Form C. 2118.

July 1916

No 5

Place	Date	Hour	Summary of Events and Information	Remarks and references to Appendices
AMPLIER	26th		Battalion in Rest Camp - Interior Economy, drill etc under Company arrangements	C.R.
— " —	27th		The 87th Bde left for HAZEBROUCK entraining at DOULLENS SOUTH - The Battalion left for DOULLENS at 1500 entrained at DOULLENS SOUTH at 1919 reaching HAZEBROUCK at 2330 from there we proceeded by train to PROVEN arriving 0230 the Bn detrained and marched into Rest Camp "L" near POPERINGHE arriving 0430.	C.R.
"L" Camp W of POPERINGHE	28th		Battalion in Rest Camp - Commanding officers parade, training of Specialists etc	C.R.
	29th		Bn "do" - Parades & training of Specialists. 1 officer and 68 other ranks joined from Base - Strength - 35 officers & 689 O.R.	C.R.
— " —	30th		Bn in Rest Camp - Church parades. Inspection of new drafts by C.O. -	C.R.
— " —	31st		Bn in Rest Camp - Parades etc training of Specialists - 2 officers joined the Bn from Base & were taken on the strength	C.R.

C. J. [illegible] Capt & Adjt for Major
Comndg 1st R. Innisk. Fus.

2449 Wt. W14957/M90 750,000 1/16 J.B.C. & A. Forms/C.2118/12.

29th Division.

87th Infantry Brigade.

1st BATTALION

ROYAL INNISKILLING FUSILIERS

AUGUST 1 9 1 6

Battalion Operation Orders attached.

1st Royal Inniskilling Fusiliers

Confidential

Vol 6

War Diary

From 1-8-16 To 31-8-16

Volume:- IV

X.16

The
Staff Captain
87th Inf: Bde.

Herewith War Diary for the month of August 1916.

Kindly acknowledge receipt

1/9/16 { C. J. Lawson Major
1st Bat Inniskilling Fus.

9

Army Form C. 2118.

August /16

No 1

Instructions regarding War Diaries and Intelligence Summaries are contained in F. S. Regs., Part II. and the Staff Manual respectively. Title Pages will be prepared in manuscript.

WAR DIARY
or
INTELLIGENCE SUMMARY

(Erase heading not required.) 1/R. Inniskilling Fus.

Place	Date	Hour	Summary of Events and Information	Remarks and references to Appendices
POPERINGHE 'L' Camp	1st		Battalion in Rest Camp. Parades, training of Specialists &c. Relieved 1/KOSB in YPRES (Reserve Billets). Entrained at POPERINGHE 20.30, arrived YPRES 21.30.	C.R.
YPRES	2nd		Bn in Reserve Billets. General cleaning up of Billets. Supplied working party of 120 men for work in front line trenches under 1/KOSB. Situation quiet.	C.R.
-do-	3rd		Bn in Reserve Billets. Inspection shelters under Coy arrangements. Training of Specialists. Supplied working party of 200 men for work in firing line. Situation quiet.	C.R.
-do-	4th		Bn in Reserve Billets. Training Specialists &c. Supplied working party 1[illegible] men. Situation quiet.	C.R.
-do-	5th		Bn in Reserve Billets. — do — . 1 officer & 150 other ranks arrived from Base. Casualties wounded other ranks 1. Strength 37 officers 722 other ranks	C.R.
-do-	6th		Relieved 1/KOSB in firing line. Relief completed at 22.30. A & C Coys in front line. D in support & X line. B in reserve in CONGREVE WALK. "Gas alert" 20.15 nothing happened. Situation quiet. Casualties nil.	C.R.
FIRING LINE	7th		General repair of trenches &c. Situation all quiet. Casualties nil.	C.R.
-do-	8th		Repair of trenches. Enemy sent over some gas shells & lacrymatory shells about 23.00 dispersing K.O.S.B. working party in STRAND & FLEET St. We sent out 3 listening patrols in front of C29 6 & C29 6 5. They reported all quiet. Situation unchanged. Casualties nil. Enemy were apparently working at their trenches at night. Various indications of this were observed. Mining was carried out by 'A' Coy in night Sub Sector.	C.R.

Instructions regarding War Diaries and Intelligence Summaries are contained in F. S. Regs., Part II. and the Staff Manual respectively. Title Pages will be prepared in manuscript.

Army Form C. 2118.

WAR DIARY
or
INTELLIGENCE SUMMARY
(Erase heading not required.)

1/1R Inniskilling Fus^s

August/16

N° 2

Place	Date	Hour	Summary of Events and Information	Remarks and references to Appendices
FIRING LINE	9th		Ordinary routine repairing trenches the situation quiet during day – Enemy made a very heavy & concentrated discharge of Gas at our lines starting 22-30 it lasted for over two hours our casualties were heavy especially in "C" Coy which was in the left sub-sector – Owing to our Lewis Gun fire being kept up, during the whole attack, on the enemy parapet & our close artillery support the enemy did not leave his trenches –	
			Casualties. KILLED 7 officers – 42 other ranks – WOUNDED 5 officers – 82 other ranks	C.R.
			DIED afterwards – 39 other ranks – Casualties all occurred from effects of Gas with the exception of a few who were killed during the bombardment of our trenches – One officer joined from the Base & was taken on the strength of the Bn.	
BRANDHOEK Camp "C"	10th		The Battalion was relieved in the line by 2/Royal Fusiliers on the night 9/10th Aug. and moved into Divisional Reserve in Camp "C", entraining at YPRES 0100.	
– " –	11th		Bn in Rest Camp – Bathing, inspections & issue of new clothing etc.	C.R.
– " –	12th		– do – Special programme of training – Training of officers & specialists –	C.R.
– " –	13th		– do – ~~Church Parade~~ 40 other ranks returned to unit Division –	
			Strength 25 officers – 487 other ranks.	
– " –	14th		Bn in Rest Camp – Work same as previously – Found camp fatigue of 100 men – 21 other ranks joined from Base & were taken on the strength of the Bn. 1 officer evacuated (gas poison).	C.R.
– " –	15th		Bn in Rest Camp – Work same as previous day.	C.R.

2449 Wt. W14957/M90 750,000 1/16 J.B.C. & A. Forms/C.2118/12.

Instructions regarding War Diaries and Intelligence Summaries are contained in F. S. Regs., Part II. and the Staff Manual respectively. Title Pages will be prepared in manuscript.

WAR DIARY
or
INTELLIGENCE SUMMARY
(Erase heading not required.) 1/R. Inniskilling Fus.

Army Form C. 2118.

Aug. /16

No 3

Place	Date	Hour	Summary of Events and Information	Remarks and references to Appendices
BRANDHOEK Camp C	16th		Bn in Rest Camp - Parades, training of Specialists etc - Staff ride for all officers, tactical scheme under G.O.C. -	C.R.
— " —	17th		Bn in Rest Camp - work same as previous day - Bathing parade in afternoon -	C.R.
— " —	18th		— do — do — One officer joined from Base -	C.R.
YPRES	19th		Took over Reserve Billets in YPRES from 1/K.O.S.B., entraining at BRANDHOEK 8-30 pm arriving about 9.15 pm. "A" Coy billeted in Town. "B" HQ. " " the Prison. "C" " " " Magazine. "D" " " Switch Canal Bank.	
— " —	20th		Strength - 25 officers, 485 other ranks. Bn in Reserve Billets at YPRES. Church parade. Supplied working party of 90 men to work on FLEET St also 7 other ranks to work at MENIN GATE -	C.R.
— " —	21st		Bn in Reserve Billets - Parades under Company arrangements - Working party 90 men FLEET St. Gas alarm 8-20 pm which turned out to be false - Our artillery bombarded Enemy's front for 2 hours starting at 3 p.m. -	C.R. / C.R.
— " —	22nd		Bn in Reserve Billets - Same as previous day - Working party 90 men on STRAND - Casualties. WOUNDED - 1 other rank -	C.R.
— " —	23rd		Bn in Reserve Billets - Training of specialists etc. Working party 90 men on STRAND - Casualties. WOUNDED - 1 -	C.R.
— " —	24th		Bn in Reserve - Work same as previous day - Working party 90 men on STRAND - 1 officer & 12 other ranks joined from Base -	C.R.

Instructions regarding War Diaries and Intelligence Summaries are contained in F. S. Regs., Part II. and the Staff Manual respectively. Title Pages will be prepared in manuscript.

WAR DIARY
or
INTELLIGENCE SUMMARY

(Erase heading not required.) 1/R. Inniskilling Fus.

Army Form C. 2118.

Aug./16
No. 4

Place	Date	Hour	Summary of Events and Information	Remarks and references to Appendices
YPRES	25th		Bn in Reserve Billets – work same as previous day – Working party 125 men digging new trench in ADMIRALS ROAD – Casualties. WOUNDED – 2.	C.R.
"	26th		Bn in Reserve Billets – Same as previous day. Working party – 60 men ADMIRALS ROAD 30 men wiring – 50 men Carrying – Casualties – nil – Strength 26 officers 490 other ranks.	C.R.
"	27th		Bn in Reserve Billets – Church parade – Rest all day – Carrying party of 160 men at night to FIRING LINE – 23 other ranks joined from Base.	C.R.
"	28th		Bn in Reserve Billets – Parade under Coy arrangements – Carrying party 160 men –	C.R.
FIRING LINE	29th		Relieved the 1/K.O.S.B. Regt. in the Right Sub-sector – Relief complete 23.00 – "B" & "D" Coys in firing line – "A" Coy in Support X line – "C" Coy in Reserve CONGREVE WALK. Proposed gas attack postponed owing to unfavourable wind –	C.R.
"	30th		FIRING LINE – Draining of trenches owing to very heavy rain. Situation normal. Casualties – nil –	C.R.
"	31st		FIRING LINE – Draining of trenches, repairing parapet & parados, wiring – Gas attack postponed owing to unfavourable wind – Casualties – WOUNDED – 1 –	C.R.

C. J. [illegible] Major
1st R. Inniskilling Fus.

2449 Wt. W14957/M90 750,000 1/16 J.B.C. & A. Forms/C.2118/12.

ECRET. Copy No.5

87TH INFANTRY BRIGADE
OPERATION ORDER NO.39

In-the-Field,
5/8/16.

1. The 1st Royal Inniskilling Fusiliers and 1st King's Own Scottish Borderers in the Right Sub-sector, and the 1st Border Regiment and 2nd South Wales Borderers in the left Sub-sector, will relieve each other on the night of the 6th/7th instant.

2. Details of relief to be arranged between Units concerned.

3. Completion of relief to be reported to these Headquarters by orderly,

4. Please acknowledge.

(Signed.) J. C. BRAND. CAPTAIN.

Issued at 1200. Brigade Major 87th Inf.Brigade.

Copies 1-2 Staff
3=2/SWB
4=1/KOSB
5=1/RIF
6=1/Borders
7=87th M.G.Coy.
8=87th T.M.B.
9=Right Bde.4th Division. (for information)
10=88th Brigade "
11=Left Group 20th Div.Art. "
12=29th Division "G". =

OPERATION ORDER. No.5

by

MAJOR J. HARDRESS--LLOYD.

Commanding 1st Battalion The Royal Inniskilling Fusiliers.

YPRES. 6/8/16

Reference Maps.
BELGIUM Sheet 28.N.W.1.20000
Trench Map. 1.10000

1. The Battalion will relieve the 1st K.O.S.B's Regt in the Right Sub-Sector tonight the 1st Company leaving here at 21.00.
Companies will proceed in the following order:-

"A" "C" "B" "D" and "HEADQUARTERS".

Method of procedure by ½ companies at 5 minutes interval.

"A"Company relieves "A"Company 1st K.O.S.B's in Right Sector.

"C" " " "D" " " " " left Sector

"D" " " "C" " " " " Support

1½ Platoons in X 4, 1½ Platoons in X 5. 1 Platoon in "S" 8.

(See Trench Maps).

"B"Company relieves "B"Company 1st K.O.S.B's in Reserve. (Congreve Walk).

2. Route: via the MENIN GATE - MENIN-POTIJIE-ROAD.
Guides will meet Companies at the X Roads I.C.4.10.

3. Lewis Gunners and Bombers will proceed with their Companies.

4. Signallers will proceed in advance and take over all telephone communications.

5. Companies to report to Battalion Headquarters by Runner when relief is completed.

6. All trench stores etc., will be taken over by Companies and receipts given, a copy of same to be sent to Orderly Room.

7. Officers' Kits, Mess Boxes etc.,M.O.Stores and Lewis Gun ammunition must be packed and ready by 21.00 at the Prison.

8. Companies will be responsible that their billets are left scrupulously clean and that all fires and lights are extinguished.

9. The strictist silence must be observed on the march.

10. In order to keep the 5 minutes interval, Company Commanders on moving off will let the next Company know.

(Signed) C. J. LENDRUM Capt.and Adjutant.

1st Batt, The Rl. Inniskilling Fusiliers.

1st Battalion The Royal Inniskilling Fusiliers

Orders for Relief. 9th August 1916

1. The Battalion will be relieved tonight by the 2/ Rl.Fusiliers about 22.00.

2. Companies will report by runner to Battn. Headquarters on completion of relief, and will march independently to the entraining point at ASYLUM, West Corner of YPRES.

3. On arrival at destination G.6.d. (Ref.BELGIUM MAP Sheet 28 N.W.) the Battalion will proceed into Rest Billets in Camp "C".

4. Officers' Kits. Mess Boxes. M.O's Stores, Camp kettles etc, must be down at Battn. H.Q. at 21.00 sharp.

5. All camp kettles, periscopes, and any other articles belonging to Companies will be retainable. All other trench stores etc., will be handed over to relieving unit, and a receipt obtained

6. All bombs and grenades in possession if Companies will be handed over by Companies.

7. One guide per Coy. and one for Headquarters will be at Prison in YPRES at 20.00 to guide relieving Companies. These guides report to Battn. H.Q. at 18.00.

(Signed) C. J. LENDRUM, MAJOR.

1st Battn. The Royal Inniskilling Fusiliers.

One Copy to each Coy.

Issued at 10 a.m.

9/8/16.

SECRET.

1st Battn. The Royal Inniskilling Fusiliers

-:-:-:-:-:-:-:-:-:-:-:-:-

OPERATION ORDER No.6. Copy No...

by

MAJOR J. HARDRESS-LLOYD

COMMANDING 1ST BATTALION THE ROYAL INNISKILLING FUSILIERS.

Reference Map
Belgium. Sheet
28 N.W.1.20,000

BRANDHOEK,
Camp "C".
19/8/16.

1. The Battalion will move into Brigade Reserve in YPRES tonight relieving the 1st King's Own Scottish Borderers. Companies will move into Billets as last time i.e.,

"A"Company	In Town	"B"Company	In Prison
"C" "	In Magazine	"D" "	In Switch Road. (Canal Bank)

2. Entraining place G.6.d.Time 9.45 p.m.

3. Parade 8 p.m. March off 8.15 p.m.

4. One representative from each Company (C.Q.M.Sgt) and one from Headquarter Company will proceed as an advance party leaving here at 5.30 p.m.

5. Officers' trench kits, M.O's Stores and Mess Boxes must be stacked outside Orderly Room at 7.p.m.

6. Guides will meet Companies at place of detrainment.

7. Lewis Gunners and Bombers will parade with their Companies.

8. Th Signalling Officer will arrange to send with the advance party 2 signallers and telephones to relieve the 1st King's Own Scottish Borderers.

Issued at 10.30. (Signed) C. J. LENDRUM. MAJOR,

1st Battn, The Royal Inniskilling Fusiliers.

Copy No.1. = Office.
2 = O.C."A"Coy.
3 = O.C."B" "
4 = O.C."C" "
5 = O.C."D" "
6 = Transport Officer
7 = Officers' Mess.

SECRET

OPERATION ORDER No.6.
BY
MAJOR J. HARDRESS-LLOYD.
COMMANDING
IST BATTALION THE ROYAL INNISKILLING FUSILIERS.

Reference Maps. YPRES Aug.29th 1916.
Belgium Sheet 28 N.W.1.20000
Trench Map 1. 10000.

1 The Battalion will relieve the 1st K.O.S.B's in the right sub-sector tonight, the 1st Company leaving here at 20.00. Companies will proceed by ½ Companies in the following order. at 5 minutes interval between Companies:-

"C"Coy. "D"Coy. "B"Coy. "A"Coy.

"C"Coy to relieve 1 Coy. of 1st K.O.S.B's in CONGREVE WALK

"D" " " 1 " " " in Right Sub-Sector.

"B" " " 1 " " " in Left Sub-Sector.

"A" " " 1 " " " in X Line.

2. Route as on the 6 instant.

3. Lewis Gunners will proceed with their Companies. Battn.Bombers will parade under Bombing Officer.

4. Signallers will proceed in advance and take over all telephone communications.

5. Companies to report to Battn. H.Q., by runner when relief is completed.

6. All trench stores etc will be taken over by Companies and receipts given. A copy of same to be sent to Orderly Room.

7. The Brigade Guard will be relieved by guards from 1st K.O.S.B's during the course of the afternoon.

8. Officers' kits, Mess Boxes etc.,M.O's Stores and Lewis Guns ammunition must be packed and ready by 21.00 at the Prison. Baggage Guard to accompany officers' kits etc.Officers' Mess
9. Sgt. and 2 Officers' servants per Coy.

9. Companies are responsible that their billets are left scrupulously clean and all fires and lights extinguished.

10. The strictest silence must be observed on the march.

11. In order to Keep the 5 minutes interval Coy Commanders on moving off will let the next Coy.know.

12. Distribution of hand carts is :- 2 for cooks stores and 1 per Coy.

(Signed) J. C. LUDLOW Lieut.for MAJOR
Commanding 1st Battn. The Royal Inniskilling Fusiliers.

The following is published forninformation of all.
<u>SCALE OF WORK</u> in future will be as follows. One man if four hours is expected to do
1. Fill 30 Sand-bags.or 2. Excavate 30 cubic feet, or 3. Erect 4 yards rapid wiring. (by day one third more should be done)
These tasks are less that ½ amount laid down by Field Engineering Manual.

29th Division.

87th Infantry Brâgade

1st BATTALION

ROYAL INNISKILLING FUSILIERS

SEPTEMBER 1916

Battalion Operation Orders attached.

Army Form C. 2118.

Instructions regarding War Diaries and Intelligence Summaries are contained in F. S. Regs., Part II. and the Staff Manual respectively. Title Pages will be prepared in manuscript.

WAR DIARY
or
INTELLIGENCE SUMMARY
(Erase heading not required.)

September /16
No 1
1/R. Inniskilling Fus.

Place	Date	Hour	Summary of Events and Information	Remarks and references to Appendices
FIRING LINE	1st		Work in trenches. Repairing parapet, wiring etc. Situation normal. Casualties: wounded 1. Gas attack postponed on account of unfavourable wind –	C.H.
— " —	2nd		Work same as previous day – Situation normal. Strength 25 officers. 486 other ranks.	C.H.
— " —	3rd		Work same as previous day – Situation normal. Casualties – nil –	C.H.
— " —	4th		— do — Gas alarm 2300 turned out to be false. Situation normal.	C.H.
— " —	5th		— do — Gas attack postponed owing to unfavourable wind –	C.H.
— " —	6th		— do — Situation normal.	C.H.
— " —	7th		— do — "C" Coy relieved "B" in firing line. Situation normal	C.H.
— " —	8th		— do — Situation normal. 1 officer & 18 o. ranks joined from Base	C.H.
— " —	9th		Battalion relieved in right sub sector by 2/Royal Fusiliers – Relief complete 22-30. On completion of relief the Bn moved into "C" Camp at BRANDHOEK – Strength 25 officers. 495 other ranks.	C.H.
BRANDHOEK "C" Camp	10th		Bn in Rest Camp – Church parades. Cleaning camp etc.	C.H.
— " —	11th		— do — Parades as per training programme; Training of specialists officers classes etc.	C.H.
— " —	12th		Bn in Rest Camp – Work same as previous day. Bathing parade.	C.H.
— " —	13th		— do — — do — 2 officers joined from Base	C.H.
— " —	14th		— do — — do — 2 officers joined from Base	C.H.
— " —	15th		— do — — do —	
— " —	16th		— do — — do — 1 officer joined from Base. Strength 29 officers. 518 other ranks.	C.H.

Army Form C. 2118.

WAR DIARY
or
INTELLIGENCE SUMMARY

(Erase heading not required.)

Instructions regarding War Diaries and Intelligence Summaries are contained in F. S. Regs., Part II. and the Staff Manual respectively. Title Pages will be prepared in manuscript.

September /16
No 2

1/R. Inniskilling Fus.

Place	Date	Hour	Summary of Events and Information	Remarks and references to Appendices
BRANDHOEK "C" Camp	17th		Battalion in Rest Camp – moved up in the evening to ELVERDINGHE and took over defences from details of the 4th Division. "A" Coy in L.8 "B" Coy ~~L.6~~ L.2. "C" Coy L.4. "D" Coy & H.Q. Coy at CHATEAU – Relief complete about 22.30 – Draft of 6 ~~Other~~ ranks arrived from Base –	[illegible]
ELVERDINGHE	18th		Worked on defences, completing new dug-outs etc – Situation normal.	[illegible]
"	19th		Work same as previous day – Battalion relieved in the evening by the NEWFOUNDLAND REGT. and proceeded to ~~Divisional~~ Brigade Reserve in YPRES – "A" Coy in Town. "B" Coy & H.Q. Coy in the PRISON – "C" Coy in MAGASIN – "D" Coy SWITCH CANAL BANK.	[illegible]
YPRES	20th		Bn in Brig: Reserve. Supplied working party for MONMOUTH TRENCH and at night a party of 160 men to carry empty gas cylinders from front line –	[illegible]
"	21st		Bn in Brig. Reserve. Supplied working party for MONMOUTH TRENCH – Parades under Coy arrangements	[illegible]
"	22nd		Bn in Brigade Reserve — do — do —	[illegible]
"	23rd		Bn in Brigade Reserve — do — Draft: 37 other ranks arrived. Strength – 29 officers. 543 other ranks –	[illegible]
"	24th		Bn in Brigade Reserve. Same work as previous day – Relieved 1/KOSB in firing line, right sub-sector, relief complete 2200. "A" & "C" Coy in front line – "B" Coy in X line. "D" Coy in CONGREVE WALK. Situation normal – Casualties – nil –	[illegible]
FIRING LINE	25th		Worked on repair of trenches, wiring, draining etc – Situation normal –	[illegible]
"	26th		Same work as previous day – Sent out patrol from "C" Coy. nothing to report –	[illegible]
"	27th		— do — Situation normal	[illegible]

2449 Wt. W14957/M90 750,000 1/16 J.B.C. & A. Forms/C.2118/12.

Army Form C. 2118.

Instructions regarding War Diaries and Intelligence Summaries are contained in F. S. Regs., Part II. and the Staff Manual respectively. Title Pages will be prepared in manuscript.

WAR DIARY
or
INTELLIGENCE SUMMARY

(Erase heading not required.) 1/R. Inniskilling Fus.

September /16

No 3.

Place	Date	Hour	Summary of Events and Information	Remarks and references to Appendices
FIRING LINE	28th		Same work as previous day. Sent out Patrols. Casualties Killed - 1 -	C.J.R.?
— " —	29th		——— do ———. Casualties Killed 1 Wounded 4. 12 other Ranks arrived from Base - Relieved by 1/R.I.R.? & proceeded to Brigade Reserve in YPRES. Companies taking over their old Billets -	C.J.R.?
YPRES	30th		Bn in Brigade Reserve. Supplied working party to R.E. at BRIDGE? - Strength 30 officers. 542 other Ranks.	C.J.R.?

C. J. [illegible] Major
1/R. Inniskilling Fus.

2449 Wt. W14957/M90 750,000 1/16 J.B.C. & A. Forms/C.2118/12.

ORDERS FOR RELIEF
B Y

MAJOR J. HARDRESS-LLOYD
COMMANDING
IST BATTALION THE ROYAL INNISKILLING FUSILIERS.

In-the-Field,
8th Sept. 1916

----

1. The Battalion will be relieved tomorrow night the 9th inst., by the 2nd Royal Fusiliers about 21.50.

2. Companies will report by runner to Battalion Headquarters on completion of relief, and will march independently to the entraining point at the ASYLUM W. Corner of YPRES.

3. On arrival at destination G.b.d. (Reference Map BELGIUM Sheet 28 N.W.) the Battalion will proceed into Rest Billets in CAMP "C".

4. All Officers kits, Mess Boxes, Medical Officers Stores, Camp kettles etc.,etc., must be down at the Battalion Dump at 20.50 sharp.

5. All camp kettles, periscopes and any other articles belonging to Companies will be retained. All other trench stores etc., will be handed over to relieving unit and a receipt obtained.

6. All bombs and grenades in possession of Companies will be handed over by Companies.

7. One guide per Company and one for Headquarters will be at the Battalion Headquarters at 19.30 to guide relieving Coys. These guides will report at Battalion Headquarters at 18.00.

8. All water-tins surplus to what was taken over will be sent to the Dump by the time notified in para 4.

(Signed) J. C. LUDLOW. Lieut.& Adjutant,

1st Battalion The Royal Inniskilling Fusiliers.

OPERATION ORDERS
BY
MAJOR J. HARDRESS--LLOYD
COMMANDING
1ST BATTALION THE ROYAL INNISKILLING FUSILIERS.
September 19th, 1916

Reference Maps.
Belgium Sheet 28 N.W.(Trench Maps).
Belgium Sheet 28.

1. The Battalion will be relieved tonight 19th instant by the NEWFOUNDLAND REGIMENT and will proceed into Brigade Reserve at YPRES, on relief of the 1st K. O. S. B's.

2. All Companies will go into the same billets as on the previous occasion that the Battalion was in Brigade Reserve.

3. Advance parties under Company arrangements, of the C.Q.M.S. and 1 man per Company will proceed to YPRES during the afternoon to take over the billets etc.

4. The Signallers will proceed in advance and take over all telephonic communications.

5. All officers' kits, mens' blankets, Mess Boxes etc, to be ready by 6 p.m. and dumped by Companies as under:-

   "A" and "C" at their Company Headquarters.
   "B"Company at the point on the road to which the Company rations were brought during the last two nights.
   "D" Company at Battn. Headquarters and to be kept carefully separate from H.Qrs kits.

6. The Brigade Guard at YPRES, consisting of 1 Sergt. 1 Lce/Cpl and 12 men and mounting at 6.30 p.m. will be found by "C"Company.

7. On completion of relief "A" and "C"Companies will march straight to their billets at YPRES, and "B" and "D"Coys will march to YPRES via BRIELEN.

8. Lewis Gunners and Bombers will proceed with their Coys.

9. Companies will report to Battn. Headquarters by runner when the relief at YPRES is completed.

(Signed) J. C. LUDLOW Lieut and Adjutant,

1st Battalion The Royal Inniskilling Fusiliers.

OPERATION ORDER NO.6.
BY
MAJOR J.HARDRESS-LLOYD
COMMANDING
1ST BATTALION THE ROYAL INNISKILLING FUSILIERS.

YPRES.
Sept.24th,1916.

Ref.Maps.
Belgium Sheet 28 N.W.120000
Trench Maps 1:10000.

1. The Battalion will relieve the 1st K.O.S.B's in the right sub-sector tonight, the 1st Company leaving YPRES at 1915. Companies will proceed by half Companies in the following order, at 5 minutes interval between Companies:-

"D"Coy, "A" Coy, "C"Coy, "B"Coy.

"D"Coy to relieve 1 Coy 1st K.O.S.B's in CONGREVE WALK.
"A" " " " 1 Coy " " " Right Sub-sector.
"C" " " " 1 Coy " " " Left " "
"B" " " " 1 Coy " " " X Line.

2. Route as on August 29th 1916.

3. Battalion Lewis Gunners will parade with their Companies. Battalion Bombers will parade with the Bombing Officer.

4. An advance party of 1 officer, the Coy.Q.M.Sgts and two men will parade at the PRISON at 1700. Signallers will proceed with this party.

5. Companies to report to Battalion Headquarters by runner when relief is completed.

6. All trench stores etc will be taken over by Companies and a receipt given. A copy of same to be sent to Orderly Room.

7. Brigade Guard will be relieved by guard of the 1st K.O.S.B's.

8. Officers trench kits, Mess Boxes etc, must be packed and ready at the Prison by 1900. Baggage party to accompany these. Officers Mess Sergt. and one officers servant per Coy.

9. All officer valises will be dumped at the PRISON by 1900 and kept carefully apart from the trench kits etc. These will be taken back by the Transport. A Baggage party of 1 man per Company to remain with these till they are put on to the Transport. They will then rejoin their Companies.

(Signed) J. C. LUDLOW LIEUT. & ADJUTANT for
MAJOR,
Commanding 1st Battalion TheRoyal Inniskilling Fusiliers

OPERATION ORDERS
by
MAJOR J. HARDRESS-LLOYD
COMMANDING
IST BATTALION THE ROYAL INNISKILLING FUSILIERS.

In-the-Field,
Sept. 29th, 1916

1. The Battalion will be relieved tonight by the 1st K. O. S. B's and will go back into Divisional Reserve in YPRES.

2. On completion of relief Companies will march straight to their billets in YPRES.

3. All trench stores will be handed over to the relieving companies and a receipt obtained for the same.

4. On completion of relief Companies will report to Battalion Hd.Qrs.

5. An advance party from each company consisting of the C.Q.M.Sgts and four men per company will proceed independently to YPRES and take over the Company billets. Company Cooks, Officers servants etc, will be included in these advance parties.

6. All officers' trench kits etc, to be at the Dump by 1900. A corporal of "D"Company has been detailed to look after the baggage.

7. A guard already detailed, will parade at Battalion Hd.Qrs at 1800 and march to YPRES in relief of the Brigade Guard at present furnished by the 1st K. O. S. B's.

(Signed) J. C. LUDLOW LIEUT. & ADJUTANT,

IST BATTALION THE ROYAL INNISKILLING FUSILIERS.

29th Division.

87th Infantry Brigade.

1st BATTALION

ROYAL INNISKILLING FUSILIERS

OCTOBER 1 9 1 6

Operation Orders etc attached.

Confidential X. 18

87/29

Vol 8

War Diary

1st Royal Inniskilling Fusiliers

1st October to 31st October 1916

Volume XX

Instructions regarding War Diaries and Intelligence Summaries are contained in F. S. Regs., Part II. and the Staff Manual respectively. Title Pages will be prepared in manuscript.

WAR DIARY
or
INTELLIGENCE SUMMARY

(Erase heading not required.) 1/In. Inniskilling Fus.

Army Form C. 2118.

October /16
No. 1

Place	Date	Hour	Summary of Events and Information	Remarks and references to Appendices
YPRES	1st		Battalion in Brigade reserve. Supplied working parties for work in front line. Parades under Company arrangements.	C.R.
— " —	2nd		Bn in Brigade reserve. Same work as previous day. 29 other ranks arrived from Base & were taken on the strength.	C.R.
— " —	3rd		Relieved by ~~4/King's Own Lancaster Regt.~~ 5th SOUTH LANCASHIRE REGT. ~~166th Brigade~~, and proceeded to "K" rest camp near POPERINGHE.	C.R.
POPERINGHE "K" Camp	4th		Battalion in rest camp. General cleaning up. Parades under Company arrangements. 2 officers struck off the strength invalided.	C.R.
— " —	5th		Battalion in rest camp. Parades under Company arrangements —	C.R.
— " —	6th		do —— —— do ——	
— " —	7th		The Battalion marched to HOPOUTRE and entrained at 10.44 am for an unknown destination. Arrived LONGEAU about 2 Am. and marched into Billets at ALLONVILLE. Strength 28 officers & 570 other ranks.	C.R.
ALLONVILLE	8th		Battalion in Billets. Parades under Company arrangements, training of Specialists &c. 1 officer & 6 other ranks joined from Base.	C.R.
— " —	9th		Battalion in Billets. Training of Specialists &c. Battalion parade. 22 other ranks joined from Base.	C.R.
— " —	10th		Battalion marched to BUIRE via QUERRIEU (about 11 miles) and took over Billets in that village.	C.R.

2449 Wt. W14957/M90 750,000 1/16 J.B.C. & A. Forms/C.2118/12.

Army Form C. ?118.

October /16

No 2

Instructions regarding War Diaries and Intelligence Summaries are contained in F. S. Regs., Part II. and the Staff Manual respectively. Title Pages will be prepared in manuscript.

WAR DIARY
or
INTELLIGENCE SUMMARY

(Erase heading not required.) 1/R. Inniskilling Fus.

Place	Date	Hour	Summary of Events and Information	Remarks and references to Appendices
BUIRE	11th		Battalion in Billets – Training of Specialists & Company parades.	[illegible]
"	12th		——— do ——— – ——— do ——— Attack practice behind Bazentin –	[illegible]
"	13th		Battalion marched to FRICOURT Camp (about 6 miles) –	[illegible]
FRICOURT CAMP	14th		Company parades, attack practice under Battalion arrangements. Strength 29 officers & 599 other ranks.	[illegible]
"	15th		Bathing parades & church parades – 1 officer struck off the strength evacuated –	[illegible]
"	16th		Attack practice under Battalion arrangements.	
"	17th		Battalion employed on road-making fatigues	
"	18th		——— do ——— do ———	
"	19th		Battalion marched to BERNAFAY Camp, where it rested for two hours, and thence to the trenches at GUEUDECOURT, relieving the 4th Worcester Rgt. One company in HILT TRENCH	[illegible]
GUEUDECOURT	20th		Draft of 24 other ranks arrived: Bn supplied parties for carrying fatigues.	[illegible]
"	21st		Relieved by 1st Border Rgt: Battalion went into reserve in SWITCH TRENCH. Killed – 2 other Ranks; Wounded 2 officers and 7 other Ranks. Strength 28 officers 629 O.R.	[illegible]
	22nd		Wounded – 12 other Ranks; Killed 1 officer and one other ranks.	[illegible]
	23rd		Bn supplied parties for carrying fatigues. Wounded 1 officer and 1 other ranks; ~~Killed~~ ~~16 other ranks missing~~.	[illegible]

2449 Wt. W14957/M90 750,000 1/16 J.B.C. & A. Forms/C.2118/12.

Army Form C. 2118.

Instructions regarding War Diaries and Intelligence Summaries are contained in F. S. Regs., Part II. and the Staff Manual respectively. Title Pages will be prepared in manuscript.

WAR DIARY
or
INTELLIGENCE SUMMARY
(Erase heading not required.)

1/Bn. R. Inniskilling Fus — October/16 — Lo 8

Place	Date	Hour	Summary of Events and Information	Remarks and references to Appendices
SWITCH TRENCH	24th		Battalion supplied parties for carrying fatigues.	JHK
— " —	25th		One officer arrived: Wounded 1 other Rank. Battalion marched to trenches and relieved 1st Border Rgt. One company in GREASE TRENCH.	JHK
GUEULECOURT	26th		1 officer joined. Wounded 3 other Ranks. Strong point begun on left of GREASE TRENCH. Battalion supplied carrying parties.	JHK
— " —	27th		Strong point continued: Battalion at work deepening communication trenches. Wounded 6 other Ranks.	JHK
— " —	28th		Strength 23 officers, 562 other Ranks. Wounded – 2 officers. Battalion relieved by Newfoundland Rgt and went into support in BULL and PIONEER TRENCHES.	JHK
BULL TRENCH	29th		Draft of nine other Ranks arrived. Killed 1 other rank, wounded 2 other Ranks. Battalion was relieved by 5th Bn. A.I.F. and marched to POMIER'S Camp	JHK
	30th		Battalion marched to Australian Camp at FRICOURT.	JHK
FRICOURT	31st		Bathing parades at VIVIER MILL	JHK

Hardress Lloyd Lt-Col.
Comdg: 1st Bn: R. Inniskilling Fus.

2449 Wt. W14957/M90 750,000 1/16 J.B.C. & A. Forms/C.2118/12.

OPERATION ORDER
BY
LIEUT-COLONEL J.HARDRESS-LLOYD
COMMANDING
IST BATTALION THE ROYAL INNISKILLING FUSILIERS.

BUIRE

October 10th,1916.

1. The Battalion will proceed by route march today to FRICOURT CAMP F.8.c. Distance about 6 miles.
2. Parade at 12.50 p.m.
3. March off at 1.5.p.m.
4. The same intervals between Companies and the same rules concerning halts will be observed as on the 10th instant.
5. Special attention must be paid by all Company Officers and N.C.O's to march discipline.
6. Officers' valises, men's Blankets, etc., must be dumped at the MAIRE (Headquarter Mess) by 10 a.m.

(Signed) J. C. LUDLOW, LIEUT.
A/Adjut. 1st Battn.The Rl.Inniskilling Fusrs.

Issued at 9 a.m.

WD

Operation Order [illegible] No. 2

by

Lieut-Colonel J. [illegible]

Reference Map

AMIENS [illegible]

Allonville

10th October 1918

I. The Battalion will march today to [illegible] (about 11 miles) via QUERRIEU, [illegible] D 20 [illegible] and Crossroads D 27 [illegible]

II. Starting point opposite Billet No 51, at 14.00.

III. Companies will fall in outside their billets at 13.45 & be ready to march off at 14.00

IV. A distance of 200 yards will be kept between Companies and 200 yards between the Transport and the Battalion

V. A 10 minutes halt will be observed each hour at 10 minutes before the hour

VI. Strict attention will be paid to march discipline especially through QUERRIEU.

VII. The rear Company will detail an officer & [illegible] to march in rear of the Battalion to pick up stragglers [illegible] will be reported by the [illegible]

VIII. Officers [illegible] [illegible] [illegible]

IX. All messages to [illegible] to the head of the [illegible]

[illegible]

[illegible]

Copy [illegible] 2 = War Diary
3 = [illegible]
4 = [illegible]
5 = [illegible]
6 = [illegible]
7 = [illegible]
8 = Transport Officer

SECRET.

The Officer Commanding,
2nd South Wales Borderers.
1st K.O.S.Borderers.
1st Rl.Innis'.Fus.
1st Border Regt.
87th M.G.Coy.
87th T.M.B.
1/1st W.Riding Fld.Co.R.E.
87th Field Ambulance.

---

1. Reference my letter No.B.203.of even date. There will be no working parties tomorrow.

2. Reconnoitring Parties will go forward as arranged and rejoin the Brigade at BERNAFAY CAMP.

3. The Brigade will march to Camp at BERNAFAY WOOD tomorrow morning probably about 10.a.m.

4. Advance Billeting Parties with bicycles will report to Brigade Headquarters at 8.a.m.

5. The Officers Commanding 1/1st W.Riding Fld.Co.R.E.and 87th Field Ambulance will receive their orders direct from Division.

6. Further orders will be issued shortly.

7. PLEASE ACKNOWLEDGE.

October 18th.1916.

Broadman
CAPTAIN.
BRIGADE MAJOR.87th INFANTRY BRIGADE.

Officer Commanding,

2nd South Wales Borderers.
1st King's Own Scottish Borderers.
1st Royal Inniskilling Fusiliers.
1st Border Regiment.
87th Machine Gun Company.

Blankets and packs will be carried by the men on the line of march to-morrow.

O.C. 2/S.W.B. will send the extra S.A.A. wagon at present with that battalion to Brigade Headquarters at [illegible] to-morrow.

O.C. 1/K.O.S.B. will hand over the extra S.A.A. wagon to O.C. 87th Trench Mortar Battery at [illegible] to-morrow.

O.C. 1/R. Innis Fus. will hand over the extra S.A.A. wagon to O.C. 87th Trench Mortar Battery at [illegible] to-morrow.

Transport lines will be taken over from [illegible] Brigade.

One guide in addition to those already detailed in B.204 of even date, will report at Brigade Headquarters, with Bicycles at [illegible] to-morrow to proceed in advance to take over these lines.

[illegible] October [illegible]. [illegible]

Urgent

R. S. M. Framingham

37th I[illegible] BDE.
No. B218
Date 21.10.16

M.S.[illegible].17763.
A.M.S.Fourth Army No.373/AMS.
XV Corps No.A"G./3118.

FOURTH ARMY.

1. A limited number of Lieutenants and Second Lieutenants are
required for Field Companies and Army Troops Companies Royal
Engineers. The names of candidates should be submitted to the
Military Secretary, General Headquarters, not later than [illegible]th
October 1916.

2. Applicants should either be (a) Territorial Lieutenants or 2nd
Lieutenants, (b) Temporarily Commissioned officers, or (c) Non
commissioned officers or men of the Territorial Force and those
Serving on engagements for the period of the War only.
Those selected will be required to attend a course of instruction
at home, after which, if they attain the requisite standard, they
will be (a) seconded in the case of Territorial officers, (b)
transferred in the case of temporary commissioned officers (but no
officer will be granted a higher rank than that of Lieutenant
on transfer), granted a temporary commission in the Royal
Engineers in the case of other ranks.
3. Only a few officers and other ranks who are very specially
qualified by their civil training or occupation, as well as being
suitable in other respects, should be recommended.
Not more than 30 candidates will be selected from France to attend
the first course., but other suitable candidates will be noted
for later courses to be held at intervals of about one month.

4. The attached form should be completed and should accompany the
applications in each case; and in the case of candidates from
the ranks Form M.T.393 should be rendered in addition.

(Sd). W.E.Peyton.Major General,
Military Secretary to C.in C.

General Headquarters,
13th October 1916.

=======================

29th Division.

==============

For necessary action. Applications should reach
this office not later than the 24th inst. [illegible] M.S.[illegible]
above should be quoted, when submitting.

(Sd) [illegible] Major,
D.A.A. & Q.M.G. [illegible]

17th October 1916.

[illegible]th Div.[illegible].

The Officer Commanding,
[illegible]

Reference [illegible] correspondence, will you
please submit the names of any officers or other ranks desirous
of applying for one of these appointments, to reach this office
by 2100 on the 22nd inst.
In the case of men from the ranks it will be noted
that form M.T.393 should be rendered in addition to the accompanying
manuscript form.

[illegible signature] CAPTAIN.
STAFF CAPTAIN, 37TH INFANTRY BRIGADE.

Oct. 20th 1916.

Rank, Initials, Name and Unit.______________________________
____
Nature and date of commission ________________.

1. Age _________.

2. Education.:-
Schools, Colleges, Universities etc, specifying time spent at each.

____

____

3. Degrees or Diplomas:-_______________________________________

4. Civil Engineering experience. Firms with which employed. Knowledge of general engineering. Organisation of labour. Building and Construction work. Roadwork. Bridge Work. Machinery and Workshops. Electricity, Survey etc.

- -

- -

- -

5. Military Training.____

____

6. Knowledge of Military Engineering __________________________

____

____

SECRET

Officer Commanding
1st Royal Inniskilling Fusiliers.

1. The following alteration is made in the relief of the 1st Royal Inniskilling Fusiliers by the Newfoundland Regiment. The Officer Commanding Newfoundland Regt. will take over from the 1st Royal Inniskilling Fusrs as follows:-

1 Company (with 4 Lewis Guns) will take over from the present Right of the 1st Royal Inniskilling Fusiliers in GREASE TRENCH to the extreme Left of GREASE TRENCH.
½ Company (with 2 Lewis Guns) will take over HILT TRENCH and the bombing post at N.20.d.4½.5.
1 Company will go into support in SUNKEM ROAD Trench finding the post of 2 Lewis Guns, 2 bombing squads and 1 section in the Gun-pits.
½ Company in Battalion Reserve in GIRD TRENCH.

2. PLEASE ACKNOWLEDGE.

27th October 1916. (Signed) BRODIE MAIR CAPTAIN,

BRIGADE MAJOR 87TH INFANTRY BRIGADE.

Operation Order (Copy. No. 3)
by
Major C. J. Lendrum
1st Batt. The Royal Inniskilling Fusiliers

"K" Camp.
Oct. 6th 1916

1. The Battalion will leave "K" Camp tomorrow 7th inst. and proceed by train to a "Southern" Destination.
2. Reveille will be sounded at 4.30 a.m. tomorrow
3. The Battalion will parade at "K" Camp tomorrow morning at 7 a.m. with the exception of "C" Coy which will proceed with the transport, and find all loading and unloading parties. The O.C. "C" Company will be notified of the hour of parade by the Transport Officer.
4. Rations will be issued to all Companies on arrival at "HOPOUTRE" the entraining centre.
5. The entrainment of all Coys must be completed by 10.14 a.m.
6. O.C. Companies are responsible for taking the necessary steps to ensure that no men leave the train, during any stops that may occur on the journey.
7. All officers' valises, kits, mess boxes Etc. must be dumped outside the Officers' Mess, "K" Camp, by 5 am sharp tomorrow morning.
8. All Lewis Gunners and Bombers will parade with their Coys.
9. All members of the Hd. Qr. Coy will join their Coys at the entraining point.
10. All huts and tents must be left clean and tidy when the Battalion marches out.
11. An issue of tea will be made before the hour of parade tomorrow morning.

J. C. Ludlow. Lieut. & Adjutant
1st Batt. The Royal Inniskilling Fusiliers

Copies 1 & 2 = War Diary
3 = Office
4 = O.C. A Coy
5 = " B "
6 = " C "
7 = " D "
8 = Transport Officer

Copy 9 = Q.M.

Operation Order. (Copy No. 2)

by

Major C. J. Lendrum

1st Batt. The Royal Inniskilling Fusiliers

"K" Camp.

Oct. 6th 1916

1. The Battalion will leave "K" Camp tomorrow 7th inst. and proceed by train to a Southern Destination.
2. Reveille will be sounded at 4.30 a.m. tomorrow.
3. The Battalion will parade at "K" Camp tomorrow morning at 7 a.m. with the exception of "C" Coy, which will proceed with the transport, and find all loading and unloading parties. The O.C. "C" Company will be notified of the hour of parade by the Transport Officer.
4. Rations will be issued to all Companies on arrival at "HOPOUTRE" the entraining centre.
5. The entrainment of all coys must be completed by 10.[illegible] a.m.
6. O.C. Companies are responsible for taking the necessary steps to ensure that no men leave the train, during any stops that may occur on the journey.
7. All officers' valises, kits, mess boxes etc. must be dumped outside the Officers' Mess, "K" Camp, by 5 am sharp tomorrow morning.
8. All Lewis Gunners and Bombers will parade with their Coys.
9. All members of the Hd. Qr. Coy will join their Coys at the entraining point.
10. All huts and tents must be left clean and tidy when the Battalion marches out.
11. An issue of tea will be made before the hour of parade tomorrow morning.

J. C. Ludlow. Lieut. & Adjutant

1st Batt. The Royal Inniskilling Fus.

Copies 1+2 = War Diary
3 = Office
4 = O.C. A. Coy
5 = " B "
6 = " C "
7 = " D "
8 = Transport Officer

Copy 9 = Qr. Mr.

29th Division.

87th Infqntry Brigade.

1st BATTALION

ROYAL INNISKILLING FUSILIERS

NOVEMBER 1 9 1 6

Battalion Operation Orders attached.

Army Form C. 2118.

WAR DIARY
or
INTELLIGENCE SUMMARY

(Erase heading not required.)

Instructions regarding War Diaries and Intelligence Summaries are contained in F. S. Regs., Part II. and the Staff Manual respectively. Title Pages will be prepared in manuscript.

November 1916 Vol.

1 Royal Inniskilling Fusiliers

Place	Date	Hour	Summary of Events and Information	Remarks and references to Appendices
FRICOURT CAMP	1st		1 Officer arrived.	[illegible]
	2nd		5 Officers & 290 other ranks joined. Transport moved to CORBIE. Draft inspected by C.O. Major [illegible] 1st Border Regt took over command of battalion in the absence of Lt Col Hardress Lloyd.	[illegible]
	3rd		Battalion marched to ALBERT and entrained for BETTENCOURT. Detrained at AIRAINES & marched to billets at BETTENCOURT. 1 Officer & 61 other ranks arrived.	[illegible]
BETTENCOURT	4th		Major R. R. Willis V.C. 2 Lancashire Fusiliers, arrived & took over command of battalion during absence on leave of Lt Col. Hardress Lloyd. Strength 31 Officers 841 O.Rs.	[illegible]
	5th		Church parade.	[illegible]
	6th		Battalion parade under R.S.M. Specialist parades under officers.	[illegible]
	7th		[illegible] parade under R.S.M.	[illegible]
	8th		[illegible] parade under R.S.M. Football A v C in the afternoon.	[illegible]
	9th		[illegible] Company parades. Route march under company arrangements.	[illegible]
	10th		[illegible]	[illegible]
	11th		[illegible] company parades.	[illegible]
	12th		[illegible]	[illegible]
	13th		[illegible] BETTENCOURT to BUIRE by motor lorries and from BUIRE to CITADEL CAMP [illegible]	[illegible]
CITADEL CAMP	[illegible]		[illegible] 2nd R.S.F. Regt [illegible]	[illegible]
CARNOY	[illegible]		[illegible] Battalion moved to GUILLEMONT.	[illegible]
	[illegible]		[illegible]	[illegible]

2449 Wt. W14957/M90 750,000 1/16 J.B.C. & A. Forms/C.2118/12.

Army Form C. 2118.

Instructions regarding War Diaries and Intelligence Summaries are contained in F. S. Regs., Part II. and the Staff Manual respectively. Title Pages will be prepared in manuscript.

WAR DIARY
or
INTELLIGENCE SUMMARY
(Erase heading not required.)

Nov

Place	Date	Hour	Summary of Events and Information	Remarks and references to Appendices
GUILLEMONT	17th		Battalion in Support trenches, improving dugouts & draining area	[illegible]
	18th		Battalion in Support same work as previous day	[illegible]
	19th		Battalion in Support trenches, working parties	[illegible]
	20th		Battalion in Front line, relieved [illegible] on Brigade front	[illegible]
	21st		Battalion in front line.	[illegible]
	22nd		[illegible]	[illegible]
	23rd		[illegible] marched to CARNOY.	[illegible]
CARNOY	24th		CARNOY [illegible]	[illegible]
	25th		Working parties [illegible] Bn strength 33 officers [illegible] OR	[illegible]
	26th		[illegible] from Base.	[illegible]
	27th		Battalion [illegible]	[illegible]
	28th		Battalion moved to Support line relieving 1st Border Regiment in Ox trench two platoons C Co in SHAMROCK TRENCH	[illegible]
	29th		In Support Line improving Communication trenches	[illegible]
	30th		Still in support furnishing working parties and salvaging stores etc Strength 33 Officers 950 other ranks	[illegible]

30th November 1916

[illegible] Lloyd Lieut-Colonel
Commdg 1st R. Inniskilling Fusiliers

2449 Wt. W14957/M90 750,000 1/16 J.B.C. & A. Forms/C.2118/12.

REALM ORDERS (Copy No. 1)
No. 3

1. REALM will relieve READY on night of 20/21/11/16

2. Detail of Relief

(a) Left Front L. .... "A" Co.
Right " .... "D" "
Support .... "B" "
Reserve .... "C" "

(b) Order of Relief & March:

	Time leaving S. Point
Left Front	4 p.m
Right	4.15 pm
Support	4.30 pm
Reserve	4.45 pm
Hd. Qrs	5 pm.

3. All trench stores will be taken over in front line trenches & handed over in present trenches. Duplicate receipt forms to be prepared beforehand & stores collected in Co. dumps in present trenches.

4. Guides from all Co's will meet incoming Battn (A) at X roads W of Camp at 4 pm. Guides will meet REALM Co's at LESBOEUFS end of Duck Walk.

Starting Point ~~[illegible]~~ level crossing on GINCHY ROAD N.E of Camp

Distance 200^x between Platoons

6/ Two days rations will be carried up.

[illegible]

Capt & Adjt
REALM

Copy No. 1 = War Diary
" " 2 = O.C. Hd Qr Co
" " 3 = " 'A' Co
" " 4 = " 'B' Co
" " 5 = " 'C' Co
" " 6 = " 'D' Co

Copy No. 1

Operation Order No. 1

by

Lt. Colonel [illegible]

Comdg [illegible]

1. [illegible] will be relieved by the [illegible] on the night of the [illegible] & will [illegible] to camp indicated by [illegible]

2. Detail of Reliefs

Left front A Co. [illegible] platoons [illegible]

Right " B " [illegible]

Left Support C " [illegible] 1 [illegible]

Right " 2 platoons B [illegible] 2 [illegible]

Company Commanders will [illegible] [illegible] a [illegible] to [illegible] H.Qrs. when relief [illegible] completed

3. All trench stores [illegible] & waterproof capes will be handed over [illegible] form [illegible] [illegible] overhead. [illegible] will be handed into Orderly Room the following morning.

4. [illegible] from all Companies [illegible] including H.Q. [illegible] battalion.

5. An advance party [illegible] [illegible] [illegible] H.Q. at 8 pm [illegible] the camp [illegible]

6. Coy. Commanders [illegible]

ons all Lewis Gun ammunition, magazines & carriers, obtaining receipts for same.

7. A Distance of 300ˣ was to be kept between platoons.

22/11/16

[illegible]
KEHLA

Copy No 1 = War Diary
2 = H. Q. Co
3 = A Co
4 = B Co
5 = C Co
6 = E Co
7 = D Co

Operation Order
by
Lieut-Col. J. Hardress Lloyd
Commdg 1st Royal Inniskilling Fusiliers

Ref. Map 1/40,000 ALBERT Nov 15th 1916

I, The Battalion will march to CARNOY CAMP at 10.30 A.M this morning, proceeding across country.
The Camp is situated at A. 8. 6

II Companies will parade outside their hutments in full marching order at 10. A.M. and will move off at 10.30 a.m as follows:-
H.Q. Coy. A. B. C. D. at an interval of 200 yds between Coys.
Starting Point Qr. Mr's Stores.

III Transport will move off the same time as the Battalion & will march via MEAULTE, MAMETZ-MONTAUBAN Road.

T O Fraser
[illegible]

29th Division.

87th Infantry Brigade.

1st BATTALION

ROYAL INNISKILLING FUSI:IERS

DECEMBER 1 9 1 6

87/29

Vol 10

+ 20

Confidential

War Diary

of

1st Bn The Royal Inniskilling Fusiliers

From 1/12/16 to 31/12/1916

Volume No 21

Army Form C. 2118.

Instructions regarding War Diaries and Intelligence Summaries are contained in F. S. Regs., Part II. and the Staff Manual respectively. Title Pages will be prepared in manuscript.

WAR DIARY
or
INTELLIGENCE SUMMARY
(Erase heading not required.)

Place	Date	Hour	Summary of Events and Information	Remarks and references to Appendices
OX TRENCH	1st		Battalion was relieved by 1st Lancashire Fusiliers and returned to CARNOY CAMP.	Ref
CARNOY	2nd		Furnished fatigue parties, and improved the drainage of camp.	Ref
	3rd		Sunday. Voluntary Divine services.	Ref
	4th		Battalion proceeded to GUILLEMONT in Brigade Reserve in relief of K.O.S.B.	Ref
GUILLEMONT	5th		Relieved the 15th Middlesex in Brigade Front line. B & C Coys Firing line, A & D Coys Supports ANTELOPE Trench	Ref
	6th		Repairing & improving communication & fire trenches.	Ref
	7th		Same work as previous day. Capt J. B. [illegible], Lt Swindells, Lt Prentice & 23 other ranks wounded – 5 other ranks killed. ~~[illegible] to CARNOY~~	Ref
	8th		Relieved by 1st Border Regiment & proceeded to	Ref
CARNOY	9th		Entrained at PLATEAU Railhead for MERICOURT.	Ref
MERICOURT	10th		Company inspections of clothing & similar work.	Ref
	11th		Battalion marched to CORBIE a distance of about 4 miles & billeted for the night.	Ref
	12th		Entrained for LONGPRE and marched from there to PICQUIGNY distance about 9 miles.	Ref
PICQUIGNY	13th		Day occupied in general clean up, attention to equipment & arms.	Ref
	14th		Battalion parades, training drill etc.	Ref
	15th		Battalion [illegible] parades, training drill etc.	Ref

2449 Wt. W14957/M90 750,000 1/16 J.B.C. & A. Forms/C.2118/12.

Instructions regarding War Diaries and Intelligence Summaries are contained in F. S. Regs., Part II. and the Staff Manual respectively. Title Pages will be prepared in manuscript.

WAR DIARY
or
INTELLIGENCE SUMMARY

(Erase heading not required.)

Army Form C. 2118.

Place	Date	Hour	Summary of Events and Information	Remarks and references to Appendices
PICQUIGNY	25th		Christmas day. Inspection of billets & dinners by C.O.	Ent
	26th		Battalion training, musketry, bombing etc	Ent
	27th		Battalion parade & company training	Ent
	28th		Same as for 27th	Ent
	29th		Same as for 28th	Ent
	30th		Battalion training	
	31st		Battalion training	

1st BATTALION. ROYAL INNISKILLING FUSILIERS.
No. 6
Date 31-12-16

F.R. Willis
Major for Lieut-Colonel
Commanding 1st Bn. The R. Inniskilling Fusrs.

REALM OPERATION ORDERS No.9. 7/12/16.

7th 12 Cancelled

1. REALM will be relieved by RASHER on the night of the 8/9th inst., on completion of relief cos., will move to quarters in the new camp [illegible].
2. An Advance Guard - C.Q.M.S. of "A" "B" "C" and a representative of HQ.Qr.Co. - will report at H. Qrs. at 9.0.a.m. on 8th. inst.
3. Cos., will detail 1 guide per platoon to report at Bn., Hd.Qrs at 8.0.p.m. These guides will not be in marching order.
4. All trench kits, mess stores, and medical stores will be stacked at the ration dump by 1.30.p.m.
5. All Lewis guns magazine carriers, magazines and ammunition will be cleaned and handed over to relieving Unit, receipts being obtained.

(Sd)C.E.Framingham Lieut.& Adjutant.

1st.Royal Inniskilling Fusiliers.

X 21

Vol XI

W/95

War Diary

of

1st Bn, The Royal Inniskilling Fusiliers

From 1st Jany, 1917 To 31st Jany, 1917

Volume I

Instructions regarding War Diaries and Intelligence Summaries are contained in F. S. Regs., Part II. and the Staff Manual respectively. Title Pages will be prepared in manuscript.

WAR DIARY
or
INTELLIGENCE SUMMARY
(Erase heading not required.)

Army Form C. 2118.

(1)

Place	Date	Hour	Summary of Events and Information	Remarks and references to Appendices
PICQUIGNY	Jany 1st		Battalion parade	Let
	2nd		Inspection by G.O.C. 29th Division. Advancing under artillery barrage practice 3 Officers joined	Let
	3rd		Battalion parades.	Let
	4th		Battalion parades Lt Col Hardress Lloyd awarded D.S.O. Capt R.O.G. [illegible] awarded D.S.O. RSM Gregory awarded D.C.M.	Let
	5th		Battalion parades, Ceremonial.	Let
	6th		Battalion parades	Let
	7th		Church parade.	Let
	8th		Inspection by Brigadier. Battalion attack practice. Capt (T. Maj) C.J.W.K. Lendrum 2Lt (T. Capt) W.E. Nicholls, No 8635 CQMS J. Hill mentioned in despatches. Lt Col Bond DSO transferred to heavy branch M.G. Corps. Maj R.R. Willis assumes command.	Let
	9th		Holiday.	Let
	10th		Instruction in Bayonet fighting	Let
	11th		Battalion parades	Let
	12th		Battalion proceeded to HANGEST by march route & entrained for MERICOURT detrained & proceeded by march route to BRESLE. Strength 41 Officers 1011 O.Rs	Let
BRESLE	13th		Companies at disposal of Co Commdrs.	Let
	14th		Battalion marched to CARNOY distance 14 miles – Brigade reserve –	Let
CARNOY	15th		Battalion proceeded to GUILLEMONT. – Brigade support.	Let
GUILLEMONT	16th		Battalion relieved 1st K.O.S.Bs in the firing line	Let
	17th		Battalion occupied firing line	Let
	18th		Relieved by 1st Border Regt & occupied quarters in CARNOY – Brigade reserve.	Let
	19th		Companies at disposal of Co Commdrs.	Let

2449 Wt. W14957/M90 750,000 1/16 J.B.C. & A. Forms/C.2118/12.

Instructions regarding War Diaries and Intelligence Summaries are contained in F. S. Regs., Part II. and the Staff Manual respectively. Title Pages will be prepared in manuscript.

WAR DIARY
or
INTELLIGENCE SUMMARY
(Erase heading not required.)

Army Form C. 2118.

Place	Date	Hour	Summary of Events and Information	Remarks and references to Appendices
CARNOY	Jany 20th		Battalion furnishing parades	[illegible]
	21st		Relieved the 1/Newfoundland Regt in front line	[illegible]
	22nd		Relieved by 1/KOSB and returned to quarters in Nov Camp CARNOY 2/Lt J. DUFF & 2/Lt R. O'CONNELL wounded 1 OR Killed.	[illegible]
	23rd		Interior economy, companies under Company commanders	[illegible]
	[illegible]		Training carried out & training of specialists	[illegible]
	[illegible]		Interior economy	[illegible]
	[illegible]		Relieved the [illegible] in the front line	[illegible]
	[illegible]		Attacked & captured two lines of enemy's trench in conjunction with the [illegible] Border [illegible] on a frontage of about 200 yards. Employed in consolidating position [illegible] them to repel enemy counter attack	[illegible]
	[illegible]		Lieut. [illegible] killed 4 officers wounded & 140 O.Rs.	[illegible]
	[illegible]		Relieved by [illegible] & proceeded to CARNOY CAMP [illegible]	[illegible]
	30th		[illegible] as far as possible	[illegible]
	31st		Relieved [illegible] and proceeded to CARNOY CAMP	

3rd Feby 1917

[illegible] Willis
Lieut. Colonel
Commdg 1 R. [illegible] Fus.

2449 Wt. W14957/M90 750,000 1/16 J.B.C. & A. Forms/C.2118/12.

REALM ADVANCE ORDERS. 20/1/17.

1. <u>REALM</u> will relieve REFORM in the right sector on the 21st instant.

2. Cos. will send in by 12 noon today a return showing their strength, the number of men they wish to leave behind, taking the state of bad boots into consideration.

3. Time of starting about [illegible] a.m. Order of March "C" "B" "D" & "A" Cos.

4. The Bn. will return to [illegible] on the 22nd.

(Sd) G. F. [illegible] Lieut.

Adjut. 1st Royal Inniskilling Fusiliers.

[illegible] ORDERS NO. [illegible]

1. [illegible]

2. [illegible]

3. [illegible]

"[illegible]" [illegible]
"[illegible]" Co. " " " [illegible]
"[illegible]" Co. " " " [illegible]
"[illegible]" Co. " " " [illegible]
"[illegible]" " " " [illegible]

4. [illegible]

[illegible]
[illegible]

5. [illegible]

[illegible]
[illegible]
by [illegible]
[illegible]
[illegible]

6. [illegible]
[illegible]

REALM Order No 4.
22. 1. 17.

---

1. REALM will be relieved by READY to-night.
2. Guides will meet the incoming Bn. at the TANK at 5 P.M. with slips as before. "A" Co will find an N. C. O. i/c of guides.
3. Cos will proceed independently to No. 2 Camp CARNOY; this camp is just beyond the Y.M.C.A. on the left going down.
4. Tea will be ready at GUILLEMONT LEFT CAMP & Pls. will see that each man has a hot drink in passing
5. Lewis Gun Amm. –
Stokes Mortar, less cling bag, Trench Stores –
Will be handed over & receipts taken. These receipts will be sent into the Orderly Room on arrival in camp
6. Reports –
Special reports on NO MANS LAND are required, showing –
(a) Distance of en. line and whether it can be easily distinguished
(b) Landmarks, if any
(c) Total number which can be accommodated pro tem in front line
(d) Position of dumps

(CONTINUED)

REALM – Order No. 4 (continued)

7. Water tins will be brought down by Cos & dumped at the Water Dump

8. Cos will report in code when relief is complete.

9. Pack cobs will be at the Dump at 2 P.M.

C Cunningham
Lieut & Adjt.
REALM.

REPORT on ACTION of 27.1.17 opposite LE TRANSLOY.

Ref. F.S.R. Part II, Para.130.

1. Orders issued and received - Copies attached.

2. Circumstances of every important period of the fight.
   (a) At ZERO it was very dark and it was impossible to take points to march on.
   (b) The barrage started slightly before the synchronised time as received by us.
   (c) Much confusion at the start owing to all four waves starting out at once in the darkness.
   (d) Owing to surprise there was little or no serious opposition from the actual front.
   (e) The whole attack of the right section inclined slightly to the left with the result that the right blocking parties missed their objective, viz., the trenches E. of the road, at T.5.
   (f) The objectives were reached without difficulty and surprise was complete.

3. Notes on the action and special points:-
   (1) Areoplane photos. are not reliable owing to camouflage employed by the enemy.
   (2) Shrapnel barrage is somewhat ineffective owing to the fact that,
      (a) Trenches are not occupied (men being in dug-outs)
      (b) The resisting power of the camouflage is great.
   (3) Our wire was most excellently cut on the right front by Essex R. and the enemy's wire by our artillery.
   (4) An en.field battery was observed about 1000x N.of point A, in the open and not being served by its gunners.
   (5) The 3rd wave, "C" co. distributed along the whole front, did not prove a success as there was lack of controland the men became attached to various waves according to their temperament.
   (6) Some implement such as a bill hook is necessary, in order to pull up the camouflage on trenches which is strongly wired down.
   (7) No fires appear to be used in German trenches but a large no. of solidified fuel tins was found.
   (8) The value of unaimed fire on a flat trajectory was proved, as the Germans have dug no communication trenches owing to the universal lack of fire from our trenches at night except by specialists.

4. Casualties -

Offrs.	W.O's (2nd Cl.)	O.R.	Total
4	2	132	138

Captures - (a) Personnel.

Offrs.	O.R.
6	200 (roughly)

(b) Material.

3 M.G's (two salved and one destroyed)
A Co.Q.M.Store with much material (in Post A)
Much ordinary salvage in Sunken Road (rifles,amm.,bombs & R.E. stores).

5. Gallant and meritorious actions of individuals -
   Sent to Div. direct who will type them and return to Bde. for signature.

[signature]

Lieut.Colonel,

Commanding 1st Battalion,The Royal Inniskilling Fusiliers.

29th January,1917.

Copy No...... REALM ORDER NO.[illegible] [illegible]. 1. 17.

1. REALM will relieve [illegible] on the night [illegible]th/[illegible]th January 1917.

2. ORDER OF RELIEF

Flanking Bombing Parties.
Stokes Gun Detachment.
"A"Co.
"B" "
"C" "
"D" "
1 offr. and [illegible] men specially detailed (4 N.C.O's) will take over and hold Posts 1-4 inclusive.

3. At ZERO on the morning of the [illegible]th REALM will attack the Enemy Trenches in the formation practised previously viz:-

1ST WAVE	2 PL.	"A"CO.	ON RIGHT.
	2 PL.	"B"CO.	ON LEFT.

MOPPING UP PARTIES IN REAR OF 1ST WAVE.

2ND WAVE	2 PL.	"A"CO.	ON RIGHT.
	2 PL.	"B"CO.	ON LEFT.

These two waves and the Mopping Up Parties will capture and consolidate the first system of trenches.

3RD WAVE "C"CO. will pass through the first two waves and will take up an outpost line as shown on the map making [illegible] into a strong point and a second strong point on the track on the right of our front with intermediate points as found necessary. The capture of [illegible] is the most important duty for this Co.

4TH WAVE "D"CO. will act according to special instructions issued.

The bearing of [illegible] from the [illegible] is [illegible]° magnetic. The general bearing of the advance is [illegible]° magnetic. These bearings should be noted [illegible] will occur in the centre of our line.

4. BARRAGE

The Barrage will move according to [illegible] issued to Cos. These must be carefully explained to all ranks.

NOTE

All 4 waves and Mopping Up Parties will advance at ZERO so as to get under the protection of the Barrage.

SPECIAL INSTRUCTIONS

Officers and N.C.O's must move in line with their men.

Bayonets will not be fixed till just before [illegible] as they must not show over the parapet.

Flares will be lit in groups of [illegible] when called for by the Contact Aeroplane. Neglect to fire these flares when called upon may lead to our being shelled by our own guns.

Smoke barrages are being used by our Artillery. These must not be confused with GAS.

6. LEWIS GUNS

Only two men per team will accompany the ASSAULT. Two men.

.(Sheet [illegible]).

5 (Cont.) will remain in our front system of trenches with half the magazines as a reinforcement. The remainder of the team being left behind.

6.. Flanking Bombing Parties will act under the instructions of the Bombing Officer and will give orders to the Stokes Guns.

M.G.Co. has told off two guns to accompany the attack. Cos. will provide protection for these if required.

WIRE. On arrival in the trenches Cos. will inspect our wire and see that it has been cut.

Fire steps will also be improved if necessary.

No Maps or Papers containing information valuable to the enemy will be taken over.

7. WATCHES

All watches will be sent to Bn. Hd. Qrs. to the Signalling Officer at [illegible] a.m. on the [illegible] instant. They will be called for at ANTELOPE [illegible] at [illegible] p.m. same day.

8. VISUAL SIGNALS

Visual Signals can be taken from front to rear.

9. AID POST

Aid Post at Old French Dugout near [illegible].

10. Reports for Bn. to ANTELOPE through Signal Office in [illegible] TR.
For Bde. to [illegible].
Companies will report by signal when ready in position for the assault, using the code word "[illegible] CHAPLIN".
This report should be sent as early as possible.
Reports are required by the Bde. every [illegible] hour starting from ZERO [illegible]. Any information should be sent in even of a negative character.

Issued at...... (Signed) [illegible] Capt. & Adjt. [illegible]

Copies Nos. [illegible] [illegible]
[illegible]
[illegible] (for information)
5 - [illegible]
[illegible]
[illegible]
[illegible] (for information)
[illegible] BDE.

REALM Orders 9/109

31st January. 1917.

REALM will be relieved by RASHER on the night of the 1st/2nd February.

Cos. will send to Bn. Hd. Qrs, ANTELOPE TRENCH, by 5 p.m., 1 guide per platoon – reliable men. These guides must be in possession of written instructions, showing where they are to guide the relieving Unit. Officers will give these guides all instructions.

All Lewis Guns, carriers, and L.G. ammunition will be brought away.

All water tins will be brought down, and dumped at the Brigade water dump. Sandbags will be securely tied round the boots.

All wounded men are to be brought to Bn. Hd. Qrs., and all dead in the vicinity of posts to be buried.

All trench stores will be handed over, and receipts obtained and handed into Orderly Room.

A certificate that all posts, with all information, has been correctly handed over, will be obtained from the Officer in Command of the relieving Co.

Cos. on relief will proceed direct to No. 4 Camp CARNOY, reporting relief complete at Bn. Hd. Qrs. ANTELOPE TRENCH. All stores will be salvaged, and lists forwarded to Orderly Room, salvage dumps being formed by Cos. in the most convenient place for removal.

[illegible] Lieut. & Adjutant
REALM.

Instructions regarding War Diaries and Intelligence Summaries are contained in F. S. Regs., Part II. and the Staff Manual respectively. Title Pages will be prepared in manuscript.

87/29

WAR DIARY
or
INTELLIGENCE SUMMARY

(Erase heading not required.)

1st R. Inniskilling Fus

Army Form C. 2118.

(1)

Vol 12

Place	Date 1917	Hour	Summary of Events and Information	Remarks and references to Appendices
CARNOY	1st		Relieved from Brigade front line by 1st BORDER Regt) & proceeded to quarters in CARNOY	[illegible]
	2nd		At CARNOY company inspections & reorganisation	[illegible]
	3rd		Same as for 2nd	[illegible]
	4th		Same as for 2nd	[illegible]
	5th		Proceeded to GUILLEMONT – Brigade Reserve – in relief of 1st KOSBo	[illegible]
	6th		Proceeded to front line in relief of 2nd S.W.Bs.	[illegible]
	7th		Front line, repairing & consolidating position	[illegible]
	8th		Relieved by 11th R.B. 20th Division & proceeded to CARNOY Camp. Lieut FRAZER wounded	[illegible]
	9th		Marched to MEAULT distance 6 miles	[illegible]
MEAULT	10th		Company inspection & general clean up.	[illegible]
	11th		Battalion training & reorganisation	[illegible]
	12th		Training of specialists & lectures to officers & NCOs	[illegible]
	13th		Battalion parades & specialist training	[illegible]
	14th		Same as for 13th	[illegible]
	15th		Battalion parades & company inspections	[illegible]
	16th		Fatigues found by battalion at MEAULT & CARNOY	[illegible]
	17th		Fatigues as on 16th	[illegible]
	18th		As for 16th & 17th Battalion marched to BRONFAY	[illegible]
BRONFAY	19th		Proceeded to FRIGICOURT	[illegible]
	20th		Relieved the 7th E.YORKS in the front line	[illegible]
	21st		Cleaning trenches strengthening position. The line consisted of a series of isolated	[illegible]

X 22

2449 Wt. W14957/M90 750,000 1/16 J.B.C. & A. Forms/C.2118/12.

Instructions regarding War Diaries and Intelligence Summaries are contained in F. S. Regs., Part II. and the Staff Manual respectively. Title Pages will be prepared in manuscript.

WAR DIARY
or
INTELLIGENCE SUMMARY
(Erase heading not required.)

Army Form C. 2118.

Place	Date	Hour	Summary of Events and Information	Remarks and references to Appendices
	21st		posts, on the right front 150x & on left front 30x to 40x from enemy front line enemy active with rifle grenades & bombs	[illegible]
	22nd		Relieved by 1st Essex & proceeded to FRIGECOURT.	[illegible]
	23rd		Marched to TRONES WOOD & entrained for BRONFAY.	[illegible]
	24th		Organising & cleaning up	[illegible]
	25th		Marched to COMBLES, Brigade support	[illegible]
	26th		Proceeded to front line in relief of 4th Worcester Regt 2 ORs killed 1 OR missing	[illegible]
	27th		Engaged in improving & strengthening posts 3 ORs killed 12 ORs wounded ~~[illegible]~~. Bn Strength 33 officers 792 ORs	[illegible]
	28th		Same as for 27th Lt Whittingham 4th R.W.F. & 2 ORs killed 9 ORs wounded 1 OR missing	[illegible]

[illegible] Lt.
for Lieut Col.
Comdg 1/R. Inniskilling Fus.

REALM ORDER No.11. [illegible]/[illegible]/17

1. ThexBattalion will march to FRICOURT today.

2. Dress fighting order, great coats rolled in oil sheet will be carried enbanderole. Water bottles to be filled.

3. Order of march "A"Co.1.30.p.m. "B"Co.1.36.p.m. "C"Co.1.42.p.m. "D"Co.1.48.p.m. A distance of 300 yards will be maintained between platoons.

4. All Kits, blankets and stores left behind will be deposited in No.32 hut.

5. All details left behind will be billeted in No. 30 hut, and rolls to be rendered to Orderly Room.

6. Lewis guns, ammunition and carriers will be carried on limbers.

7. Cookers and water carts will accompany the Bn.

8. All trench kits etc., will be loaded on transport by 12.0.noon.

9. All Public money, Company Conduct sheets etc., will be handed over to Quartermaster and receipts handed into Orderly Room.

10. This order cancels No.10.

(Sd) G.E.Fr[illegible] Lieut. & Adjutant.

REALM ORDER No.12. 11/[illegible]/17.

The Bn.,will move into the front line trenches tonight in relief of 7th.E.Y.

ORDER OF RELIEF.

C.Co.and 3 Lewis guns will relieve "A"Co.7th.E.Y. Posts 1 to 7.
"D"Co.and four Lewis guns will relieve "C"Co.7th. E.Y. Posts 10 to 18a.
2 Platoons "A"Co.& 2 Lewis guns to Canary trench in relief of 2 platoons "D"Co.7th.E.Y.
2 Platoons "A"Co. & 1 Lewis gun BETTYETR in relief of "B"Co.7th.E.Y.
"B"Co.& 2 Lewis guns reserve in relief of "[illegible]"Co. 7th.E.Y.

3. ORDER OF MARCH.

"C"Co.& 2 Platoons "A"Co.	6 .p.m.
"D"Co.	6.10.p.m.
2 Platoons "A"Co.	6.20.p.m.
"B"Co.	6.30.p.m.

4. Guides will meet Cos.,on road by Bn.,Hd.Qrs 7th. E.Y.

5. Completion of relief will be reported by runner to Bn.,Headquarters.

6. A list of all trench stores taken over will be forwarded to Orderly Room as soon as possible after relief.

7. O.C.Cos.,will be held responsible for the reliability of their guides.

8. Intelligence reports,Casualty Returns,Effective Strength and Variation in Strength Return & Programme of work will be rendered to Orderly Room by 7.0.a.m.daily.

All trenches and posts to be improved and maintained in a sanitary condition.

Cos., will draw water from water dump on the way to the front line.

The Lewis Gun Officer will arrange for the disposal of Lewis Guns in accordance with para [illegible] of this order.

Salvage dumps will be formed and O.C."B"Co. will arrange for carrying parties, O.C.Coc., will [illegible] these parties direct to O.C."B"Co.

. Absolute silence will be maintained during course of relief. No smoking to be allowed.

(Sd) G.E.Framingham Lieut. & Adjutant.

1st.Royal Inniskilling Fusiliers.

REALM ORDER No. [illegible]. [illegible]/8/17.

1. REALM will be relieved by REDAN on night of 22/23rd. instdnt.

2. Cos.and Stokes Mortar will arrange to have relia ble guides each with written instructions showing Co.and post at Bn.Hd Qrs. at 5.0.p.m.

3. A correct list of all trench stores handed over will be rendered to Orderly [illegible] on completion of relief.

4. Cos.,will carry down all empty water tins, on no account are any of these tins to be left in the trenches or posts.
These tins will be dumped at the water [illegible].

5. All trenches and postse to be left in a clean and sanitary condition.

6. All wounded men are to be brought. Cos.,requiri assistance will apply to the nearest company.

7. On relief Cos.,will proceed independently to FRICOURT occupying the same area as before.

8. Companies will report completion of relief to Bn.Hd Qrs.,in code. Code word for each Co.,will be notified.

9. Co.Commanders will submit a full report on the state of the posts and trenches [illegible], with suggestions for strengthening and linking up o all isolated posts by [illegible] on the [illegible]th.ins

10. All [illegible] guns, [illegible] will be brought out of the line.

11. O.C.'C'Co. will detail a party for the Stokes Mortars.

(Sd)G.[illegible].Fremingham Lieut.& Adjt[illegible].
1st.Royal Inniskilling Fusiliers.

Codes words for Companies to report compl
tion of relief.

"A" COMPANY.	ANCHOR.
"B" COMPANY.	BILLOW.
"C" COMPANY.	CAMP.
"D" COMPANY.	DUMP.

REALM ORDER No.14. 22/2/17

1. The Battalion will march to TRONES WOOD and entrain for BRONFAY FARM tomorrow.

2. <u>Order and hour of March.</u>

"D" Co.	10.0.a.m.
"C"Co.	10.6.p.m.
"A" Co.	10.12.a.m.
"B" Co.	10.18.a.m.

A distance of 200 yards will bw maintained between platoons. The train is due to leave TRONES WOOD at 1.0.p.m. but should there be any delay with the train. Companies may continue the march.

3. All kits and stores to be carried by transport will be dumped at the cookers by 9.0.a.m. also Lewis guns and ammunition. The Lewis Gun Officer will detail a party to accompany Levis Guns. 1 N.C.O and 3 men.

4. Breakfast at 8.0.a.m., Dinners on arrival at BRONFAY.

5. All trenches and dugouts to be left thoroughly clean.

(Sd) G.E.Framingham Lieut.& Adjutant.

1st.Royal Inniskilling Fusiliers .

REALM ORDER No.15. 24/2/17.

1. REALM will march to COMBLES tomorrow 25th.inst.

2. Order of march:-

"B"	Company.	2.0.p.m.
"C"	"	2.6.p.m.
"D"	"	2.12.p.m.
"A"	"	2.18.p.m.

Dress fighting order, great coats will be carried in waterproof sheet.

3. All trench kits and stores will be stacked at the Qr.Mr's Stores by 12.30.p.m.

4. All surplus stores and kits will be stacked in the Qr.Mr's Stores during the morning.

5. Lewis guns and ammunition will be carried on limbers.

6. An advance party of C.Q.M.S's and one man per Co., under 2/Lt.T.E.Jones. will leave Orderly Room at 9.0.a.m. tomorrow.

7. All Public money will be handed to 2/Lt.R.W.W. Stephenson and receipts obtained, all secbet documents in possession of Cos.,to be returned to Orderly Room by 9.30.a.m. and applied for on return from trenches.

8. Four sandbags per man will be carried. These will be worn round the legs going to and during the time the Battalion is in the line.

9. Every man is to be in possession of two pairs of socks. Co.Commanders will make a careful inspection.

10. Attention is directed to Bn.Order Nos.186 & 188 d/- 24th.inst., which will be stricly adhered to on all occasions going to and returning from trenches. (Sd)G.E.Framingham Lieut.& Adjutant.
1st.Royal Inniskilling Fusiliers.

REALM ORDER No.16. 27/2/17.

1. REALM will be relieved by REDAN on the night o 28/1st about 7.30.p.m.

2. <u>Order of march.</u>

Reserve 1 Company
Support 1 Company less 2 Platoons.
LEFT FRONT 13 Posts 4 Platoons.
RIGHT FRONT 9 Posts CANARY 6 Platoons.
Stokes Mortar.

3. A requisite number of guides per Co. will report at Bn.Hd Qrs.,at 6.0.p.m. with written instructions showing location of their posts.

4. Companies on relief will proceed to FRIGICOURT and occupy same areas as before.

5. All Lewis gun-ammunition will be brought out,also empty water tins, on no account will any of these tins be left in posts or trenches.

6. Completion of relief will be reported by telephone in code to Bn.Hd.Qrs.,Code word issued with these orders.

7. All wounded men to be brought down,Companies requiring assistance will apply to the nearest Company.

8. All trenches and posts to be left in a sanitary condition with dry standings for incoming unit.

9. A certificate will be obtained from each Co.Cmdr., of relieving unit, that all posts have been handed over correctly.

10. Receipts for all trench stores handed over will be forwarded to Orderly Room.

<u>Code Words.</u>

"A" Company. ANCHOR.
"B" " BILLOW.

P.T.O.

"C" Company.	CAMP.
"D" "	Dump.

(Sd) G.E.Franingham Lieut.& Adjutant.

1st.Royal Inniskilling Fusiliers.

X 23

WO 13

War Diary

of

1st Bn. The Royal Inniskilling Fusiliers

From 1st March 1917 To 31st March 1917

Instructions regarding War Diaries and Intelligence Summaries are contained in F. S. Regs., Part II. and the Staff Manual respectively. Title Pages will be prepared in manuscript.

WAR DIARY
or
INTELLIGENCE SUMMARY

(Erase heading not required.)

Army Form C. 2118.

Place	Date	Hour	Summary of Events and Information	Remarks and references to Appendices
	March 1st		In firing line improving & strengthening position. Relieved by 2nd ESSEX REGT. and ordered to retake & hold GREEN HOWARD TR and to improve same & dig a communication trench, this was successfully accomplished and the battalion was withdrawn to FRIGICOURT at 2 am on the 2nd	
FRIGICOURT	2nd		Marched to COMBLES and was conveyed in lorries to VILLE	
	~~2nd~~		Arrived about 9 pm & was billeted for the night	
VILLE	3rd		Marched to LANEUVILLE and occupied billets. Battalion engaged in cleaning & tidying up after a strenuous period in trenches	
LANEUVILLE	4th		Companies reorganising & arranging for a period of training	
	5th		Same as for the previous day.	
	6th		Battalion training, inoculating etc	
	7th		Training of specialists & general organisation of battalion	
	8th		Battalion training & lectures	
	9th		do do	
	10th		do do	
	11th		do do	
	12th		do do	
	13th		do do	
	14th		do do	
	15th		do do	
	16th		do and 1 officer 25 men joined from base	
	17th		do do	

2449 Wt. W14957/M90 750,000 1/16 J.B.C. & A. Forms/C.2118/12.

Instructions regarding War Diaries and Intelligence Summaries are contained in F. S. Regs., Part II. and the Staff Manual respectively. Title Pages will be prepared in manuscript.

WAR DIARY
or
INTELLIGENCE SUMMARY
(Erase heading not required.)

Army Form C. 2118.

(2)

Place	Date	Hour	Summary of Events and Information	Remarks and references to Appendices
LANEUVILLE	18th		Inspection of billets & [illegible]	[illegible]
	19th		Marched to [illegible] a distance of 10 kilometres and entrained for AIRAINES. Arrived about 10pm	[illegible]
			Battalion billeted	[illegible]
AIRAINES	20th		Battalion reorganisation & general clean up	[illegible]
	21st		Company training under Co Comdrs	[illegible]
	22nd		- do - do -	[illegible]
	23rd		Battalion training	[illegible]
	24th		[illegible] parade	[illegible]
	25th		Divisional parade	[illegible]
	26th		Brigade exercise	[illegible]
	27th		Battalion exercise	[illegible]
	28th		Marched to PICQUIGNY	[illegible]
	29th		FLESSELLES Major J. SHERWOOD KELLY CMG DSO assumed command of battalion vice Capt R R WILLIS VC	[illegible]
	30th		BONNEVILLE	[illegible]
	31st		Rest for the day & general clean up	[illegible]

J Sherwood-Kelly Major

Comdg 1st R Innisk Fus

X 24 87/39

Confidential

Vol 14

War Diary

of

1st Bn, The Royal Inniskilling Fusiliers

From 1st April, 1917 To 30th April, 1917

Volume 25

Instructions regarding War Diaries and Intelligence Summaries are contained in F. S. Regs., Part II. and the Staff Manual respectively. Title Pages will be prepared in manuscript.

WAR DIARY
or
INTELLIGENCE SUMMARY
(Erase heading not required.)

Army Form C. 2118.

(1)

1/R. Inniskilling Fus

Place	Date	Hour	Summary of Events and Information	Remarks and references to Appendices
BONNEVILLE	Apr 1st		Battalion marched to OUTREBOIS	[illegible]
	2nd		" LUCHEUX. Draft of 1 officer & 102 ORs joined battalion	[illegible]
	3rd		Training by companies. Advancing under barrage	[illegible]
	4th		[illegible]	[illegible]
	5th		Battalion marched to ETREE WAMIN. Draft of 110 ORs joined battalion	[illegible]
	[illegible]		[illegible] Battalion strength officers 34 ORs 931. Draft of 10 ORs.	[illegible]
	8th		[illegible] to MONCHIET	[illegible]
MONCHIET	9th		[illegible] gas etc	[illegible]
	10th		Draining and improving camp.	[illegible]
	11th		Training	[illegible]
	12th		Marched to ARRAS resting for three hours before proceeding to FEUCHY brigade reserve.	[illegible]
FEUCHY	[illegible]		Battalion moved into brigade support line & occupied the trenches lately captured [illegible] communication W of WANCOURT.	[illegible]
	[illegible]		In support repairing & improving trenches	[illegible]
	15th		[illegible] in support [illegible] on left flank of brigade, C Co in support of [illegible]	[illegible]
	[illegible]		[illegible] MONCHY [illegible] Lieut AYLMER & 5 ORs	[illegible]
	[illegible]		[illegible] 35 casualties	[illegible]
	[illegible]		[illegible] by D Co in "no man's land" 200 yds in advance	[illegible]
	[illegible]		[illegible] Gordon Highlanders & marched to ARRAS battalion billeted in [illegible] joined battalion	[illegible]
ARRAS	[illegible]		[illegible] work.	[illegible]

2449 Wt. W14957/M90 750,000 1/16 J.B.C. & A. Forms/C.2118/12.

Army Form C. 2118.

Instructions regarding War Diaries and Intelligence Summaries are contained in F. S. Regs., Part II. and the Staff Manual respectively. Title Pages will be prepared in manuscript.

WAR DIARY
or
INTELLIGENCE SUMMARY

(Erase heading not required.)

1/R. Inniskilling Fus

(2)

Place	Date	Hour	Summary of Events and Information	Remarks and references to Appendices
ARRAS	21st		Resting & general clean up.	
	22nd		Battalion proceeded to front line in front of MONCHY LE PREUX & drew up in position for an advance on the morning of 23rd	
	23rd		At 4.45 am the battalion advanced under a heavy barrage and occupied the first German trench, this position was consolidated & held under a very heavy hostile artillery fire. Casualties 1 officer killed [illegible] officers wounded	
	24th		Battalion remained in captured position and was relieved by the Royal Scots & proceeded to ARRAS.	
	25th		Battalion marched from ARRAS to DUISANS	
	26th		Continued march from DUISANS to LATTRE ST QUINTEN	
	27th		Marched from LATTRE ST QUINTEN to SAULTY	
SAULTY	28th		Reorganization of platoons & refitting of battalion. Capt J.REDENT, M.C. joined battalion	
	29th		Divine Service	
	30th		Battalion training, bombing & Lewis gun instruction	

W. Cunningham, Lt for Lieut Col.
Comdg 1/R. Inniskilling Fus.

2449 Wt. W14957/M90 750,000 1/16 J.B.C. & A. Forms/C.2118/12.

BATTALION ORDER No.6. 5/4/17.
:-:-:-:-:-:-:-:-:-:-: :-:-:-:

(1) The Battalion will march to SOMBRIN tomorrow via GRAND RULLECOURT.

(2) Brigade Starting Point. Road junction 88 yds., N of T in GRAND RULLECOURT 10.3.a.m.

(3) The Battalion Starting Point. Cross roads immediately W of S in ETREE WAMIN STATION.9.0.a.m

(4) The Battalion will be formed up ready to march by 8.54.a.m.on the ST.POL road in the following order - Drums A.B.& C Company on BERLANCOURT Road. "D"Company will join the Battalion as it passes the cross roads W of the Station. The head of the Battalion at the junction of St.POL & BERLANCOURT Roads.

(5) All kits & stores will be stacked at the Qr.,Mr's Stores by 7.15.a.m.

(6) Billeting party under 2/Lt.E.C.L.Jones will leave at 7.0.a.m.

(7) Steel helmets will be worn by all ranks including billeting parties on the line of march.

(8) All billets to be clear ready for inspection by 8.0.a.m.

(9) A distance of 500 yads will be observed between Battalions & 200 yards between other Units.

(Sd) G.E.Framingham. Lieut.& Adjutant.
1st.Royal Inniskilling Fusiliers.

BATTALION ORDER No. 7. 6/4/27.

:-:-:-:-:-:-:-:-:-: :-:-:-:

(1) The Battalion will march tomorrow. (destination unknown).

(2) Parade ready to march off at 9.0.a.m. in the following order. Drums. C. D. A. B.

(3) Kits and stores to be stacked at the Qr.,Mr's Stores by 7.15.a.m.

(4) Billeting party to be ready to march by 8.0.a.m.

(5) Billets to be ready for inspection by 8.0.a.m.

Further instructions will be issued later.

(Sd) G.E.Framingham. Lieut. & Adjutant.
1st. Royal Inniskilling Fusiliers.

BATTALION ORDER No. [illegible]

-:-:-:-:-:-:-:-:-:-:-:-:-:-:-:-:-:-:-

Ref. Map. Sheet 51c. 1/[illegible]

(1) The Battalion will march to [illegible] via BAILY, & [illegible].

(2) Dress, Marching Order, blankets and [illegible] will be carried on the man. Steel helmets will be worn.

(3) The Battalion, less [illegible], will [illegible] in the field adjoining the theatre, [illegible] be formed up in [illegible] ready to [illegible] will join the Battalion at the [illegible] of Brigade Headquarters.

(4) Order of March. [illegible] will be attached to each Company [illegible].

(5) Brigade starting point [illegible] Junction [illegible] distance of [illegible] yards will be observed between Battalions & [illegible] yards between Battalions and their Transport.

(6) All kits, stores etc., will [illegible] Mr's Stores by [illegible].

(7) All billets to be left [illegible] ready for inspection [illegible].

(8) Reveille [illegible]

([illegible]) [illegible] Capt. & Adjutant.

[illegible]

SECRET.

Copy No. 8

87th INFANTRY BRIGADE
ORDER No. 10.

Ref. Maps.
1/40,000 Sheet 51.c.
1/100,000 LENS Sheet.

In the Field,
30th April, 1917.

1. The 87th Infantry Brigade Group will march tomorrow to WANQUETIN.

2. Movement will be in accordance with March Table attached.

3. 1st Line Transport will accompany Units.

4. The following distances will be observed -
   500 yards between Battalions and battalions and their transport.
   200 yards between other units and other units and their transport.

5. ACKNOWLEDGE.

Issued at 1800

J. Brodie[illegible] Captain,
Brigade Major, 87th Infantry Brigade.

Copies to:-
Staff 1-5.
S.W.B. 6.
K.O.S.B. 7.
1/R.Innis.Fus.
1/Border Regt.
87th M.G.C.
87th T.M.B.
87th Bde.Sigs.
W.R.Fld.Co.R.E.
87th Fld.Amb.
No.3.Co.Train.
29th Division."G".

Confidential. X

Vol 15

War Diary

of

1st Battn R. Inniskilling Fusrs

from

1st May 1917 to 31st May 1917

Volume 27

No 27

Instructions regarding War Diaries and Intelligence Summaries are contained in F. S. Regs., Part II. and the Staff Manual respectively. Title Pages will be prepared in manuscript.

WAR DIARY
or
INTELLIGENCE SUMMARY
(Erase heading not required.)

1/R Inniskilling Fus.

Army Form C. 2118.

Place	Date	Hour	Summary of Events and Information	Remarks and references to Appendices
SAULTY	May 1st	6am	March to WANQUENTIN & go into Billets.	
WANQUENTIN	2nd	5.00pm	" " ARRAS " "	
ARRAS	3rd	7.5am	Take up position in old German trenches on OBSERVATION RIDGE (H 31 B to H 25 D) the division being in reserve to VI Corps.	
"	4th	12 Noon	March back to billets in ARRAS.	
"	5th		Interior economy.	
	6th		" " & Divine Service.	
"	7th	10.15a	March to DUISANS. Draft 2 offrs 20 OR.	
DUISANS	8th–12th		Training. Brigade Sports.	
	13th	5.15pm	March to ARRAS	
ARRAS	14th	8.30pm	March from ARRAS to front line & take over from 1st Gordons vide Bn orders No 16 & dispositions attached.	
In trenches	15th–18th		Officer patrols go out nightly. Enemy holds HOOK TRENCH. Snipers active & intermittent shelling. 4 Killed 8 wounded 1 missing	
	19th	1900	Attack carried out in accordance with attached B.O. 17. The attack fails owing to severe casualties from M.G. fire. Centre party reach their objective but are outnumbered. Lieut Aitchison effect a lodgement in HOOK TRENCH with about 20 men but nothing more is heard of them. Casualties. Capt Osman, 2Lt McGrane, Lt Hepworth killed, 2Lt O Somers died of wounds, 2Lt Glancy & Lt Springer Wd & missing, Lieut Hall missing, Lt Aitchison Wd & missing, 2Lt Graham wounded. OR 192 K.W.&M.	

2449 Wt. W14957/M90 750,000 1/16 J.B.C. & A. Forms/C.2118/12.

No 27

Instructions regarding War Diaries and Intelligence Summaries are contained in F. S. Regs., Part II. and the Staff Manual respectively. Title Pages will be prepared in manuscript.

WAR DIARY
or
INTELLIGENCE SUMMARY
(Erase heading not required.) 1/R. Inniskilling Fus: 2

Army Form C. 2118.

Place	Date	Hour	Summary of Events and Information	Remarks and references to Appendices
			1917 MAY	
	20th		Relieved by 16th Middlesex march to ARRAS.	JRCW
ARRAS	20th/28th		Training	JRCW.
	29th			
	29th		Orders received re capture of HOOK TRENCH vide Bde Order No 18. This order is cancelled.	JRCW
	30th		Training	JRCW
BROWN LINE	31st		Move into Brigade Reserve in BROWN LINE N4a vide BO. No 19.	JRCW

J. Sherwood-Kelly Lieut Col:
1/R. Inniskilling Fus:

2449 Wt. W14957/M90 750,000 1/16 J.B.C. & A. Forms/C.2118/12.

BATTALION ORDER No.13. 2/5/17.

(1) The Battalion will march to ARRAS today, via WARLUS & DAINVILLE.

(2) Parade at 5.50.p.m. in the Camp ready to march off.

(3) Dress:- Marching Order, blanket & great coat will will be carried on the man. Steel helmets will be worn.

(4) Brigade starting point, K 28,d.3.5. will be reached by 6.26.p.m. No halts will be observed East of the N & S line through DAINVILLE Church. There will be no halt at 5.50.p.m.

(5) Guides from billeting parties sent forward will meet the Battalion at the PORTE D'AMIENS.

(6) All kits, stores etc., will be stacked at the Qr.,Mr's Stores by 4.30.p.m.

(7) The N.C.O's and men detailed to remain at ARRAS will be formed up as a separate unit & march in rear of the Battalion.

(8) Huts are to be left in a thoroughly clean & sanitary condition and ready for inspection by the C.O. at 5.0.p.m.

(9) On arrival in ARRAS companies will arrange to draw battle stores and be prepared to move at an hours notice.

Lt.& Adjutant.

1st.Royal Inniskilling Fusiliers.

REALM ORDER No. 8. 5/3/17.

1. REALM will relieve READY at GUILLEMONT, today.
2. The Battalion will parade at [illegible].30.p.m. [illegible] march to CARNOY light meter guage railway, there to entrain.
3. Dress Fighting Order, great coats will be worn.
4. All surplus stores, blankets, kits etc will be stacked at the Qr.Mr's Stores.
5. All Officers' Kits medical and mess stores accompanying the Bn., will be stacked at the Qr. Mr's Stores by 1.30.p.m.
6. Cos. will render to Orderly Room as soon as possible states showing number of men proceeding and nominal rolls of men left behind.
7. Lewis guns and ammunition, Coolers and trench kit will be taken to [illegible] by Regimental Transport. Cos. will detail 1 Lewis gunner to accompany these stores.
8. Corporal [illegible] will proceed to GUILLEMONT at 10.0.a.m. to take over the duties of [illegible] during the stay of the Battalion.

(Sd) [illegible] Frankington Lieut. & A[illegible]
[illegible] Royal Inniskilling Fusiliers.

BATTALION ORDER No.14 6/5/17.
:-:-:-:-:-:-:-:-:-: :-:-:-:

Ref.Map. 1/40,000. Sheet 51. B & C.

(1) The Battalion will march to DUISANS tomorrow the 7th.Inst.

(2) Brigade starting point:- Road junction G.26 b 7.9.

(3) Battalion parade at 10.15.a.m. & march off in the following order, Drums. "D" "A" "B" "C"

(4) Dress,Marching order with blanket & steel helmets.

(5) All kits and stores to be stacked at Qr., Mr's Stores at 9.0.a.m.

(6) Billets to be clear & ready for inspection at 10.0.a.m.

(7) Ist.Line transport will accompany Battalion.

(8) A distance of 500 yards will be observed between Battalions & 200 yards between Companies & between Battalion Transport.

(9) Billeting party will leave at 8.0.a.m.& report at the Town Major's Office DUISANS at 10.0.a.m. The Quartermaster will proceed with this party.

(Sd) J.R.C.Dent.
Capt.& Adjutant.
Ist.Royal Inniskilling Fusiliers.

SECRET.

Copy No. 7

87th INFANTRY BRIGADE ORDER NO. ~~12~~ 14.

Reference Map:-
1/40,000
Sheet 51 B & C.

May 6th, 1917.

1. The 87th Infantry Brigade Group will march to DUISANS tomorrow the 7th.inst.

2. Movement will be in accordance with the attached March Table.

3. The following distances will be maintained:-

   Between Battalions 500 yards.
   " Companies and between Battalions and their Transport 200 yards.
   Between other Units and other Units and their Transport 200 yards.

4. 1st Line Transport will accompany Units.

5. ACKNOWLEDGE.

Brodie [illegible]
CAPTAIN.
BRIGADE MAJOR.87th.INFANTRY BRIGADE.

Issued at 1145.

Copies 1-3.=Staff.
4.=War Diary.
5.=2/S.W.B.
6.=1/K.O.S.B.
7.=1/R.Innis.Fus.
8.=1/Border Regt.
9.=87th M.G.Company.
10.=87th T.M.Battery.
11.=87th Signals.
12.=87th Fld.Amb.
13.=No.3.Coy.Train.
14.=West Rdg.Fld.Co.
15.=86th Bde.
16.=88th Bde.
17.=29th Division.'G'.

BATTALION ORDER No.15. 13/5/17.

Reference Map 1/40,000. Sheet 51 B & C.

(1) The Battalion will march to ARRAS today, via Dry weather track.

(2) <u>Brigade Starting Point.</u> Railway arch at L 15 a 5.4.

(3) Time of Parade:- 5.15.p.m., ready to march off.

Dress:- Marching Order with Steel helmets.

Order of March:- Drums, "A" "B" "C" "D". A distance of 200 yards will be observed between Companies, and between Bn., & Transport.

(4) First Line Transport will accompany Battalion.

(5) One piper will march with each Company.

(6) Kits will be stacked at the Qr.,Mr's Stores by 4.0.p.m.

(7) Blankets to be rolled in bundles of 10, and stacked at the Qr.,Mr's Stores by 12.0.noon.

(8) Huts to be clear and ready for inspection by 5.0.p.m.

(9) There will be no halt at 5.50.p.m.

[illegible signature] Captain & Adjutant.
Ist.Royl Inniskilling Fusiliers.

BATTALION ORDER. No.16. 14/5/17.

Ref.Map 51 B.N.W.& S.W. & 51 B S.W.2.
1/20,000 1/10.000.

(1).The 1/R.Innis.Fus., will relieve the 1st.Gordons Highlanders. & 10th R.W.F., in the front line on the night of the 14/15.May.

)2)."C" & "D" & 1 platoon of "B" Company each will occupy the firing line from O 8 a 8.9. to S.E. corner of twin copse (O 2 b 05.20)."C" Co.on the right "D" on the left.

(3)."A" Co. & 1 platoon of "B" (under command of Capt Williams). will occupy SHRAPNEL TRENCH from GRAPE TRENCH. to CANNISTER TRENCH.

(4). Bn.,Hd.,Qr., will be at O 1 c 9.2.
Bde " " " " " N 5 a Central.

(5). The Bn will parade ready to march off at 8.30 p.m. in the following order.Bn Hd Qrs "D" & 1 Platoon of "B", "C" & 1 platoon of "B", "A" & 1 platoon of "B".

(6). DRESS. Marching order and steel helmets and mackintosh sheets.
Tools and Lewis Guns will be carried.
Blankets will be rolled and stacked at Q.M.Stores

(7). 1 guide per platoon & Bn Hd Qrs.will be at N.4. a 4.7. (Brown Line) at 10.p.m.

(8).All spare kits to be stacked at the Qr Mr Stores

(9). 1 days ration will be carried on the man.

(Sd) J.R.C.DENT.
Capt & Adjutant
1st Royal Inniskilling Fuslrs.

SECRET. Copy No. 8.

2

87th INFANTRY BRIGADE ORDER No.16.

Ref.Maps.51.B.,N.W.& S.W.
1/20,000 and Special Trench Map. May 14th.1917.

1. The 87th Infantry Brigade will relieve the 76th Infantry Brigade in the line on the night of 14th/15th May as follows:-
The 1st ROYAL INNISKILLING FUSILIERS will take over the firing line from O.2.a.8.9.to the S.E.Corner of TWIN COPSE(O.2.b.05.20.) with 2¼ Companies relieving the 1st GORDON HIGHLANDERS and 10th ROYAL WELSH FUSILIERS. The remaining 1¾ Companies will take over SHRAPNEL TRENCH from GRAPE TRENCH to CANISTER TRENCH from the 1st GORDON HIGHLANDERS and 10th ROYAL WELSH FUSILIERS. K.O.S.B.
1st ~~xxxxxxxxxxxxxx~~ (plus 1 Company 2/S.W.BORDERERS) will take over the firing line from the S.E.Corner of TWIN COPSE to BIT LANE (exclusive) with 2¼ Companies plus 1 Company S.W.B.from the 10th ROYAL WELSH FUSILIERS and the 8th KING'S OWN (R.L.)REGT.the remaining 1¾ Coys. will take over SHRAPNEL TRENCH from CANISTER TRENCH (exclusive) to LID TRENCH (inclusive) from the 10th ROYAL WELSH FUSILIERS and the 8th KING'S OWN (R.L.) REGIMENT.
The 2nd SOUTH WALES BORDERERS/will take over the MONCHY DEFENCES (less 1 Coy).
from the 7th K.S.L.I.placing 1 Coy.in ORCHARD TRENCH and 2 Companies in EAST TRENCH.
The 1st BORDER REGIMENT will relieve the 2nd SUFFOLK REGIMENT in the BRWON LINE.
Battalion Headquarters will take over as follows:-
1/R.Innis.Fus.from 1/Gordon Highlanders at O.1.c.9.2.
2/S.Wales Bords.from 7/K.S.L.I.at O.1.c.3.9.
1/K.O.S.B.from the 8th K.O.R.L. N.6.b.8.4.
1/Border Regt.from 2/Suffolk Regt.at N.4.a.4.7.

2. The 87th TRENCH MORTAR BATTERY will relieve the 76th TRENCH MORTAR BATTERY.

3. The Officer Commanding 2nd SOUTH WALES BORDERERS will place 1 Company at the disposal of the Officer Commanding 1st KING'S OWN SCOTTISH BORDERERS.

4. Guides (1per Platoon and 1 per Battn.Hd.Qrs) will at the 2nd SUFFOLK REGIMENT'S Headquarters in BROWN LINE at N.4.a.4.7.at following times:-

1st K.O.S.B.(plus 1 Coy.2/S.W.B.)	at 9-15.p.m.
1st R.Innis.Fus.	at 10.p.m.
2nd S.W.B.(less 1 Coy.)	at 10-45.p.m.
1st BORDER REGT.	at 11-30.pm.

5. Battalions will take their Battalion complement of picks and shovels.

6. Brigade Headquarters will be established at N.5.a. central.

7. Completion of reliefs will be reported to Brigade Headquarters.

8. ACKNOWLEDGE.

Issued at 0930.

Broadwood
CAPTAIN.
BRIGADE MAJOR.87th.INF.BRIGADE.

Copies 1-3.=Staff.
4.=War Diary.
5.=File.
6.=2/S.W.B.
7.=1/K.O.S.B.
8.=1/R.Innis.Fus.
9.=1/Border Regt.
10.=87th M.G.Co.
11.=87th T.M.B.
12.=87th Signals.
13.=87th Fld.Amblce.
14.=W.R.Fld.Co.R.E.
15.=No.3.Co.Train.
16.=86th Bde.
17.=88th Bde.
18.=76th Bde.
19.=29th Division.'G'.

R. I. Fus.

926.B.79.

14.5.17

Scale 1:10000

Yards

Monchy

Musket Trench

Rifle Farm

Rifle Tr.

Halbard Tr.

Chain Trench

Devils Tr.

Devils Trench

Cartridge Tr.

Keeling Copses

Haversack Tr.

Tree Trench

Magnet

Tower

Jack Wood

Wood Trench

Orange (Approx)

S. Street

Sword Lane

Orange Hill

Arrowhead Copse

Twin Tr.

Twin Copses

Cigar Copse

B. des Aubepines

Fontaine des Chiens

B. du Sart

Canister Tr.

MONCHY les-Preux

East Tr.

Shrapnel Tr.

Dale Tr.

Grape Tr.

Hill Tr.

INFANTRY HILL

Green Lane

Hook Tr.

Puppy Tr.

Vine Lane

Dragoon Lane

Hussar Lane

Pick Trench

Spade Tr.

Bayonet Trench

31

32

6

12

7

REALM.

Ref Map – 51. B. SW.2. 1·10,000.

Dispositions –

Front Line – O.8.a.8.9 to O.2.b.05.20.
Equally divided between C & D
Companies C Coy on the right
D " " " Left.
Strength D Coy 4 off 153 O.R – No M.G. 5 Lewis G.
" C " 5 off 147 O R – 1 " 5 Lewis G.

Support line. "A" Coy. 2 M.G.
Strength 6 officers 136 O.R & 6 Lewis G.
from GRAPE TRENCH to CANNISTER TR.
(inclusive)

N.B. The Batt. is organized into 3 Coys of
4 Platoons each –

H.Q – 4 officers
Aid Post – N.12.b.8.7. (in VANE LANE)

In Case of attack the Front Line
will be held –

15/5/17

[signature] Lt Col
O.C. 1st Royal Inniskilling Fusiliers

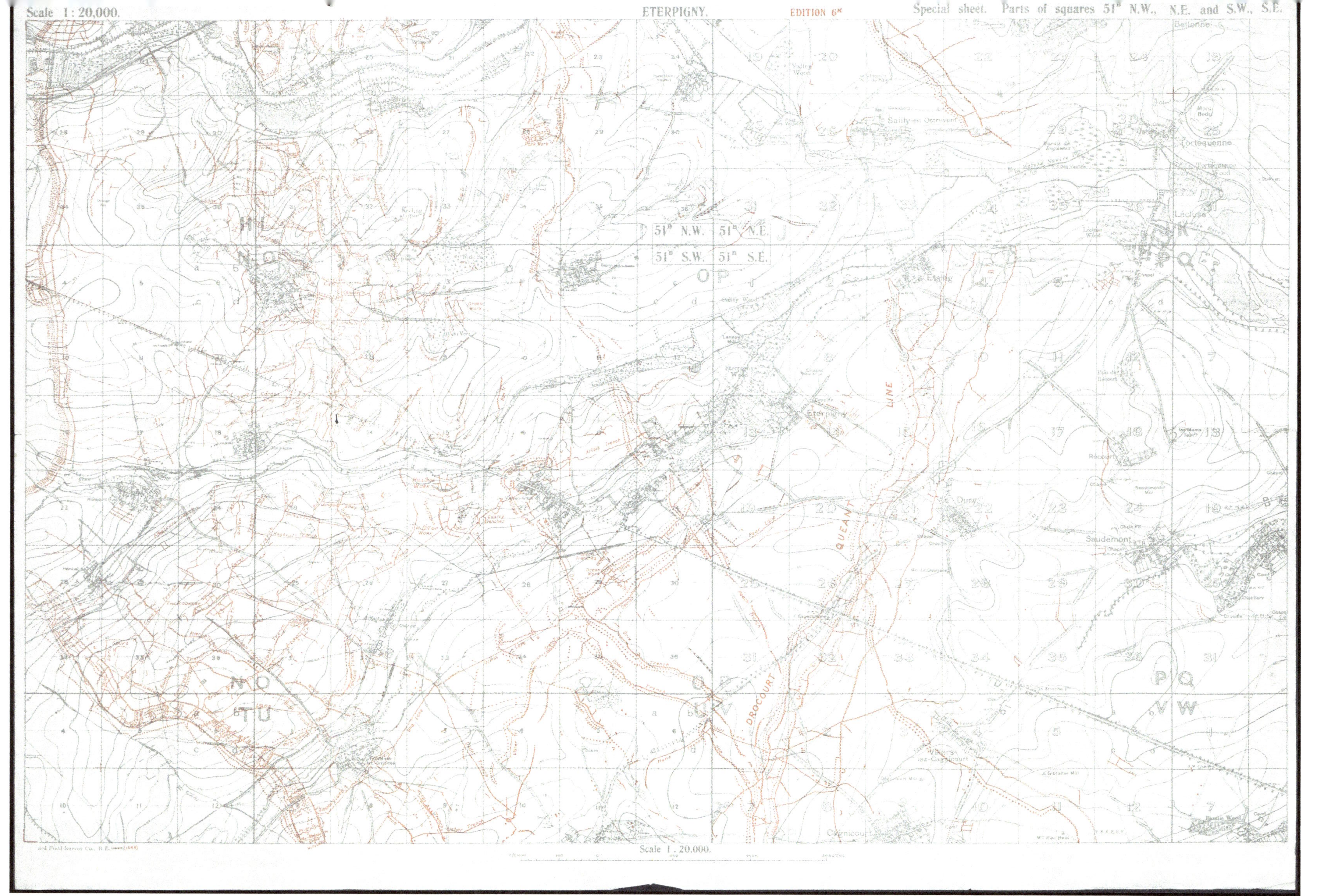

Scale 1 : 20,000.
ETERPIGNY.
EDITION 6[K]
Special sheet. Parts of squares 51[B] N.W., N.E. and S.W., S.E.
51[B] N.W.
51[B] N.E.
51[B] S.W.
51[B] S.E.
Bellonne
Sailly-en Ostrevent
Tortequenne
Lécluse
Etaing
Eterpigny
Dury
Saudemont
Recourt
Villers lez-Cagnicourt
Cagnicourt
QUEANT
DROCOURT
LINE
Scale 1 . 20,000.

SECRET.   Copy No. 8 .

87th INFANTRY BRIGADE ORDER No.19.

May 17th.1917.

Ref. Map attached.

1. On May 19th at a Zero hour to be notified later the 29th Division have been ordered to capture INFANTRY HILL and the BOIS des AUBEPINES in conjunction with the 56th Division (on our Right) who will cooperate and occupy those parts of LONG TRENCH and HOOK TRENCH which lie within their Area.

2. The 87th INFANTRY BRIGADE will attack objectives shewn in RED and BLUE on attached Map, the 167th INFANTRY BRIGADE (Hd.Qrs.N.10.d.3.7) cooperating on our Right by attacking portion of the objective within the 56th DIVISION Area.

3. The attack will take place under cover of an intense Artillery Barrage which will open at Zero in the RED Line. It will lift at Zero plus 5 minutes and advance at the rate of 50 [100] yards 4 [2] minutes to the BLUE Line from which it will lift at Zero plus 10 minutes. At Zero the Troops will leave their Trenches and get as close to the barrage as possible in order to enter the enemy's trenches immediately the barrage lifts. Details of this Creeping Barrage will be forwarded later.

4. The assault will also be covered by a Machine Gun Barrage details of which will be issued later.

5. At Zero, if the wind is favourable, 'J' Company, Royal Engineers will discharge LIEVENS PROJECTORS in the BOIS DU VERT and the SUNKEN ROAD in O.3.c. North of the BOIS DU VERT.
The trenches from I.32.d.2.6.to I.32.a.0.7.and the Valley beyond will be treated with Smokes and " 4" Mortars.

6. ACTION. The attack will be carried out by 6 Platoons of the 1st ROYAL INNISKILLING FUSILIERS on the Right and 2 Platoons 1st BORDER REGIMENT (plus 1 Company 2nd SOUTH WALES BORDERERS) on the Left.
At Zero the Artillery Barrage will drop on the RED Line when the attacking troops will leave the trenches and get right close up under the barrage.
At the same time the Officer Commanding 2nd SOUTH Wales Borderers will send ½ a Company from ORCHARD TRENCH to garrison SNAFFLE TRENCH. This ½ Company will come under the orders of the Officer Commanding 1st BORDER REGIMENT, on arrival there.

/The 2nd

B.O. 19/2
18/5/17

SECRET.

The Officer Commanding,
2nd South Wales Borderers.
1st K.O.S.Borderers.
1st R.Innis.Fus.
1st Border Regt.
87th M.G.Company.
87th T.M.Battery.
29th Division.'G'.

In continuation of 87th Infantry Brigade Order No.19 dated 17th May.1917 the following are the Trench Mortar arrangements.

3" Stokes Mortars will be placed as follows:-

Position Target.		Target.
1 Gun.	O.2.c.3.5.	Area round SUDDEN Road in O.2.d. Rapid fire from Zero for 30 seconds.
1 "	O.2.c.3.45.	
1 "	O.2.c.3.75.	
1 "	O.2.c.5.30.	
2 Guns	O.2.c.9.83.	Northern end BOIS DES AUB EPIN S. To fire rapid from Zero to 0.5.
" "	O.2.b.00.00.	
1 Gun	O.2.c.95.05.	INFANTRY HILL COPSE To fire rapid from Zero to 0.5.
1 "	O.2.c.97.10.	
1 "	O.2.d.0.15.	
1 "	O.2.d.0.25.	

Two guns from O.2.b.0.0. will go forward after the enemy barrage has ceased to the Strong Point in the N.E.Corner of BOIS DES AUBEPINES. Each gun to go forward with 50 rounds.

ACKNOWLEDGE.

Brodie...

CAPTAIN.
BRIGADE MAJOR.87th.INFANTRY BRIGADE.

May 18th.1917.

The 2nd SOUTH WALES BORDERERS will also send Two Companies from EAST TRENCH to garrison SHRAPNEL TRENCH from our Right Boundary to ARROWHEAD COPSE. The remainder of the 1st BORDER REGIMENT will hold TWIN TRENCH from the S.E. Corner of TWIN COPSES to about O.2.a.3½.?.and 1 Company 1st ROYAL INNISKILLING FUSILIERS will hold the Old Firing Line from our Right Boundary to the S.E.Corner of TWIN COPSES.The remaining two Platoons may be used as Carrying Party to the assaulting Platoons
At O.4.5 The Barrage will lift and advance at the rate of 50 yards per minute to the BLUE LINE where it will remain until O.10.when it will lift and Strong Points will be dug as follows:-

(a). By the 1st ROYAL INNISKILLING FUSILIERS:-

at O.2.d.10.2½.(Strength 2 Platoons)
at O.3.c.2½.6. (1 Platoon).
at O.2.d.10.0. (2 Platoons).

(b). By the 1st BORDER REGIMENT:-

at O.2.b.2.4½.(1 Platoon).
at O.2.b.6.9. (3 Platoons).
and in CIGAR COPSE at about I.32.d.1.0.(2 Platoons)
also at I.32.c.7.3.(1 Platoons).

(c). By the 2nd SOUTH WALES BORDERERS :-

On the North side of BIT LANE at about I.32.c.3.4. (Strength 1 Company) with a Post on the S.side of the Road at I.32.c.2.5.

The 1st ROYAL INNISKILLING FUSILIERS will leave 1 Platoon to Mop-Up in HOOK TRENCH which will afterwards reinforce the Strong O.3.c.2½.6.

7. The 1st KING'S OWN SCOTTISH BORDERERS will hold themselves in readiness to move at Zero and will send 2 Companies at Zero plus 2 hours up into EAST TRENCH.

8. Communication Trenches will be dug by the 1/2nd MONMOUTH Pioneer Battalion from I.2.d.1.3.to I.2.a.9.3.and from I.2.Central to I.2.b.6.0. Working on these trenches from the front line backwards.
Guides will be detailed by the 1st ROYAL INNISKILLING FUSILIERS to meet these parties at the Junction of HILL TRENCH and CANISTER TRENCH at 11.p.m.
The 2nd SOUTH WALES BORDERERS will join up SNAFFLE Trench with DEVILS TRENCH by continuing the Communication Trench along the South Side of BIT LANE.

9. Each man will carry the following:-
4 Sandbags.
1 Ground flare per two men.
3 S.O.S.Signals per Platoon.
50% will carry either a Pick or a Shovel.

10. A Contact Plane will be in the air shortly after dawn on the 20th.inst. Troops will light flares when the plane calls for them either by sounding a KLAXON Horn or firing White Lights.

/11.

11. The 1st KING'S OWN SCOTTISH BORDERERS will detail 3 parties each of 1 N.C.O. and 3 men to form STRAGGLERS' Posts at FEUCHY CHAPELLE X Roads and X Roads H.29.c. 3.1. and on road at N.3.b.9.5.

12. There will be an Advanced Dressing Station at N.5.a.6.3. with a combined Regimental Aid Post at ~~N.5.a.6.3.~~ 6.d ?

13. Prisoners will be sent to the Cage at H.~~33.b.6.8.~~ 27 c 37. where they will be handed over to the ~~APM~~ A.P.M.

14. Watches will be synchronised at Brigade Headquarters at 9.a.m. and 5.p.m. on the 19th. instant.

15. ACKNOWLEDGE.

Issued at 1900.

Brodie Mair
CAPTAIN.
BRIGADE MAJOR. 87th. INF. BRIGADE.

Copies 1-3. = Staff.
4. = War Diary.
5. = File.
6. = 2/S.W.B.
7. = 1/K.O.S.B.
8. = 1/R. Innis. Fus.
9. = 1/Border Regt.
10. = 87th M.G.Co.
11. = 87th T.M.B.
12. = 87th Sigs.
13. = 87th Fld. Ambce.
14. = W.R. Fld. Co. R.E.
15. = 88th Bde.
16. = 86th Bde.
17. = 167th Bde.
18. = 29th Division 'G'.

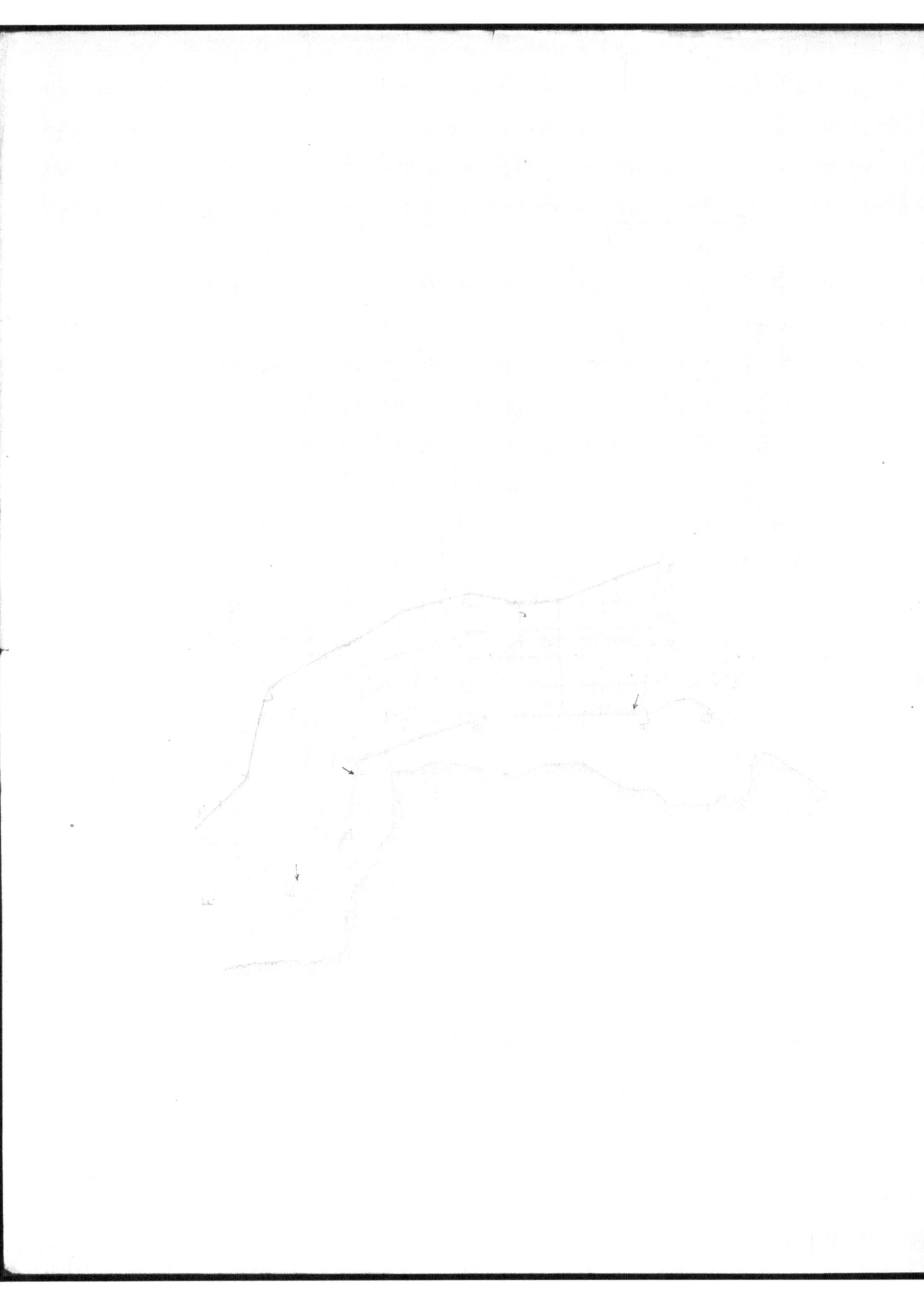

Battalion Order No ~~16~~ 17

Reference map attached.

1. C & D Companies (6 platoons) will carry out an attack on Blue line on the night of the 19th under cover of intense barrage which will open at Zero (to be notified later) on the red line

2. Strong points will be made as follows. –

at O 2 d 10.2½ — 2 Platoons C. Co. (Capt Osman)

" O 3 c 2½.6. — 1 Platoon C
" D
(2Lt Graham)

" O 2 d 10.9. — 2 Platoons D (2Lt Clancy)

3. 1 Platoon of B Co will follow the assaulting Companies & thoroughly mop up HOOK TRENCH. When the OC. Platoon has satisfied himself that this is done & the hostile barrage has quietened, he will return to HILL TRENCH & carry up wire & knife rests from dump at O 2 d 1.4. to S.P. O 2 d 10.2½

3 (Contd). The remaining 2 Platoons B Co will act as carrying party for S.Ps O 3 c 2½ 6 + O 2 d 10.9. They will assist in digging + wiring these strong points
The carrying parties will not go forward till enemy's barrage has quietened.
After wiring is completed B Co will return to HILL TRENCH as garrison

4. At zero A. Co will move into + garrison HILL TRENCH.

5. Barrage will open at zero on the red line + lift at zero + 5 + advance at the rate of 100x in 2 minutes to Blue Line from which it will lift at zero + 10

6. Gas will be discharged at zero if wind is favourable

8. Each O.C. S.P + 1 NCO will carry a bicycle lamp to be lighted + placed facing present line

9. A Coy will provide two parties of 8 men each to report to MG

B.

Co. One party to meet Lieut Outwin at 6 pm 19th at junction of CANISTER & SHRAPNEL TRENCH & one to NCO i/c MG Co at 6 pm 19th at junction of GRAPE TRENCH & SHRAPNEL TRENCH

10 The 1/2 Monmouths will dig two CTs to outer SPs. A Co will send two guides to meet these parties at junction of VINE & SHRAPNEL TRENCHES. One party will be directed via SHRAPNEL & CANISTER TRENCH & one via GRAPE TRENCH

11. Position of Bn HQ will be notified later.

issued at 1200 to Co
19/5/17.

J R Edwards Capt Adjt
1/R. Innis Fusiliers

SECRET.

Copy No.___

87th INFANTRY BRIGADE ORDER No. 20.

In the Field,
20th May, 1917.

Ref. 29th Division
Trench Map, 1/100,000.

1. The 87th Infantry Brigade will be relieved in the right sector of the line tonight 20th/21st May. Relief to be complete by dawn 21st May.

2. The 1st Royal Inniskilling Fusiliers will be relieved by the 16th Middlesex Regiment in the right subsector of of the line.
The 1st Border Regiment will be relieved by the 1st Lancashire Fusiliers in the left subsector of the line.
The 2nd Royal Fusiliers will relieve the 2nd South Wales Borderers in the MONCHY DEFENCES.
The 1st Royal Dublin Fusiliers will relieve the 1st King's Own Scottish Borderers in the Strong Points , D.E.F. and G., The remainder of the Royal Dublin Fusiliers will go into the BROWN LINE.

3. The 87th Machine Gun Company will be relieved by a similar unit of the 88th Infantry Brigade, under arrangements to be made between Officers Commanding concerned, but will leave 1 gun in each of the four Strong Points D.E.F. and G.

4. The 87th Trench Mortar Battery will be relieved by the 88th Trench Mortar Battery under arrangements to be made between Officers Commanding concerned.

5. Units will hand over all maps, Trench Stores etc., but will take out their complement of Regimental picks and shovels.

6. After relief Units will march to ARRAS.

7. ACKNOWLEDGE.

Brodie[?]man

Captain,
Brigade Major, 87th Infantry Brigade.

Issued at ______

Copies 1-5. Staff.
6. S/I.T.B.
7. 1/K.O.S.B.
8. 1/R. Innis. F.
9. 1/Border Regt.
10. 87th M.G.Coy.
11. 87th T.M.Bty.
12. 167th Infantry Bde.
13. 88th Infantry Bde.
14. 29th Division "G".
15. 87th Field Amb.
16. [illegible] Fd. Co.

SECRET. BATTALION ORDER No. 18. 26/5/17.

BATTALION-ORDER-No:18.:

I. The 29th.Division has been ordered to capture HOOK TRENCH in conjunction with the 37th.Division twith a view to the eventual occupation ofeINFANTRY HILL.
The 86th.Brigade are carrying out the attack on night of 29/30th.May,at a Zero hour to be notified later.

2. The 87th.Brigade (less 2nd.S.W.Bs & Ist.K.O.S.Bs who move into BROWN LINE on evening of 29th.May.) remain in Divisional Reserve in ARRAS.

3. The Battalioh will be ready to move at an hour's notice.

(Sd) J.R.C.Dent.
Captain & Adjutant.
Ist.Royal Inniskilling Fusiliers.

Copies to - Staff.
- War Diary.
- O.C.Companies
- QUartermaster.
- Transport Officer.

SECRET. Copy No. 6.

87th INFANTRY BRIGADE ORDER No.21.

May 28th.1917.

1. The 29th Division has been ordered to capture HOOK TRENCH in conjunction with the 37th Division with a view to the eventual ~~capture~~ occupation of INFANTRY HILL.

2. The 86th Infantry Brigade with the assistance of a Battalion of the 112th Infantry Brigade will attack HOOK TRENCH from the block at O.8.b.2.1.to the Northern end of the trench at O.2.b.4.0.on the night of the 29th/30th May at a zero hour to be notified later.

3. 12 Guns of the 87th Machine Gun Company have been placed at the disposal of the G.O.C.86th Infantry Brigade for the operation.

4. Four Stokes Mortars of the 87th Trench Mortar Battery have been placed at the disposal of the G.O.C.86th Infantry Brigade and 2 Mortars at the disposal of the 88th Infantry Brigade.

5. The 87th Infantry Brigade (less 2nd South Wales Borderers and 1st King's Own Scottish Borderers) will remain in Divisional Reserve in ARRAS and will be ready to move at 1 hour's notice.
The 2nd SOUTH WALES BORDERERS and the 1st KING'S OWN SCOTTISH BORDERERS will proceed to the Brown Line at dusk on theovening of the 29th May., taking over the trenches occupied by the 16th MIDDLESEX REGIMENT.

6. ACKNOWLEDGE.

Brodie [signature]
CAPTAIN.
BRIGADE MAJOR.87th INFANTRY BRIGADE.

Issued at 1500.

Copies to - Staff.
- 2/S.W.B.
- 1/K.O.S.B.
- 1/R.Innis.F.
- 1/Border R.
- 87th M.G.Co.
- 87th T.M.B.
- 86th Inf.Bde.
- 88th Inf.Bde.
- 87th Sigs.
- 29th Division.'G'.

SECRET. Ist.Royal Inniskilling Order No.10. Copy.No.2.
30/5/17.

I. The Battalion will move into the BROWN LINE this evening & occupy that portion vacated by the Ist.K.O.S.Bs.

2. Hd.Qrs.,"C" & "D" Cos.& 2 Platoons "A"Co. will parade at 8.30.p.m. & Pass the starting points road junction G 29 central at 9.0.p.m.

3. "B"Co. & I Platoon "A"Co.(under 2/Lt.Austin) will take over strong Points D.E.F. & G. Parade at 7.15.p.m. & report at Ist.K.O.S.B.Hd.Qrs. in BROWN LINE at 9.15'p.m.where they will be met by guides.

4. Dress Marching Order. Water Bottles to be filled. One day's ration will be carried. Each man will carry four sandbags.

5. Transport Officer will arrange to carry Lewis Guns & Picks & Shovels & medical equipment, on Transport.

6. All billets to be thoroughly cleaned & ready for inspection at 8.0.p.m.

Issued at 4.45.p.m.

Copy. I. Staff.
2.& 3. War Diary.
4.5.6.7. O.C."A" "B" "C" "D".
8. Transport Officer.
9. Quartermaster.
10. Medical Officer.

(Sd) J.R.C.Dent.
Capt.& Adjutant.
Ist.Royal Inniskilling Fusiliers.

SECRET. Copy No. 8.

87th INFANTRY BRIGADE ORDER No.22.

May 31st.1917.

1. The 87th Infantry Brigade will relieve the 88th Infantry Brigade tonight. The relief to be complete by daylight 1st June.

2. (a) The 1st KING'S OWN SCOTTISH BORDERERS will take over the right sub-sector of the Line from GRAPE TRENCH (inclusive) to the S.E.Corner TWIN COPSES from the 1st Lancashire Fusiliers placing 2½ Companies in the firing line and 1½ companies in SHRAPNEL TRENCH.
   (b) The 2nd SOUTH WALES BORDERERS will take over the left subsector of the line from the S.E.Corner of TWIN COPSES up to but exclusive of BIT LANE from the 1st Royal Dublin Fusiliers placine 3 companies in the firing line and 1 company in SHRAPNEL TRENCH.
   (c) The 1st BORDER REGIMENT will take over the MONCHY DEFENCES from the 2nd South Wales Borderers placing 1 Company in ORCHARD TRENCH, 2 Companies in EAST TRENCH and 1 company in the new trench at S.E.Corner of MONCHY.
   (d) The 1st ROYAL INNISKILLING FUSILIERS will go into that portion of the BROWN LINE vacated by the 1st KING'S OWN SCOTTISH BORDERERS placine 1 platoon in each of the Strong Points 'D', 'E', 'F' and 'G'.

3. GUIDES (1 per platoon and 1 per Battalion Headquarters) from the 1st Lancashire Fusiliers will meet the 1st King's Own Scottish Borderers on the track just S of 88th Infantry Brigade Headquarters (N.5.a.Central) at 9-45.p.m.
   Guides from the 2nd South Wales Borderers will meet the 1st Border Regiment at the same place at 10-15.p.m.
   Guides from the 1st Royal Dublin Fusiliers for the 2nd South Wales Borderers will report at 2nd South Wales Borderers'Headquarters at 9-15.p.m.under arrangements to be made by the 88th Infantry Brigade.
   The Officer Commanding 1st KING'S OWN SCOTTISH BORDERERS will arrange to have guides for 'D', 'E', 'F' and 'G' Strong Points at his Headquarters in the BROWN LINE at 9-15.p.m.

4. Units will take up their own Picks and Shovels and all trench stores etc.will be taken over.

5. The 1st BORDER REGIMENT will pass the Road Junction at G.29.central at 8-30.p.m.and the 1st ROYAL INNISKILLING FUSILIERS at 9.p.m.(The platoons of the 1st Royal Inniskilling Fusiliers going to 'D','E', 'F' and 'G' Strong Points should report at Headquarters 1st King's Own Scottish Borderers in BROWN LINE at 9-15.p.m.

6. The 87th Machine Gun Company and the 87th Trench Mortar Battery will relieve similar Units from the 88th Infantry Brigade under arrangements to be made between Officers Commanding Units concerned.

/7.

87th Infantry Brigade Order No.22.Contd.

7. Units will report Relief Complete to Brigade Headquarters at N.5.a.central by wire. The Surname of the Officer Commanding Unit will be used as a Code word to indicate that the relief of the Unit is complete.

8. ACKNOWLEDGE.

Issued at 1500.

Brodie Mau

CAPTAIN.
BRIGADE MAJOR.87th INFANTRY BRIGADE.

Copies 1-3.=Staff.
4.=War Diary.
5.=File.
6.=2/S.W.B.
7.=1/K.O.S.B.
8.=1/R.Innis.Fus.
9.=1/Border Regt.
10.=87th M.G.Co.
11.=87th T.M.B.
12.=87th Bde.Sigs.
13.=86th Bde.
14.=88th Bde.
15.=29th Division.'G'.

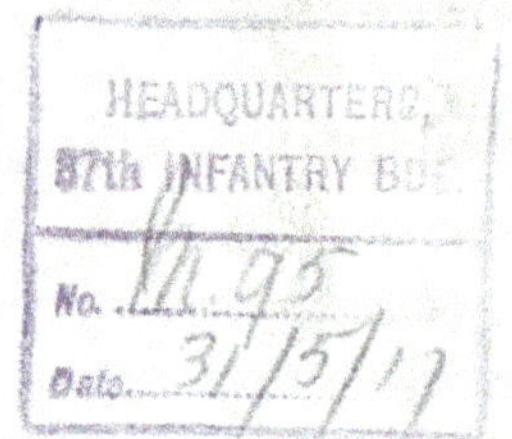

S E C R E T.

29th DIVISION ADMINISTRATIVE ORDERS NO. 14.

Reference General Staff Order No. 124 regarding relief of Division :-

1. BILLETS. A list of billets in the BERNAVILLE-CANAPLES Area is attached. (Location Table No.22).

2. TRANSPORT. Brigade Groups will move by Tactical Trains in accordance with a Time-table to be issued later. Four lorries for baggage will be provided for each Brigade Group.

1st Line Transport and Train Companies will stage at BERNEVILLE, (5 miles S.W. of ARRAS), and LUCHEUX. Transport of the 88th Brigade Group will move to BERNEVILLE on evening of 3rd, that of 87th Brigade Group on evening of 4th June.

1st Line Transport and Train Companies will march as a Brigade Unit under the Brigade Transport Officer or Staff Captain, who will see that march discipline is maintained, advance parties sent forward, men properly billeted and horses picketed out.

Billets at BERNEVILLE will be obtained from the Town Major; at LUCHEUX from the Maire.

Mounted personnel of Divisional Headquarters, S.A.A. Section, and 18th Mobile Veterinary Section will march with Brigade Groups to which they are allotted in General Staff Order No.124.

3. RATIONS, For the day of entrainment and following day will be carried with personnel by rail. Rations for the day after that will be issued direct to billets by the Supply Column.

1st Line Transport will carry one day's supplies for themselves the day they move. Supply wagons will carry two day's supplies for the 1st Line Transport of their Groups.

4. ADVANCE PARTIES, of the 86th Brigade Group will be sent forward by lorry and on bicycles from BERNEVILLE on 2nd June, 1917. Those of 88th and 87th Brigade Groups will move by the trains carrying the 86th Brigade Group on the 3rd June. All parties will take three day's rations with them.

5. WATER TINS up to the recognised establishment will be carried on 1st Line Transport and Train wagons, etc.. All surplus tins will be evacuated at once to Supply Railhead, ARRAS, under Brigade arrangements. The S.A.A. Section will supply 5 G.S. wagons for this purpose to report at IVORY DUMP and 5 G.S. Wagons at ALADIN CAVE, both at 10 a.m. on the 30th instant.

6. AMMUNITION. Full establishments of S.A.A., Grenades, Picks and Shovels will be carried on 1st Line Transport.

The following practice ammunition has been asked for in the back area :-

S.A.A.	4000 rounds per Bn.	Flares	400 per Bn.
Grenades No.5	800 " " "	S.A.A.	30,000 rds.per M.G.Coy.
" No.23	800 " " "		
" No.24	800 " " "	Stokes Ammn.	100 rds. per Battery.
Pistol Ammunition	1 Box per Bn.		
Ring Charges	80 rds. per Bty.	Stokes (blank)	400 rds. per Battery.

The C.R.E. will also make arrangements in advance to procure R.E. Stores for training.

P.T.O.

7. TOWN MAJORS. There are no permanent Town Majors in the Area except at CANDAS. Billets elsewhere will be arranged with the Maires, and a temporary Town Major appointed in each village.

8. BATHS are available as follows :-

BERNAVILLE	12 Sprays.	
BOISBERGUES	12 "	
CANDAS	16 "	(Under the Town Major).
MONTRELET	12 "	

The Divisional Baths Officer will arrange for personnel with the A.D.M.S. and Clothing from the FREVENT Laundry.

9. REINFORCEMENTS.from the XVIIIth Corps Depot will join by train from ST. POL, detraining at CANDAS on the 6th June, 1917. Time guides should report at CANDAS will be notified later.

10. LEAVE PARTIES up to and including the 5th June will be left behind in LEVIS Barracks. Lorries will be arranged to convey them to AUBIGNY daily. A nominal roll of Officers and men left behind will be sent by Brigades and Divisional Troops to the Divisional Disbursing Officer at LEVIS Barracks. (Lieut. E.T. BUTLIN).

From 6th June inclusive the Divisional Disbursing Officer will be transferred to CANDAS and all leave parties will go from that station.

11. PERSONNEL. Traffic Control men and Salvage Section will be relieved and withdrawn on 2nd June to ARRAS.

The Burials Party, Officers and personnel at Dumps, etc. as per Appendix 1, will also be relieved on the 2nd June and will rejoin their Units.

Personnel at Divisional Baths, Grande Place, will be relieved on 4th June and travel by train with 87th Brigade on 5th under arrangements to be made by Baths Officer.

12. The 3rd Division will NOT be taking over the Transport Lines of the 29th Division. Before the latter are vacated they must be thoroughly cleaned up. All tents will be struck under Brigade arrangements and handed over to corresponding Brigades of the 3rd Division. Receipts for all tents and for all Trench and Area Stores will be collected and sent to Divisional Headquarters, "Q" Branch.

13. A C K N O W L E D G E.

Lieut.Colonel,

30th May, 1917. A.A. & Q.M.G., 29th Division.

Appendix to 29th Division Order No. 121.

The arrangements for the Artillery barrage are as follows :-

At Zero a barrage will be placed on the line A.B.C.D.E.

The fall of the barrage is the signal for the troops to leave the trenches, and at Zero, the troops advance from our front line, and get as close to the barrage as possible.

If troops reach the barrage, before it commences to creep back, they should kneel down; they must not however lie down.

At 5 minutes after Zero (i.e. 0.5.) the barrage will lift 100 yards off the front line, thus enabling our troops to enter the enemy's front line trenches.

The barrage will creep back at the rate of 100 yards every two minutes, reaching the second objective at 0.7. and lifting off it at 0.10. From here, it will creep to the line H.J.K.L.M. at the rate of 100 yards every two minutes.

The barrage will continue on the line H.J.K.L.M./in bursts for one hour (i.e. till 0 plus 1 hour 15 mins.) to enable the troops to consolidate.

Should the S.O.S. call (a succession of Red Very Lights) be made, while our troops are consolidating the second objective, a barrage will be placed on the line H.J.K.L.M.

-o-o-o-o-o-o-o-o-o-

MARCH TABLE.

Unit.	From.	To.	General route.	Starting Point.	Time.	Remarks.
?.Bdg.Fld.Co.	LA HERLIERE.	WANQUETIN.	SAULTY-BARLY-FOSSEUX.	Road junction V.9.b.7.8.	6.55.a.m.	Units at ST.AMAND to march to SAULTY by GAUDIEMPRE - Halts U.24.b.7.7. and cross roads at V.8.c.9.0.
87th M.G.Company.	" "	"	"	"	7-0.a.m.	
No.3.Co.Train.	" "	"	"	"	7-5.a.m.	
87th Fld.Amb.	" "	"	"	"	7-10.a.m.	
1/K.O.S.Bordrs.	ST.AMAND.	"	"	Cross Roads on ST.AMAND.-GAUDIEMPRE Road.200 yards N.W. of ST.AMAND Church.	6-0.a.m.	Units at LA HERLIERE to march to SAULTY via Road junction at V.9.b.7.8.
2/S.W.Bordrs.	"	"	"	"	6-15.a.m.	and road junction V.9.a.7.4.
1/Border Regt.	SAULTY.	"	"	500 yards N,.of Road junction V.2.b.1.7.on SAULTY-BARLY Road.	8-25.a.m.	Troops from LA HERLIERE will not observe halt at 8-50.a.m.
1/R.Innis.Fus.	"	"	"	"	8-35.a.m.	Troops not to enter BAVINCOURT BIENVILLERS-POMMIER or BERLES-AUX-BOIS.
Bde.H.Q.) Bde.Sigs.) T.M.B.)	"	"	"	"	8-45.a.m.	

MARCH TABLE.

Unit.	From.	To.	Via.	Starting Point.	Time.	Remarks.
Bde.Sig.Sec.) 87th Bde.H.Q.) 87th T.M.B.)	ARRAS.	DUISANS.	Dry Weather Track(see attached sketch).	Road Junction G.26.b.7.9.	10-30.a.m.	There will be no halt until 11-50.a.m.
87th M.G.Co.	"	"	"	"	10-35.a.m.	
1/Border Regt.	"	"	"	"	10-40a.m.	
1/R.Innis.Fus.	"	"	"	"	10-58.a.m.	
1/K.O.S.B.	"	"	"	"	11-16.am.	
2/S.W.B.	"	"	"	"	11-34.a.m.	
W.R.Fld.Co.R.E.	"	"	"	"	12.midday.	
87th Fld.Amb.	"	"	"	"	12-7.p.m.	
No.3.Co.Train.	"	"	"	"	12-14.p.m.	

min Bron (?) X.126

Vol 116

War Diary

of

1st Battalion

R. Inniskilling Fusiliers

1st – 30 June 1917

Volume XXVIII

Volume No 28

Instructions regarding War Diaries and Intelligence Summaries are contained in F. S. Regs., Part II. and the Staff Manual respectively. Title Pages will be prepared in manuscript.

WAR DIARY
or
INTELLIGENCE SUMMARY

(Erase heading not required.)

1/R Inniskilling Fus. No 1.

Army Form C. 2118.

JUNE 1917

Place	Date	Hour	Summary of Events and Information	Remarks and references to Appendices
BROWN LINE	1st		Battalion is relieved by 7th KSLI vide B.O. No 20 & go into billets in ARRAS. Casualties 2 W.	JRCW
	2-4.		Training. 1st Line Transport moves to BERNEVILLE en route to FIENVILLERS. vide B.O. 21. Strength 2nd B213. 29 Officers 615 O.R.	JRCW
	5.		Battalion entrains for FIENVILLERS vide B.O. 21. Arrive in billets 3 pm.	JRCW
FIENVILLERS	6		Training. Draft 1 Officer (2Lt W.J.W. McCulloch) 26 O.R.	JRCW
	7		" " 19 O.R.	JRCW
	9		" Strength B213. 30 Officers 647 O.R.	JRCW
	10.11		" Draft 1 Officer (2Lt R.M. Callaghan) 29 O.R.	JRCW
	12.13.14		" " 73 O.R.	JRCW
	15.16		" Strength B213. 31 Officers 736 O.R.	JRCW
	17		" Draft 1 Officer (2Lt E.A.V. Laurence) 13 O.R.	JRCW
	17-23.		" Strength B213. 32 Officers 732 O.R. Lieut A.C. Lendrum, 2Lts McS Aitcheson & 2Lt McC. Despard join 22nd	JRCW
	23-25		Training	
	26th		Leave for PROVEN vide B.O. No 22 attached	JRCW
	27th		Arrive PROVEN & go into camp.	JRCW
	27.28		Relieve 13 RWF in front line vide B.O. No 23.	JRCW
	29th		Quiet day except for intermittent shelling of Canal Bank. 2Lt Hunter Killed. 2Lt Barnett wounded 1 O.R. K 1 W.	JRCW
	30th			JRCW

2449 Wt. W14957/M90 750,000 1/16 J.B.C. & A. Forms/C.2118/12.

Instructions regarding War Diaries and Intelligence Summaries are contained in F. S. Regs., Part II. and the Staff Manual respectively. Title Pages will be prepared in manuscript.

WAR DIARY
or
INTELLIGENCE SUMMARY
(Erase heading not required.)

Army Form C. 2118.

1st Royal Inniskilling Fus. No2

Place	Date	Hour	Summary of Events and Information	Remarks and references to Appendices
	29th		with 4.7 Guns and 5.9 HE at interval. AIRCRAFT Hostile activity very marked – single aeroplane flew over our front line at altitude of 500ft on several occasions. At 6.30 pm. nine enemy aircraft painted with rainbow colours flew down our line in a S. direction at a great height. At ?.? pm the enemy machines came over but was driven back by our AA MG and triplanes. MOVEMENT No enemy movement was observed throughout the period. MISCELLANEOUS About 20 rifle grenades received at HELM TRENCH	C.O.B.
	30th 15 31st		B2B. Ration strength 24 Officers 623 OR. Hostile Artillery activity less than usual. ~~When~~ Two enemy seen in front line trench at 2000, bearing 352° True from Post 23., distance 300x. Canal Bank heavily shelled from 0100 – 0115 & 0300 – 0320. Casualties nil.	J.R.D.

2449 Wt. W14957/M90 750,000 1/16 J.B.C. & A. Forms/C.2118/12.

Secret

1/R. Inniskilling Fus. Order No 20.
1st June 1917.

.1. The Battalion will be relieved by the 7th K.S.L.I. this evening.

.2. O.C. A, C + D will be ready to move off at 9 pm.
Limbers will be at Bn HQ ready for loading at 9 pm
O.C. D Co will arrange a party to load up Picks + Shovels + Salvage.

.3. O.C. B Co will arrange for guide for Strong Points, D.E.F+G to be at Bde HQ. at 9.15 pm.

Picks + Shovels + Lewis Guns will be carried down to Bn HQ where they will be loaded on a limber.

4. Trenches to be left clean + in a sanitary condition + receipts obtained for all trench stores handed over.

.5. O.C. Cos will report "relief complete" to adjutant at Bn HQ.

6. Bn will go into Billets in Arras in barracks near "big bell".

Issued at 4 pm

J C Owen / Capt & Adjt
1/R. Inniskilling Fus

SECRET. Copy No. 8.

87th. INFANTRY BRIGADE ORDER No. 25.

June Ist. 1917.

I. The 87th. Infantry Brigade will be relieved by the 8th. Infantry Brigade on the nights of the 1st/2nd and 2nd/3rd. June, 1917, as follows:-

(a) On the night of the 1st/2nd June 1917.
The IST. BORDER REGIMENT will be relieved in the MONCHY DEFENCES by the 2nd. Royal Scots.
THE IST. ROYAL INNISKILLING FUSILIERS will be relieved in the BROWN LINE and in the Strong Points "D" "D" "F" "G" by the 7th. K.S.L.I.
GUIDES (I per Company and I per Battalion Headquarters) from the Ist. Border Regiment will meet the 2nd. Royal Scots, on the track just South of 87th. Infantry Brigade Headquarters at 9.45.p.m.
The Officer Commanding Ist. Royal Inniskilling Fusiliers will arrange to have guides for the Strong Points "D" "E" "F" "G" at these Headquarters at 9.15.p.m.
The 87th. Machine Gun Company and the 87th. Trench Mortar Batteru. will be relieved by similar units of the 8th. Infantry Brigade under arrangements to be made mutually between Officer Commanding Units concerned.

(b) On the night of the 2nd/3rd. June. 1917.
THE IST. KING'S OWN SCOTTISH BORDERERS will be relieved by the 8th. EAST YORKS in the right sub-sector.
THE 2nd. SOUTH WALES BORDERERS will be relieved by the IST. ROYAL SCOTS FUSILIERS in the left sub-sector.
GUIDES. (I per platoon), I per Battalion Headquarters and I for Regimental Aid Post) from the 2nd South Wales Borderers will meet the Ist. Royal Scots Fusiliers at the point where the dry weather track meets the CAMBRAI ROAD, about 300 yards WESY og FEUCHY CHAPEL Cross Roads at 9.0.p.m., and from the IST. KING'S OWN SCOTTISH BORDERERS for the 8th. East Yorks at the same place at 9.45.p.m.

2. Units will detail as many Officer guides as possible.

3. Units will broing out their Battalion compliment of picks & shovels but will hand over all maps, trench stores etc.

4. After relief Units will return ot billets in ARRAS.

5. Units will report relief complete to these Headquarters. The surname of the Unit Commander will be the code word intimating that the relief of the Unit is complete.

6. The Command of the right sector will pass from the Brigadier General Commanding 87th. Infantry Brigade to the Brigadier Commanding the 8th. Infantry Brigade on completion of relief.

7. Acknowledge.

(Sd) Brodiemair.
Captain.
Brigade Major, 87th. Infantry Brigade.

S E C R E T.

29th DIVISION ADMINISTRATIVE ORDERS No.14

APPENDIX II

TIME TABLE OF TRAINS 3rd, 4th & 5th June, 1917.

U N I T.	Entraining Station.	Date.	Time.	Detraining Station.
86th Brigade Group.				
2 Battalions	BEAUMETZ RIVIERE	3rd	10 a.m.	FIENVILLERS CANDAS
86th M.G. Company	" "	"	"	" "
88th Fld.Ambulance	" "	"	"	" "
86th Brigade H.Q.	" "	"	11 a.m.	" "
2 Battalions	" "	"	"	" "
86th T.M. Battery	" "	"	"	" "
497 (Kent) Field Coy.	" "	"	"	" "
Adv.Parties 87th & 88th Brigade Groups	" "	"	"	" "
87th Brigade Group.				
2 Battalions	ARRAS	5th	10 a.m.	FIENVILLERS CANDAS
87th M.G. Company	"	"	"	" "
87th T.M. Battery	"	"	"	" "
87th Fld.Ambulance	"	"	"	" "
87th Brigade H.Q.	"	"	11 a.m.	" "
2 Battalions	"	"	"	" "
1/2nd Monmouth Regt.	"	"	"	" "
88th Brigade Group.				
2 Battalions	ARRAS	4th	10 a.m.	FIENVILLERS CANDAS
88th M.G. Company	"	"	"	" "
88th T.M. Battery	"	"	"	" "
29th Divl.Reserve Coy.	"	"	"	" "
29th Divl.Band	"	"	"	" "
2 Battalions	"	"	11 a.m.	" "
510 (London) Field Coy.	"	"	"	" "
89th Fld.Ambulance	"	"	"	" "
29th Divisional H.Q.	"	"	"	" "
29th Divl.Traffic Control	"	"	"	" "

On arrival at CANDAS the 88th and 89th Field Ambulances will proceed to billets in accordance with Location List No.22 already issued.

Brigades will be responsible for entraining and detraining the whole of the Brigade Groups.

Loading parties will be at the entraining point one hour and troops quarter-of-an-hour before the departure of trains.

Captain A. GEE, M.C. will remain in ARRAS until the entrainment of all Units is completed to represent Divisional Headquarters and render to Brigades any assistance necessary. Similarly, Captain T.C. BELL, will be present during the detrainment.

Advance parties should have guides with bicycles at Detraining Station to guide units to billets.

Acknowledge.

[signature]

Captain,

1st June, 1917.

D.A.A.G., 29th Division.

87th BRIGADE ADMINISTRATIVE ORDER.

1. ADVANCED PARTIES.

Advanced Parties of 1 Officer and 6 Other Ranks per Battalion, and a corresponding number for smaller Units, will move by train from BERNAVILLE at 11-a.m., 3rd June. These parties will take bicycles with them, and will carry 3 days rations.

The Officer or N.C.O. in charge of each party will report to REAR BRIGADE HEADQUARTERS, 23 RUE de TURENNE, ARRAS, at 6-p.m. tonight for further instructions. The senior Officer will be in charge.

2. ENTRAINMENT.

(a) The time of entrainment of each unit will be in accordance with Movement Table attached to Brigade Order No. 24.

(b) Surplus Baggage (except as stated in para. 4) will be carried on the train, and will be moved to the Entraining Point by lorry, and together with the Loading Party will be at the Entraining Point 1 hour before the departure of the Train.

(c) Units will take their dixies with them on h the train, as Water Carts and Cookers will move by road on the 4th June.

(d) Rations for the day of entrainment and following day will be carried with the personnel by rail. Rations for the day after will be issued direct to billets by Supply Column.

3. DETRAINMENT.

The Advanced Parties will send guides to the Station to conduct Units to their billets.

4. LORRIES.

To take surplus stores to the Entraining Point, and from the Detraining Point lorries are allotted as follows:-

87th Brigade Headquarters.	1 Lorry.
87th Machine Gun Company.) 87th Trench Mortar Batty.)	1 Lorry.
2nd S.W.Borderers.) 1st Border Regiment.)	1 Lorry.
1st K.O.S.Borderers.) 1st R. Innis. Fusrs.)	1 Lorry.

In addition each Unit mentioned above may send half a lorry load direct by road to billets on the 5th June.

5. WATER TINS.

Units will carry 100 Water Tins in the crates on Limbers and Water Carts.

6. AMMUNITION.

Full establishment of S.A.A., Grenades, Picks and Shovels will be carried in 1st Line Transport.

7. 1st LINE TRANSPORT.

(a) The 1st Line Transport will move by road under the Command of , Capt. LANGLEY R.E. Lieut. DAVIES 2nd South Wales Borderers will be attached for duty to . Captain LANGLEY. R.E.

(b) The Officer Commanding the Transport will be responsible for the March Discipline, billeting etc., on the line of march. He will obtain billets at BERNEVILLE from the Town Major, and at LUCHEUX from the MAIRE.

(c) Personnel 1st Line Transport will carry 1 days rations. Supply Wagons will carry 2 days rations for the 1st Line Transport of the Group.

(d) The Officer Commanding Transport will send a Billeting Party forward each morning. (Note. Chimneys of Cookers must be kept down, on the line of march).

8. TEMPORARY TOWN MAJORS.

On arrival in new Areas Temporary Town Majors will be appointed by Units as follows :-

FIENVILLERS	by	the	1st Royal Innishilling Fusiliers.
AUTHEUX	"	"	1st King's Own Scottish Borderers.
VACQUERIE	"	"	West Riding Field Coy. R.E.
LE MEILLARD	"	"	1/2nd Monmouth Regiment.

9. BATHS.

Baths are established at the following places :-

BERNEVILLE	12 Sprays.
BOIS BERGUES	12 Sprays.
CANDAS	16 Sprays.

Permission to use these Baths will be given on application to Brigade Headquarters except in the case of CANDAS where the Town Major should be applied to.

10. Attention is drawn to 29th Divisional Administrative Order No. 14, as regards reinforcements and leave parties.

[signature]

Captain,
Brigade Major, for
Staff Captain, 87th Infantry Brigade.

2nd June, 1917.

SECRET. Copy No. 8.

87th INFANTRY BRIGADE ORDER NO.24.

2nd June, 1917.

Ref. 1/100,000
Map Sheet No.11.

1. The 87th Infantry Brigade Group (less No. 3 Company Train the 455th (West Riding) Field Company R.E., and 1st Line Transport) will move by rail to the CANDAS Area, on June 5th.
The 455th (West Riding) Field Company R.E., No. 3 Company Train, and all 1st Line Transport will move by road on June 4th.

2. All movement will be in accordance with the Movement Table attached.

3. Administrative Order written in conjuhction with 29th Divisional Administrative Order No. 14 already issued to Units, are attached.

4. ACKNOWLEDGE.

Brodie Mair
Captain,
Brigade Major, 87th Infantry Brigade.

Issued at 1800.

Copies. 1-5- Staff.
6. 2/S.W.B.
7. 1/K.O.S.B.
8. 1/R. Innis. Fus.
9. 1/Border Regt.
10. 87th M.G.Coy.
11. 87th T.M.Bty.
12th 87th Bde Sigs.
13. 87th Field Ambulance.
14. No. 3 Coy., Train.
15. West Riding Field Coy.
16. 1/2nd Monmouth Regt.
17. 29th Division 'G'.
18. 29th Division 'Q'.

SECRET. COPY No 2

1st. ROYAL INNISKILLING FUSILIERS ORDER No. 31.

3rd.Dec.1917.

Reference 1/100,000.
LENS II.

(1) The Battalion (less 1st.Line Transport) will move to FIENVILLERS on the 5th.inst.

(2) Place of Entrainment, ARRAS Station 9.40 a.m.
Train leaves 10.0 a.m.
Place of Detrainment CANDAS.

(3) Time of parade will be notified later.

(4) Dress Marching Order, steel helmets. Water bottles to be filled.

(5) The 1st.Line Transport will move by road on the 4th.inst, under orders of Captain LAMBLIN, M.C.
Starting point G 20 b 0.0. at 7.0 a.m.

Issued at [illegible]

Copy 1. Staff.
2 & 3. War Diary.
4.5.6.7. O.C.Cos.
8. Transport Officer.
9. Qr.Mr.

Capt.& Adjutant.
1st.Royal Inniskilling Fusiliers.

MOVEMENT TABLE.

(A) ENTRAINMENT.

Unit.	Date.	To be at Arras Station at:-	Train Leaves.	Detraining Station.	Location of Billets.
87th Machine Gun Coy.	5th.	9-40 a.m.	10-[illegible].m.	FIENVILLERS-CANDAS.	FIENVILLERS.
87th T.M.Bty.	5th.	"	"	"	"
1st K.O.S.Bords.	5th.	"	"	"	AUTHEUX.
1st R. Innis.F.	5th.	"	"	"	FIENVILLERS.
87th Field Amb.	5th.	"	"	"	LE MAILLARD.
87th Bde Headqrs.	5th.	10-40a.m.	11-[illegible].m.	"	FIENVILLERS.
2nd S.W.Bords.	5th.	"	"	"	CANDAS.
1st Border Rgt.	5th.	"	"	"	CANDAS.
1/2nd Monmouth Regt.	5th.	"	"	"	LE MAILLARD.

(B) TRANSPORT.

Date.	From.	To.	Order of March.	Starting Point.	Time.	REMARKS.
June 4th.	ARRAS.	BERNEVILLE.	87th Brigade Headquarters.	Road Junction G.26.b.9.9.	3-p.m.	Distance of 100 yards to be observed between Units.
" "	"	"	2nd South Wales Bords.	"	3-2.p.m.	
" "	"	"	1st K.O.S.Borderers.	"	3-5.p.m.	
" "	"	"	1st R. Innis. Fusrs.	"	3-8.p.m.	
" "	"	"	1st Border Regiment.	"	3-11.p.m.	To march on 4th via Dry weather Track to DAINVILLE-WARLUS.
" "	"	"	1/2nd Monmouth Rgt.	"	3-14.p.m.	
" "	"	"	87th Machine Gun Co.	"	3-17.p.m.	
" "	"	"	West Riding Fd. Coy.	"	3-20.p.m.	
" "	"	"	87th Field Ambulance.	"	3-25.p.m.	
" "	"	"	No.3 Company Train.	"	3-28.p.m.	
June 5th.	BERNEVILLE.	LUCHEUX.	Time of start, order of march etc, to be detailed by O.C. Column.			
June 6th.	LUCHEUX.	CANDAS AREA.				

SECRET.

Copy No. 7

87th INFANTRY BRIGADE ORDER No. 25.

Ref. Map.
1/100,000.
LENS 11.

In the Field.
25-6-1917.

1. The 87th INFANTRY BRIGADE GROUP (less the 455th West Riding Field Company R.E.) will move by Rail on June 26th and 27th 1917.

2. 1st and 2nd Line Transport will accompany Units on the journey.

3. Units will carry the current day's rations on the man and Supply Wagons will carry One day's Rations.

4. All Movements will be in accordance with the Movement Table attached.

5. First Train due to arrive at PROVEN at 2340.

6. Administrative Orders are attached.

7. ACKNOWLEDGE.

Issued at 0700.

C. G. Murray. CAPTAIN.
for BRIGADE MAJOR. 87th INF. BRIGADE.

Copies 1-3. = Staff.
4. = War Diary.
5. = File.
6. = 2/S.W.B.
7. = 1/K.O.S.B.
8. = 1/R. Innis. F.
9. = 1/Border Regt.
10. = 87th M.G. Company.
11. = 87th T.M. Battery.
12. = 87th Bde. Signals.
13. = 87th Field. Ambulance.
14. = No. 3. Company Train.
15. = 86th Inf. Bde.
16. = 88th Inf. Bde.
19. = 29th Division 'G'.
20. = 29th Division 'Q'.
21. = R.T.O., DOULLENS.
22. = R.T.O. HOPOUTRE.
23. = R.T.O. PROVEN.

87th INFANTRY BRIGADE ADMINISTRATIVE ORDER.

ENTRAINMENT.

1. Entraining Stations will be DOULLENS NORTH and DOULLENS SOUTH.

Detraining Stations will be PROVEN and HOPOUTRE.

2. (a) All Trains consist of 1 "Officers" Carriage, 17 Flat Trucks, and 30 Covered Trucks.

(b) Each Flat Truck will take an average of 4 axles.
Each Covered Truck will take an average of 40 men, or 6 H.D. Horses, or 8 L.D. Horses or Mules.

(c) No personnel will be allowed in the Brake Vans at each end of the train, or on the roofs of the trucks. No Covered trucks should be used for baggage, as it restricts space avaliable for personnel.

3. (a) INFANTRY BATTALIONS. Transport will arrive at the Entraining
(1) Station 3 hours before the departure of the train, and the personnel 1½ hours.

(b) OTHER UNITS. will arrive complete 3 hours before the departure of the train.

(ii) A Complete Marching Out State showing the number of men, horses, G.S. Wagons, Limbered G.S. Wagons, and 2 wheeled Wagons, and bicycles, will be sent down with the transport of each Unit, so that accommodation can be checked by the R.T.O. Limbered G.S. Wagons will be counted as two 2 wheeled wagons on the state.

(iii) Supply and Baggage Wagons will accompany Units, Supply Wagons carrying 1 days' rations. Units will carry current days rations on the man for the journey.

(iv) Entrainment of all Units will be completed ½ and hour before time of the departure of train.

(v) Breast Ropes for Horse Trucks will be provided by Units. Ropes for lashing vehicles on the Flat Trucks will be provided by the Railway.

(vi) Picquets will be detailed for duty at all stops, for each end of the train.

4. ENTRAINMENT PARTIES.

The 88th Brigade are supplying Working Parties for Entraining Duties at DOULLENS NORTH and DOULLENS SOUTH, throughout the whole Entrainment.

5. DETRAINING PARTIES.

Offrs.	O.Rks.	To be detailed by	From Party in Train No.	For Duty At.	Remarks.
2.	100.	O.C.[illegible]	1.	HOPOUTRE.	To Detrain Trains Nos. 1, 4, 7 & 10.
2.	100.	O.C.1/Border R.	3.	PROVEN.	To Detrain Trains Nos. 3, 6 & 9.

The Senior Officer in Charge of the above parties will report to the R.T.O. at HOPOUTRE and PROVEN respectively. The 88th Brigade will relieve 87th Brigade parties on arrival of trains Nos. 12 & 13.

Administrative Order Contd.

6. 2nd Lieutenant J.OLIPHANT. 1st K.O.S.Borderers is detailed as Brigade Entraining Officer.

7. Units will take every available Water Tin in their possession on Limbers and Water Carts.

8. LORRIES. Lorries to take Surplus Stores to the Entraining Point are allotted as follows:-

87th Brigade H.Q.	1 Lorry.
87th M.G.Company.) 87th T.M.Battery.)	1 Lorry.
2nd S.W.Borderers.) 1st Border Regt.)	1 Lorry.
1st K.O.S.Borderers.) 1st Rl.Innis.Fus.)	1 Lorry.

Lorries will be available at Brigade Headquarters at (on 26th) 10.a.m. Officers Commanding Units will arrange mutually the hours at which they will use the lorries and will arrange to have guides at Brigade Headquarters accordingly.

June 25th.1917.

[signature]
CAPTAIN,
for BRIGADE MAJOR.87th INFANTRY BRIGADE.

SECRET.

Copy. No. " "

25/6/17.

IST. ROYAL INNISKILLING ORDER NO. 22.

Ref. Map 1/100,000.
LENS II.

(1) The Battalion will move to PROVEN on the 26th. instant.

(2) The Battalion (less "A" Co.) will parade at 8.45.p.m. on the 26th. inst. to march to DOULLENS for entrainment to PROVEN. Train No. 9. leaves at 0119. 27th. inst.

(3) "A" Company will parade at 0045 27th. inst. for ditto. Train No. 12 leaves at 0519.

(4) Ist & 2nd. Line Transport will parade at 1030 26th. for ditto. Train leaves at 0119. 27th. inst.

I Cooker & team will entrain with "A" Co. Train leaves at 0519. 27th. inst.

(5) Entrainment will be completed ½ an hour before the departure of the train.

(6) Transport Officer will hand in a complete Marching Out State of the Battalion including men, vehicles & horses to the R.T.O. on arrival at DOULLENS SOUTH.

(7) Billets will be thoroughly clean & ready for inspection by 1945 26th. inst. O.C. "A" Company will arrange to inspect his own billets.

Copies to I. C.O.
2. Adjutant.
3 & 4. War Diary.
5 6 7 & 8. Companies.
9. Qr. Mr.
10. T. Officer.
11. M.O.

2/Lieut. & A/Adjutant.
Ist. Royal Inniskilling Fusiliers.

MOVEMENT TABLE (Contd).

No. of Train.	Unit.	Date.	Time.	ENTRAINING STATION.	DETRAINING STATION.	REMARKS
7.	2nd South Wales Bordrs. less 1 Coy.	26th June 1917.	2319.	DOULLENS NORTH.	HOPOUTRE.	
10.	1 Coy. 2nd S.W.B. with 1 Cooker and Team. 87th Fld. Ambulance. 1 Coy. 4/Worcrs. with 1 Cooker and Team. Mobile Vet. Section.	27th June 1917.	0319.	DOULLENS NORTH.	HOPOUTRE.	
9.	1st R. Innis. Fus. less 1 Coy.	27th June 1917.	0119.	DOULLENS SOUTH.	PROVEN.	
12.	1 Coy. R. Innis. Fus. with 1 Cooker and Team. 88th Bde. H.Q. 88th Signal Sect. 88th T. M. B. 88th M. G. Co.	27th June 1917.	0519.	DOULLENS SOUTH.	PROVEN.	

MOVEMENT TABLE.

No. of Train.	Unit.	Date.	Time.	ENTRAINING STATION.	DETRAINING STATION.	REMARKS.
1.	87th Bde.Hd.Qrs. Sign. 1 Section. M.G.Company. T.M.Battery. 1 Company 1st K.O.S.B. with 1 Cooker and Team.	June 26th 1917.	1519.	DOULLENS NORTH.	HOPOUTRE.	
3.	No.3 Coy.Train. 1 Company 1st Border Regt. with 1 Cooker and Team. Salvage Coy. Employment Coy. & Q.Divl. Train.	26th June 1917.	1719.	DOULLENS SOUTH.	PROVEN.	
4.	1st K.O.S.B. less 1 Coy.	26th June 1917.	1919.	DOULLENS NORTH.	HOPOUTRE.	
6.	1st Border Rgt. less 1 Coy.	26th June 1917.	2119.	DOULLENS SOUTH.	PROVEN.	

P.T.O.

87th INFANTRY BRIGADE ORDER NO. 26.

Ref. Map :-
1/40,000 Sheet 27.
1/20,000 Sheet 28 N.W.

1. The 87th Infantry Brigade will relieve the 113th Infantry Brigade in the ZWAANHOF SECTOR, commencing on the night of the 27th/28th June. Relief to be complete by dawn on the 29th June.

2. Reliefs will take place as per attached table.

3. All trench maps, stores, etc. will be taken over and a receipt given.

4. The 87th Machine Gun Company and 87th Trench Mortar Battery will relieve similar units of the 113th Brigade under arrangements mutually between Commanding Officers concerned.

5. Units proceeding to the forward area on the night of the 27th/28th will move up with one day's rations and filled waterbottles.

6. ~~Forward~~ Formed bodies of troops will not move East of the ELVERDINGHE-YPRES Road before 10 p.m.

7. ACKNOWLEDGE.

Captain,

26th June, 1917. Brigade Major, 87th Infantry Brigade.

Copies to :-
2nd S.W.Borderers.
1st K.O.S.Borderers.
1st R.Innis.Fusrs.
1st Border Regiment
87th Bde.Signal Section.
87th Machine Gun Coy.
87th Trench Mortar Battery.
113th Infantry Brigade.
38th Division 'G'.
29th Division 'G'.

Movement Table

Unit	From	To	Via	To Relieve	Remarks
By night 27/28 June					
1st R. Innis. Fus. B & D Co.	Camp [illegible]	Canal Bank [illegible]	[illegible] at [illegible] [illegible] at [illegible]	2 Cos. 13/R.W.F.	Guides 1 per Co. will meet Units at Detrainment Point.
By day 28 June					
1st R. Innis. Fus. B & D Co.	Canal Bank	Right Sub-Sector		2/Cos. 14/R.W.F.	Details to be arranged with Officers Commanding Units concerned.
By night 28/29 June					
1st R. Innis. Fus. [illegible]	Camp [illegible]	Canal Bank [illegible]	[illegible]	1/R.W.F. [illegible]	Guides will meet Units at [illegible]

MOVEMENT TABLE.

UNIT.	from	To	Via	To relieve	Remarks.
(a) Night 27th/28th June 1st Border Regiment	Camp	CANAL BANK. H.Q. C.13.c.00.15	Entrain at INTERNATIONAL CORNER 9.30 pm. Detrain at B.8.c.	15/R.W.F. (in support).	Guides (1 Per Hd.Qrs. & 1 per Coy.) will meet units at detrainment point.
1st R.Innis.Fusrs. (less 2 Companies).	Camp	CANAL BANK H.Q. C.19.c.c45.15	- do -	2/Coys. 13/R.W.F.	
87th M.G.Coy. 87th T.M.Bty.	Camp	CANAL BANK. C.19.c.4.2.	By road via INTERNATIONAL CORNER Road Junction B.23.a.3.1. - DROMORE CORNER - HOSPITAL FARM - DAWSONS CORNER		Guides will meet Units at DAWSONS CORNER.
By Day 28th June. (b) 1st Border Regiment	CANAL BANK	Left Sub-Sector		14/R.W.F.	Details to be arranged with Officers Commandin Units concerned.
1st R. Innis.Fusrs. (2 Companies).	" "	Right Sub-Sector		13/R.W.F. 2 Coys.	
87th M.G. Coy.	" "	Firing Line		Similar Units	
87th T.M.Battery	" "	Firing Line		of 113th Bde.	
By night 28th/29th June. (c) Brigade H.Q.	Camp	CANAL BANK HQ.C.19.c.4.2.	By Road (route as above).	113th Bde.H.Q.	Guides will meet Units at DAWSONS CORNER.
1st K.O.S.Borderers	Camp	CANAL BANK HQ C.19.A.01.45	"	14/R.W.F. (in support)	
1st R.Innis.Fusrs. (2 Companies).	Camp	CANAL BANK.	"	13/R.W.F. (2 Coys.)	
2nd S.W.Borderers.	Camp	L.2 Works. (B.23.a.)	"	16/R.W.F. (in support).	

Copy 2

1/R. Inniskilling Order No 24.

28/6/17.

I. B & D Coys will relieve two Coys 13 R.W.F in front line & Support Line. Relief will commence at 5.30 pm.

II. All movement will be carried out via HUDDERSFIELD TRENCH in parties of 10 at 60 yds distance

III. Completion of relief will be reported to Bn HQ by code.

IV. Acknowledge

1 & 2 War Diary
3 O.C. B Co
4 " D Co.

J.C. Wenk Capt Adjt
1/R. Inniskilling Fus

SECRET.   Copy No."3"

Ist.Royal Inniskilling Fusiliers Order No.23.

Ref.Map 1/40,000. Sheet 27.   1/20,000. Sheet 28. N.W.
No.23.

(1) The Battalion will relieve the 13th.Royal Welsh Fus., in the right sub-sector of the ZWAANHOF SECTOR commencing on the night of 27 - 28th.- relief to be complete by dawn the 29th.

(2) Relief will take place as per attached table.

(3) All Trench Maps, Stores etc.,will be taken over & a receipt given.

(4) "B" & "D"Cos.,proceeding to the forward area on the night of the 27 - 28th. will move up with one day's rations and filled waterbottles.

(5) Formed bodies of troops will not move EAST of ELVERDINGHE - YPRES ROAD before 10.0.p.m.

Copies to I. C.O.
2. Adjt.
3 & 4. War Diary.
5.6.7.8. Cos.
9. Qr.Mr.
10. T.Officer.
11. M.O.
12. A/Adjt.

J.Cowen Capt
~~2/Lt.& A/~~Adjutant
Ist.Royal Inniskilling Fusiliers

Captain Stokes.

[illegible] Patrols to go out tonight at

I. 11.30.p.m.

No.I. 2/Lt.Despard and eight O.R. I have given him his instructions.

No.2. (a) 2/Lt.Davidson and eight O.R. are to go out from Post 25 on a bearing of 61° (True Bearing)
His object is to create a diversion and draw away the enemy's attention from No.I. patrol.(ii) To definitly locate the post which fired on Lt. Jones patrol last night.

(b) These Officers are to write their own reports and render them direct to me.

(c) The men for these patrols are to be chosen from those who were picked at PENTVILLERS for the Raiding Party.

2. The remainder of the men (24) who were chosen for the Raiding Party are to parade under Lt.Aitcheson at any convenient time after dark and practise in front of BULLY Trench -
They are to practise, getting quickly out of the trench, crawling quietly and in the proper [illegible] keeping touch and formation in the dark, passing orders etc.

3. Will you and Lt.Londrum render to the Adjutant by noon tomorrow nominal rolls of the N.C.O's and men who are chosen for the Raiding Party, a total of 40 men.

Major.

30/6/17. Comdg.Ist.Bn.,The Royal Inniskilling Fusiliers.
8.10.p.m.

"A" Form.

MESSAGES AND SIGNALS.

Army Form C. 2121.
(In pads of 100.)

No. of Message..............

Prefix .... Code .... m.	Words.	Charge.	This message is on a/c of:	Recd. at .... m.
Office of Origin and Service Instructions.	Sent		.... Service.	Date ....
	At .... m.			From ....
	To			
	By		(Signature of "Franking Officer.")	By ....

TO O.C. 1/Border Regt

Sender's Number.	Day of Month.	In reply to Number.	AAA
* SM 310	10		

Please hasten your Reply for the [illegible] Report

[illegible]

T. W. Ross Capt

From 1/[illegible]

Place

Time

The above may be forwarded as now corrected. (Z)

Censor. Signature of Addressor or person authorised to telegraph in his name.

* This line should be erased if not required.

(2195.) Wt. W 12932/M1294. 375,000 Pads. 1/17. H. W. & V., Ld. (E. 818.)

Ref.Map St.JULIEN. 1/10,000.

DISPOSITIONS FRONT LINE "B"Co. (2 Offrs.100.O.R.)

Posts.	Map Reference.	Strength.
Post 23.	c.14.a 20.00.	2 N.C.O's. 7 Riflemen. 3 Lewis Gunners.
Post 24.	c.13.b.90.15.	I N.C.O. 5 Riflemen. 3 Lewis Gunners.
Post 25.	c.13.b.80.50.	I N.C.O. 5 Riflemen. 3 Lewis Gunners.
Post 26.	c.13.d.~~25~~.35.	~~3 Signallers,~~ I.N.C.O. 3 Riflemen, 3 Lewis Gunners.
("B"Co.Hd.Qrs. ("D"Co.Hd.Qrs.	c.13.d.60.70.	3 Signallers. 2.W.O.Class II. 2 Cooks (Officers) 5 Servants. 8 Runners.
Rem.of Co. in	NILE TRENCH.	(I Anti Aircraft L.G.Teams. 4 Stretcher Bearers.

N.B. Post 26 is not held by day.

DISPOSITIONS SUPPORT LINE "D"CO. (3 Offrs. 100 O.R.) BULLY TRENCH

BULLY POST.	c.13 d 65.80.	I N.C.O. 3 Riflemen. 3 Lewis Gunners.
BUTT 15.	c.13 d 65.00.	I N.C.O. 3 Riflemen. 3 Lewis Gunners.
BUTT 16.	c.13 b 50.10.	3 Lewis Gunners.

N.B. These posts are held by night only. Rem.of Co. in BULLY TRENCH.

DISPOSITIONS OF RESERVE. (0 Offrs. 220.O.R.)

"A" & "C" Cos.	CANAL BANK. c 19.c 45.16.
Bn.,Hd.,Qrs.	CANAL BANK. W.side of Canal.

Major.

29/6/17. Commanding Ist.Battalion The Royal Inniskilling Fusiliers.

Army Form C. 2118.

87/29

WAR DIARY
or
INTELLIGENCE SUMMARY

(Erase heading not required.)

Instructions regarding War Diaries and Intelligence Summaries are contained in F. S. Regs., Part II. and the Staff Manual respectively. Title Pages will be prepared in manuscript.

1/R Inniskilling Fus No 1.

Vol 17

Place	Date	Hour	Summary of Events and Information	Remarks and references to Appendices
Trenches.	July 1st		Quiet day. Canal Bank shelled intermittently.	[illegible]
	2nd		Relieved by 2nd/SWB & go into Brigade Reserve. vide B.O. No 24.	[illegible]
			Capt W Howard & 2/Lt J.E. Nelson joined.	
	2nd–5th		Working parties in front line digging HELM TRENCH & carrying parties to front line. Enemy put salvoes into Camp on nights of 3rd & 4th at 10.30 pm. Two wounded.	[illegible]
	5th & 6th		Relieved by 4th Worcesters & 1 Essex vide B.O. No 25.	[illegible]
	7–13th		Training. B213 Strength 7th 32 O. 720 O.R. ration Strength 23 O. 610. O.R. 2/Lt W.A. Armstrong joined 8th 2/Lt C.G. [illegible] 9th	[illegible]
	13th		Brigade moves up into Support lines vide B.O. 26.	[illegible]
	14th		Working parties. B213 14th 33 O 742. O.R. Ration strength 28 O 602. O.R	[illegible]
	14th to 19th		Working parties occasionally shelled & a few casualties occurred. 1 O. 4 O.R. K. 30 O.R. W. 2/Lt Despard killed by our own guns in X Line on 19th. Lt Col. Sherwood-Kelly wounded	[illegible]
P2 Area.	19th		Move back to PROVEN AREA Vide B.O. 27.	[illegible]
	20th		Training.	
	21st		B213. 32 Officers 708 O.R. Ration strength 26. O 605. O.R.	[illegible]
	22-26		Training. Lt Rumley (SR) & 2Lt D.C. Osborne (SR) reported for duty 26th inst	[illegible]
	27		Moved to training area 27/D12c & bivouaced for the night.	[illegible]
	28		Took part in Brigade Scheme for attack. Strength 34 O. 704 O.R's Ration strength 26 O. 628 OR's Returned to Camp same evening.	[illegible]
	29		Training.	
	30		Brigade moves up into Divisional Support in Forest Camp area vide BO 28	[illegible]

2449 Wt. W14957/M90 750,000 1/16 J.B.C. & A. Forms/C.2118/12.

Army Form C. 2118.

WAR DIARY
or
INTELLIGENCE SUMMARY
(Erase heading not required.)

Instructions regarding War Diaries and Intelligence Summaries are contained in F. S. Regs., Part II. and the Staff Manual respectively. Title Pages will be prepared in manuscript.

1st R Innis Killing Fus No 2

Place	Date	Hour	Summary of Events and Information	Remarks and references to Appendices
Trenches	31/7/17		The Battalion went on a working party East side of the Canal worked on road: STEAM MILL 28/B6d3.3 to Railway 28/C1c7.3. Left FOREST CAMP area at 18.30 returning at 22.30 Casualties during work: 2/Lt W.E. Cunning Killed 5 O.R. Killed 1 OR. D of W. 18 W. Work was done on ground captured from the Germans during the morning Zero hour being 3.50 a.m.	[illegible]

[signature] Lieut. Colonel
Commanding 1st R. Inniskilling Fusiliers

2449 Wt. W14957/M90 750,000 1/16 J.B.C. & A. Forms/C.2118/12.

SECRET. Copy No."4"

IST.ROYAL INNISKILLING FUSILIERS ORDER No.24.

2/7/17

Map Reference.
St.JULIEN 28 N.W.2.

(1) The Battalion will be relieved by the 2/S.W.B.,on 2nd. July 1917, and go into camp vacated by 2/S.W.B.,Wood B.23.a.

(2) Relief will be carried out by sections commencing at 2.0.p.m., a distance of 60^x being maintained.

(3) Cos.,in front line will move out via HUDDERSFIELD TRENCH, & Bridge 6 B, & Cos.,in reserve via Bridge 6 B.

(4) Guides will not be necessary. Arrangements have been made for points to direct Cos.,to Camp. First point will be at E end of Bridge 6 B.

(5) All petrol tins, mess stores etc.,to be stacked at Bn.,Hd.,Qrs.,by 1.30.p.m.

(6) All trench stores to be handed over & receipts obtained & forwarded to Orderly Room on arrival in Camp.

(7) Trenches & Dug-outs must be left thoroughly clean & in sanitary condition.

Copies to I. C.O.
2. Adjt.
3 & 4. War Diary.
5.6.7.8. Cos.
9 S.W.B.

[signature]
Capt.& Adjutant.
Ist.Royal Inniskilling Fus.

SECRET.

87TH. INFANTRY BRIGADE ORDER No.27.

I. The following relief will take place on the 2nd. July. The relief to be carried out during daylight.

(a) The 2/S.W.B. will relieve the I/R.Innis.Fus., in the right sub-sector and will take over from the I/Border Regt. , from the present left of the I/R.Innis.Fus. up to but exclusive of Post 43.

(b) The I/K.O.S.B. will relieve the I/Border Regt., from Post 43 to Post 42. (Present left boundary. Reliefs will be carried out by arrangements to be made mutually between C.O's concerned.

2. After relief the I/R.Innis.Fus. & 1/Border Regt., will go into the trenches etc., vacated by the 2/S.W. Borderers & I/K.O.S.B. respectively.

3. All trench stores will be handed over.

4. The boundaries between Battalions will be from Post 43 to post 31. (both inclusive to left subsector) thence along southern side of BARNSLEY ROAD.

5. ACKNOWLEDGE.

(Sd) Brodiemair. Captain.
Bde.Major.
87th. Infantry Brigade.

SECRET. Copy No. " "

IST.ROYAL INNISKILLING FUSILIERS NO.25.

Ref Map Sheet 37.

(1) The Battalion will be relieved in L 2 WORKS ~~by the 4th Worcester Regt.~~, on the nights of the 5/6th. & 6/7th.

(2) Relief will be in accordance with attached movement table.

(3) On the nights of relief all Officers Kits, Mess Stores, Lewis Guns etc., will be stacked near the Cookhouse by 9.0.p.m.

(4) Camp must be thoroughly clean before relief.

(5) Guides will be arranged by the Adjutant

Capt.& Adjutant.

5/7/27. Ist.Royal Inniskilling Fusiliers.

MOVEMENT TABLE.

Date.	Unit.	From	To	On Relief By
Night 5/6th.	Hd.Qrs. "B"& "D"Cos. Parade at 10.0.p.m.	L.S.Works.	Corps Staging Area.	4th.Worcester Regt.(less 2 Cos.)
Night 6/[illegible]	"A" & "C"Cos. Parade at 10.0.p.m.	L.W.Works.	Corps Staging Area.	Ist.Essex Regt.

A distance of 200 yards will be observed between Companies, & between Companies & Headquarters.

SECRET. Copy No." "

Ist.Royal Inniskilling Fusiliers Order No.26.

Reference Map Sheet 28 N.W.
1/20.000.

13/7/17.

I. The 87th.Brigade will become the Brigade in Support. The Battalion will relieve the 16th.Middlesex Regt. on the night of the 13/14th.

2. Relief will be carried out in accordance with attached table.

3. The Battalion will parade at 6.45.p.m.

4. Route via INTERNATIONAL CORNER - DROMORE CORNER thence by Track No.9.to BRIDGE JUNCTION - DAWSONS CORNER - WOOD B.17.c.

5. "A"Company will break off at BRIDGE JUNCTION. Guides will meet "B" & "D"Cos.at WOOD B.17.c

6. An interval of 200 yards between Cos.will be observed. Order of March.A.B.D.C.& Hd.Qrs.

7. Relief complete will be reported to Bn,.Hd.Qrs.by Runner.

8. All Officers Kits & Surplus stores will be stacked at Qr.Mr.Srores by 6.0.p.m.

Copy No.I. Staff.
2 & 3 War Diary.
4 5 6 7 Cos.
8. M.O.
9. T.O.
10.Qr.Mr.
11. 16th.Middlesex.

[signature]
Capt.& Adjutant.
Ist.Royal Inniskilling Fus.

MOVEMENT TABLE.

Date.	Unit.	From	To	Relief of
13th July.	Bn. Hd. Qrs. & "C" Co.	CAMP.	Wood S.W. of DEAD MAN FARM Hd. Qrs. at B.17.c.2.1.	Hd. Qrs. & Detachment 16th. Middlesex.
	"A" Co.	"	ELVERDINGHE.	"D" COMPANY.
	"B" & "D" Cos.	"	X LINE B.18.d. Between TALANA & HULL FARM.	"B" & "C" Cos. 16th. Middlesex.

SECRET. COPY No.9.

[illegible]th. INFANTRY BRIGADE INSTRUCTIONS No. I.

Ref. Maps. July [illegible]th. 1917
1/10.000. Sheets 28 N.W. and 20 S.W.4.
1/20.000. Sheets 28 N.W. and 20 S.E.

1. The XIVth Corps in conjunction with troops on the North and South will attack the enemy on a date and at an hour Zero to be notified later.

2. The 29th Division will be in Corps Reserve in rear of the Guards Division.
The 38th Division will be attacking on the right of the Guards and the 1st French Division on the left.

3. The boundaries, objectives and hour of advance of the attacking troops are as follows. -

GUARDS DIVISIONAL BOUNDARY.
South.
From CANAL BANK at B.18a. [illegible] thence along NORTH side of railway.
North.
From CANAL BANK at [illegible]

Brigade Boundary.
B.12. [illegible]
[illegible]

OBJECTIVES. (including objectives of the French on our left and the 38th Division on our right both of which will be co-operating at the same time).
Blue Line. [illegible]
[illegible] (leave at [illegible]
Zero plus [illegible]
1.40.
Black Line. [illegible]
(leave at [illegible]
Zero Plus. [illegible]
Green Line.
(leave at T. [illegible]
Zero Plus [illegible]

Dotted Green Line. [illegible]

Red Line. [illegible]
[illegible]

4. (a) The Green Line is the main objective for the first days operations but the capture of the passages of the STEENBEEK are also of great importance.
If opportunity offers ground further East up to and including the RED LINE should be occupied provided that this can be done without launching troops against organised and occupied positions without adequate artillery support and preparations.
(b) Inpursant of the above regards Divisions are attacking the BLUE BLACK AND GREEN LINES on a two Brigade front. The Third Brigade being utilised for capturing passages over the STEENBEEK and establishing a line (Dotted Green Line) on the E Bank of the river.

(c) As soon as the passages of the STEENBEEK are secured Cavalry Patrols will push forward under order of the XIV Corps to discover the position and state of enemy. Tactical points secured by the Cavalry will be consolidated by the Guards Brigade. If opportunity offers all ground up to the RED LINE is to be occupied ans consilidated.

Brigade Instructions Contd.

5. The Guards Division will construct the following strong points:-
(a) T.30.d.9.8.
(b) On both flanks of [illegible].
(c) On the line U.25.[illegible] - ABRI Farm - [illegible] Farm.

6. The Guards Division will be in Liaison with the French Di- [illegible]
S.W. Corner of Wood 14. [illegible]
[illegible] Farm.
E. Corner of Wood 16. [illegible]
[illegible] Farm.
~~E. Corner of Wood [illegible]~~ [illegible] Colombo Farm.

7. 45 mats will be placed across the Canal by the Guards Division. These will be supplemented by at least 10 patrol tin floating bridges to take Infantry in file. Troops must not attempt to cross the CANAL except on bridges or mats as the bottom is soft and muddy.
[illegible] Pontoon Bridge and [illegible] Pontoon Bridge are both reserved for artillery wheeled traffic.
[illegible] Bridge is reserved for Infantry [illegible] traffic.

8. A list of landmarks in so far as [illegible] opposite the Guards Division Area which are visible from the left Bank of the CANAL is attached. Battalion Staffs and [illegible] should make themselves conversant with them. [illegible] will notify these headquarters [illegible] in the Guards Area in order that arrangements [illegible] made for their reception.

9. There will be a Divisional Collecting Station [illegible] at [illegible] Farm (B.[illegible]) and the Corps Cage at [illegible]

10. There will be an advanced dressing station [illegible] (B.23.[illegible]) and in the [illegible]
[illegible] Farm ([illegible])
Canal by Clearing Stations will be [illegible]:-
[illegible]
[illegible]
[illegible]
Also a Corps Dressing Station [illegible]

11. At Zero the Brigade will be concentrated [illegible]

12. Dumps will be [illegible] as follows:-
Right [illegible] Brigade Dump.
[illegible]
Left [illegible] Brigade Dump.
[illegible]
Left [illegible] Brigade [illegible]
[illegible] [illegible]
[illegible] and Water. [illegible]
R.E. Stores. [illegible]

13. At Zero [illegible] will be as follows.
[illegible] [illegible]
[illegible] [illegible]
[illegible] Division. [illegible]
[illegible]
[illegible] Battalions. [illegible]
Rights [illegible]
[illegible] Battalions.
[illegible] [illegible]

SECRET.

Copy No. "2"

1st. ROYAL INNISKILLING FUSILIERS ORDER No. [illegible]

19 [illegible]/17.

Ref. Maps. 1/20.000.
Sheets 27 - 28.

1. The 29th. Division will be relieved in the ZWAANHOF SECTOR commencing on the 19/20th. July.
On completion of relief the 29th. Division will be in Corps Reserve.
The Battalion will move to Camp in PROVEN AREA ([illegible]) today. Hd. Qrs. at 27/F 3.a.8.3.

2. There will be no [illegible] of relief.

3. Companies will move off at 10 p.m. [illegible] or any road may be used but units going WEST must give way to those going EAST.

4. Transport Officer will arrange transport & Companies will leave a small party to load up Lewis Guns, stores etc. These parties will accompany transport to Camp.

5. Report arrival in Camp.

[signature] Capt. & Adjutant.
1st. Royal Inniskilling Fusiliers.

SECRET. Copy No. [illegible]

57th. INFANTRY BRIGADE INSTRUCTIONS No. [illegible]

(This cancels Instructions 1 and 2, and extract from Division letters attached to 57th. Infantry Brigade Instructions No.1 and 2.)

JULY [illegible]

Ref. Maps.
Sheets:- [illegible]

1. GENERAL.

(a) The [illegible] Division will be attacking on the right of the [illegible] Division and the French on the left.

(b) Boundaries of the [illegible] Division are as follows:-

South. From [illegible] at [illegible], thence along North side of railway.

North. From [illegible] at [illegible]

(c) OBJECTIVES including the Objective of the French on the left and the [illegible] DIVISION on the right.:-

BLUE LINE. [illegible]
(Leave at Zero plus [illegible])

BLACK LINE. [illegible]
(Leave at Zero plus [illegible])

[illegible] LINE. [illegible]
(Leave at Zero plus [illegible])

[illegible] [illegible]

RED LINE. [illegible]

The main objective of the first day's operations will be the [illegible] LINE, [illegible] up to and including the [illegible]. Once the [illegible] patrols will be pushed forward to [illegible] positions and [illegible] of the enemy [illegible] will [illegible].

(d). The following [illegible] Division, the [illegible] the [illegible].

(e). A list of landmarks [illegible] you.

2. [illegible]. [illegible] must be reconnoitred by Battalions [illegible]. [illegible] will be placed across the [illegible] supplemented by at least [illegible] Infantry in file. [illegible] placed in conspicuous [illegible] to a [illegible] position [illegible] Bridge.

These Bridges will be numbered 1 - 16 from Right to Left.
BOESINGHE and CATUS Pontoon Bridges are reserved for Artillery Wheeled Traffic.
CRAPOURILLOT Bridge is reserved for Infantry "UP" Traffic, including Pack animals and transport.
It is of the greatest impottance that all traffic Regulations are observed.

3. EQUIPMENT.
(a). Each Battalion will have one Stokes Mortar Detachment.
(b). Each Company 12 S.O.S. Rifle Greenade.
(c) Each Platoon 1 Bill-Hook, 1 Long Handle Wire Cutter.
(d). Each Lewis Gun Section 32 Drums in haversacks.
(e). Each man will carry oneJs days rations plus Irion Rations, plus unexpended portion of the days rations.
Two Hand grenades, 2 sandbags.
(f). 50% will carry one Aeroplane Flare.
(g). 25% will carry a pick or shovel. These are surplus to Battalion picks and shovels which will remain in Transport until required.
(h). All Officers will wear the same clothes as their men, and will carry compases.
(i). Distinguishing Marks (S.S.135, Sect.32.) will be worn by all ranks.
(j) Packs and greatcoats will be stored under arrangements to be notified later.

(4). COMMUNICATIONS.
(i). On no accoount will any Earth Return Circuit be employed. Metalic Power only to be used.
(ii). All Runners will be instructed to carry their messages in the top right hand pocket of their jacket.
(iii). Two pairs of pigeons will be issued daily to Battalions Messages sent by pigeon will be in "Clear".
(iv). Attention is drawn S.S.148. Messages handed in to Wireless Station will be in B.A.B. Code.
(v). Contact Patrol Machines will be marked with two BLACK ordinaryx recangular flags, attached to and projecting from the lower plane each side of the fusilage.
(vi). Flares are not to lit until called for when as far as possible they should be lit in groups of three.
(vii) Ground sheets, panels and code letters will be laid out at each Battalion Headquarters.

(v) DUMPS- Dumps will be established as follows:-
S.A.A. and Grenades. - at B.17.a.8.2. and B.10.b.2.1.
RATIONS and WATER. - at B.10.a.5.7. and B.11.a.3.5.
R.E. Stores - at JOYEUSE FARM and at B.11.c 9.8.

(6) PRISONERS. Units will send back to Divisional Collecting Station at B.10.d.5.2. all prisoners, obtaining a receipt from the A.P.M. All receipts for prisoners handed over for the 24 hours ending 12 will be sent to Brigade Headquarters each afternoon. Attention is drawn to I.G.101/8 dated 10th. July. (already issued).

(7) MEDICAL. Advanced Dressing Stations are situated at OLD MILL (B.15.a.1.5.) and in MAIN STREET, BOESINGHE Village, also xxxkx Walking Wounded Post in BLEUET FARM (B.10.c.3.1.).
3 extra stretchers per Battalion has been issued.x
(8) Attention is drawn to 38th Division C.G.S.38/33, already issued.

SECRET. Copy No. 4

1st. ROYAL INNISKILLING FUSILIERS ORDER No. [illegible].

JULY 30th. 1917.

Reference Maps:-

28 N.W.) 1/20,000.
27 N.E.)

28 N.W.2.) 1/10,000.
28 N.W.4.)

1. An attack will be made on enemy lines. Objectives and Boundaries have already been issued. Zero day will be 31st.July 1917.

2. The 29th.Division will be in support of the GUARDS Division.

3. The Battalion parade at [illegible] p.m. and move to the Forest [illegible] tonight. Camp II. (A.12.b.) Starting point Cross Roads [illegible] [illegible] p.m.

4. Dress:- Marching Order.

5. 1st.Line Transport will accompany Unit.

6. All Lines gained will be consolidated and will become line of resistance.

7. On Zero day the Battalion will be placed under command of G.O.C. [illegible] Division and will return to Brigade Command on completion of work that day.

8. After Zero, the Battalion will be ready to move at [illegible] notice.

9. Watches will be synchronised from a Watch to be taken round by a Staff Officer on "Z" minus one (1) day.

Copies to 1. C.O.
2. Staff.
3-4. War Diary.
5-8. Companies.
9. Q.M.
10. T.Officer.
11. S.Officer.
12. O/C. [illegible]

Captain & Adjutant.
1st.Royal Inniskilling Fusiliers.

Copy No.8.

SECRET.

87th INFANTRY BRIGADE ORDER No.34.

Reference Maps:-
Sheet N.W.)1/20,000
" S.W.)
" N.W.2.)1/10,000
" S.W.4.)

1. An attack will be made on the enemy lines on the date and at a Zero hour to be notified later.

2. The 29th Division will be in support of the Guards Division.

3. Previous to Zero day the 87th Brigade will be concentrated in the FOREST CAMP Area.
Movements will be in accordance with March Table attached.

4. The Objectives and Boundaries have already been issued,

5. All lines gained will be consolidated and will become lines of resistance

6. The 2nd SOUTH WALES BORDERERS and 1st ROYAL INNISKILLING FUSILIERS are placed under the Command of the C.R.E.29th Division.
These two Battalions will take their Orders direct from the C.R.E. 29th Division, after the arrival of the Brigade in the FOREST CAMP Area
(Details of work required have already been issued)
The 1st Bn THE BORDER REGIMENT is placed at the disposal of the GUARDS DIVISION, and will work on Zero day under their orders.
These three Battalions will return to the Brigade Command on completion of their work on Zero day.

7. After zero Units will be prepared to move at short notice.

8. The S.O.S.Signal will be coloured Rifle Grenade bursting into 2 Red and 2 Green Lights.
No other signals will be employed, except flares showing the position of Infantry to Contact Aeroplanes when called for, either by (a)sounding of "A"on the Klaxon Horn, or(b)A White Very Light.

9. Watches will be synchornised from a watch taken round by a Staff Officer on "Z"minus one(1)day.

SECRET. Copy No.3.

87th INFANTRY BRIGADE ADMINISTRATIVE INSTRUCTION No.2.

This cancels Administrative Instruction No.1.

July 30th 1917.

1.BRIGADE DUMP. The Brigade Dupm for men's packs,surplus kits, etc will be dumped there on notification from Brigade Headquarters.

2.CAMP WARDENS. All Units will leave one Warden in charge of their Camp in the P.2 Area.each warden will be rationed by his Unit up to and including 2nd August after which date they will call at Brigade Headquarters (P.2.Area)daily for their rations.

In addition the Officer Commanding the 1st KING'S OWN SCOTTISH BORDERERS will detail a Corporal to report to Brigade Headquarters at 5.p.m. 30th inst.He will take charge of the Brigade Headquarter Camp and will see that the rations are distributed.

3.LEWIS GUNS AND VICKERS GUNS.

If a Lewis Gun or Vickers Gum gets damaged or lost the Unit concernd will send a "PRIOITY"wire to Brigade Headquarters.

4.WATER.

(a)Forward points for men.

(i)Material transport and men will be held ready to carry the two mains from ELVERDINGHE across CANAL and establish forward WATER Points on E Bank of Canal one main being taken over each Bridge.

(ii)Later two mains mentioned above will be carried forward to LANGEMARCK.

(iii)Marterial and Transport and parties will be held ready to carry the LAUNDRY LINE forward by BARD CAUSEWAY establishing Water Points in HUDDLESTONE ROAD and near LIEVRE Cabarat

Forward Water Points for Horses.

(i).4-600 gallon troughs and 4 L & E Pumps will be erected at ELVERDINGHE CHATEAU.

(ii)2-600 gallon troughs and 2 L & F. Pumps will be erected at HULLS FARM.

(iii)The YPERLEE will be dammed about B.18.b.9.9.and 4-600 gallom troughs erected.

(iv)4-600 gallon troughs and 4 L & F Pumps will be erected at BOESINGHE CHEATU.

(v)In addition to the above arrangements,a water siding has been built where the Broad Gauge Railway cuts the ONDANK WOSTEN Road about A.6.d.2.2.Water Lorries and carts will refill here from tanks filled by Water Train.But this supply is only to be used in ~~emergex~~ emergency i.e.of the piped water schemes fail from any cause.

(b) A second water bottle per man will be issued laterx with sling.

5.SALVAGE. The Corps Salvage Dump will be at INTERNATIONAL CORNER, and the Divisional Dump at N Side at CACTUS BRIDGE on the E side of the CANAL.Units will make a Battalion Dump and will send back salvage material on their transport toBrigade Transport from where it will be be taken to the nearest Dump.

6-CASUALTIES. Estimated Casualties will be reported as soon as possible.The Daily Casualty Wire will be sent as before and the names of officers must be given.

7.REINFORCEMENTS. Reinforcements will go to Corps Depot and will not normally join their units until they come out of the Line.

8.MISCELLENEOUS.

Pack Saddles,Grenades,Flares,S.O.S.Signals etc will be issued later.

29th.Division No.C.G.S.73/7.

Landmarks and strong points in sequence from the North.

	BEST SEEN FROM	ALSO SEEN FROM.
CAPREE FARM.	O.P.I.Belgian O.P.at B.5.c.I.5. Tree at B.5.c.25.05.	O.Ps.N.and E. of BOESINGHE.
2 Strong Points Concrete B.6.a.3.2.	-Do-	-Do-
WOOD 14.	All O.Ps. in or E. of BOESINGHE.	No.I.Tree B.5.c. and Belgian.O.P.
STRONG POINTS IN WOOD 14. BOIS FARM.	O.P.I.Belgian.O.P. at B.5.c.I.5. Tree at B.5.C.25.05.	O.Ps.N.and E.of BOESINGHE.
WOOD 16.	Parts of from WAALKRANZ TREE.	WAALKRANZ HEDGE and partially from No.I and DOCTOR's HOUSE.
BOIS DE IABRI.	WAALKRANZ TREE and FOREUSE	
WOOD 15.	All O.Ps.in or E.of BOESINGHE	No.I.
STRONG POINTS IN WOOD 15.		
BOIS DE CRAPOUILLOTS.	Post 15 (B.6.c.5.4.	All O.Ps.on or E of BOESINGHE

	BEST SEEN FROM.	ALSO SEEN FROM.
MILL) STEAM MILL)	O.Ps. in Houses E. of BOESINGHE CHATEAU.	Most of BOESINGHE O.Ps. No. I. O.P. JOYEUSE (STEAM MILL only).
BRICK PILLAR (FOREST LODGE)	O.Ps. E. of BOESINGHE.	POST 36.
GENERAL FARM	JOYEUSE Post 36. (C.7.c.6.3.)	Periscope Tree in C.7.c.
ARTILLERY WOOD.	All O.Ps. in or E. of BOESINGHE.	JOYESUE CHEAPSIDE.
UN-NAMED HOUSES.	POST 36.	O.Ps. S. of BOESINGHE.
THATCHED HOUSSE.	O.Ps. in Gouse E. of BOESINGHE CHATEAU Only partially seen through ARTILLERY WOOD.	Most of BOESINGHE O.Ps.
CANON FARM.) PAISASADE FARM)	Post 36 & JOYESUW.	Periscope Tree in C.7.c.
CABLE HOUSE) ABZAC HOUSE)	X Line E.1[illegible].d.7.3.) JOYEUSE.) JOYEUSE.)	Most of BOSENGHIE. O.Ps.

APPENDIX "A"

ARRANGEMENTS FOR AEROPLANE CONTACT PATROLS.

Marking of Contact Patrols.

1. Each Contact Aeroplane will be marked with two Black rectangular flags (2.ft. by 1.ft.3.ins.) attached to and projecting from the lower plane, from each side of the Fuselage.

Signals for Aeroplanes.

2. The Signal from the Contact Aeroplane for the Infantry to light flares will be either:-
(a) A Succession of "As". in Morse Code on KLAXON Horn or daylight signalling lamp.
(b) A series of White lights.

FLARES.

3. Infantry will show their positions to the Contact aeroplanes by lighting Green flares. As far as possible these flares should be lighted in bunches of threes. No flares will be lit until called for.

Marking of H.Q.rs.

4. Brigade and Battalion H.Qs. will be marked by Ground sheet of authorised shape, with the code letters of the Unit laid out with the white strips alongside of it. These letters should be [illegible] in depth.
Signalling to aeroplanes will be done by [illegible].

Dropping Stations.

5. The Corps Dropping Station will be at Corps Headquarters.
All Dropping Stations will be clearly marked with a white X made from [illegible].
Each Dropping Station will have signallers in attendance to acknowledge the receipt of messages by waving flags.

2 Battalions Left) Dug Outs Left of X Line.
Guards Bde.)

14. The provisions of sections XXX page 58 of S.S.135 will be strictly couplied with.
Of the numbers participating in the operations one half will be sent to the Corps Reinforcement Camp.
Units will render a return to this office by 6.0.p.m. the 21st.inst.,of the numbers to be left behind (a) In Divisional Area. (b) To go to Corps Reinforcement Camp.

15. The S.O.S.Signal will be a coloured rifle grenade bursting into two red and two green lights. No other light signals will be shewn except flares showing positions of Infantry to contact patrols.

16. The leading troops will shew their positions to Contact Aeroplanes when demanded
(a) By KLAXON Horn
(b) By a series of White Lights.
Detail instructions are attached.

17. ACKNOWLEDGE.

(Sd) BRODIE BLAIR.
CAPTAIN.
BRIGADE MAJOR 87th. Infantry Brigade.

Issued at 2000.

War Diary

of

1st Battalion Royal Inniskilling Fusiliers

From 1.8.14 to 31.8.14

Volume

No 30

Army Form C. 2118.

WAR DIARY
or
INTELLIGENCE SUMMARY
(Erase heading not required.)

Instructions regarding War Diaries and Intelligence Summaries are contained in F. S. Regs., Part II. and the Staff Manual respectively. Title Pages will be prepared in manuscript.

Volume 30 — 1/R Inniskilling Fus. No. 1

Place	Date	Hour	Summary of Events and Information	Remarks and references to Appendices
Forest Area	Aug. 1st–2nd		Reorganizing + improving Camp 11.	[illegible]
	3rd		Brigade move back to Proven 2 Area vide BO 35.	[illegible]
Proven 2 Area	4th		Training. B213 Strength. 32 O. 690 OR Ration Strength 25 O. 567 OR	[illegible]
	5–6th		Training	[illegible]
	7th		Brigade move up into Divisional Reserve in Forest Camp Area	[illegible]
Forest Area			To occupy Camp Ballantyne Forest Vide BO. 36	[illegible]
	8–10th		Improving camp, draining roads and training	[illegible]
	11th		Bn move up to Support in right sector vide BO No 31 + disposition	[illegible]
	12th		Bn take over front line trenches in Right Sector vide BO 32 + disposition	[illegible]
			Enemy shelled blockhouses during [illegible] and [illegible] but fire was [illegible] [illegible] wounded [illegible] Aeroplanes were active. [illegible] attacked [illegible] balloon [illegible] hostile [illegible] height and were driven off by our [illegible]	[illegible]
			B213 Strength 11th inst 33 O. 744 OR Ration Strength 25 O. 560 OR	[illegible]
			[illegible] in the early hours of the morning. They [illegible] direction and wandered into our advance Posts across the [illegible] Hostile artillery [illegible] Headquarters shelled [illegible] Aeroplanes again [illegible] large flights and at lower [illegible] [illegible] hostile patrol of 5 men were driven off from [illegible] across the STEENBEEK after a brief encounter. Enemy casualties unknown. Enemy dump was blown	

Instructions regarding War Diaries and Intelligence Summaries are contained in F. S. Regs., Part II. and the Staff Manual respectively. Title Pages will be prepared in manuscript.

Army Form C. 2118.

WAR DIARY
or
INTELLIGENCE SUMMARY

(Erase heading not required.) 1/R. Inniskilling Fus. No 2.

Place	Date	Hour	Summary of Events and Information	Remarks and references to Appendices
			up opposite our front. Casualties. 3 O.R. wounded 2 O.R. missing	
			2/Lt G.E. Farningham joined 29th Div. Depot Bn 12/8/17. 2/Lt W.A. Armstrong	[initials]
			sent to 87th Fd Ambulance sick 12/8/17. Lt Bloodworth with six guides	
			guided R.E. working parties to sites for bridges on our front. see B.O. G81/14 att.	
	14th		Bn moves back to Bivouac 1 B'gd. as per B.O. No 33 attached.	
	15th		Bn move up to ABRI WOOD area to get into place of assembly for the attack. Zero hour being 4.45 pm 16th. Bn HQ are S.E. corner of Abri Wood. B Coy. at FOURCHE FARM, A, C & D at SAULES FARM.	[initials]
	16th		At about 10.30 am orders to move up & take over whole original front of Division. A & B occupy original line E of STEENBEEK from U 27 b 9.7 to U 20 b 6.6. C & D are in support on W side of river C at SENTIER FARM D at TUFFS FARM U 27 b 1.5. Bn HQ move to CAPTAINS FARM. The attack was successful & all objectives gained	[initials]
	~~17th~~	9.30 pm	Move forward to take over the new front line from 2 Cos. SWB, 1 Co Border Regt 1 Co KOSB. Dispositions as follows. Front line (Red line) occupied by A, C & B Cos. U15 central to U16 c 15.50. D Co in support at U15 d 8.2. Bn HQ at WIJENDRIFT U21 a 6.3.	
	17th		There are no enemy West of the BROENBEEK. Enemy's aircraft are continually over our lines at a low altitude & fire into our front line. Enemy does not appear to have any organised line of defence just East of the BROENBEEK. He seems disorganised & can be seen running from shell hole to shell hole when our Lewis guns get on to him. We are in touch with the 8th Regt. French on our left at U15 central & receive messages from the Commandant & chef de bataillon (attached).	

2449 Wt. W14957/M90 750,000 1/16 J.B.C. & A. Forms/C.2118/12.

Army Form C. 2118.

WAR DIARY
or
INTELLIGENCE SUMMARY
(Erase heading not required.)

1/R Inniskilling Fus. No 3.

Instructions regarding War Diaries and Intelligence Summaries are contained in F. S. Regs., Part II. and the Staff Manual respectively. Title Pages will be prepared in manuscript.

Place	Date	Hour	Summary of Events and Information	Remarks and references to Appendices
	17th		Enemy's artillery enfilade our front line from the south, + sends salvos over at intervals. Our guns retaliate with effect. An officer's patrol crosse the BROENBEEK + bombs a dugout at about U15 b 45.45. No Germans are found although seen there during the day. Another patrol reconnoitres the BROENBEEK from U15 b 35 to U15 b 6.3. + finds no bridges. The river appears to be like a serie of shell holes full of water + impassable without bridge.	
	18th		No incidents of importance. Enemy artillery more active. Relieved by 16th Middlesex vide Bde. O. No 35. Total Strength 30ff 629OR Ration Strength 20ff 499OR	

Instructions regarding War Diaries and Intelligence Summaries are contained in F. S. Regs., Part II. and the Staff Manual respectively. Title Pages will be prepared in manuscript.

WAR DIARY
or
INTELLIGENCE SUMMARY

(Erase heading not required.)

Army Form C. 2118.

1st R Inniskilling Fus (?)

Place	Date	Hour	Summary of Events and Information	Remarks and references to Appendices
26th (?)			on our front. Casualties Lt Bloodworth wounded 5 OR killed 4 OR wounded	
27th			[illegible] quiet during the morning but increased in volume until it reached great violence during the afternoon when the Corps on our right was attacking. The enemy barrage was [illegible] and very erratic and composed of very heavy shells. Enemy aircraft conspicuous by its absence. Bn relieved by the Border Regt and 1 Platoon of Scots Guards vide Bn Order No 44. attached. Casualties Lt G.A. [illegible] W. OR 10 W. 10 R [illegible]	[illegible]
28th			Entrained at [illegible] at 17.00 for [illegible] to PLURENDON (?) CAMP vide Bn Order No 44.	
29th			Cleaning and draining Camp. Capt Williams rejoined with 10th Corps [illegible] with a draft of 35 OR. 2Lt [illegible] [illegible] [illegible] and attached to [illegible]	[illegible]
30th			Reorganization of the Battalion	
31st			Training of Battalion, improving camp & refitting	

31/8/17

[signature] Lt Col
Comdg 1st R Inniskilling Fus

2449 Wt. W14957/M90 750,000 1/16 J.B.C. & A. Forms/C.2118/12.

X 29

87/39

Confidential

Vol 19

War Diary

of

1st Bn The Royal Inniskilling Fusiliers

From 1st Sept. 1917 To 30th Sept. 1917

Volume 30.

Volume 20

Instructions regarding War Diaries and Intelligence Summaries are contained in F. S. Regs., Part II. and the Staff Manual respectively. Title Pages will be prepared in manuscript.

WAR DIARY
or
INTELLIGENCE SUMMARY

(Erase heading not required.)

Army Form C. 211

1st R. Inniskilling Fusiliers

Place	Date	Hour	Summary of Events and Information	Remarks and references to Appendices
[illegible] CAMP	1/9/17		Training – Ceremonial Parades	[illegible]
	2/9/17		Church Parade – Sports: Cross country run	
	3/9/17		Ceremonial Parade before Divisional General	
	4/9/17 – 6/9/17		Training. [illegible] Moore reported for duty on [illegible] 6/9/17. Bn Sports held on the 6/9/17	[illegible]
" "	7-9-17		Training. 4/Lt. H.J. Kirkman evacuated to England.	[illegible]
" "	8-9-17		Leave for HERZEELE – vide B.O. No 45 d/6:9:17 (attached) Strength B.213 30 Officers 623 O.R	[illegible]
HERZEELE	9-9-17		Training	[illegible]
"	10-9-17		Training	[illegible]
"	11-9-17		Training – vide B.O. No. 46 d/8:9:17 (attached.) Draft arrival 3 N.C.O's + 19 men	[illegible]
"	12-9-17		Leave for PLURENDON CAMP – vide B.O. No. 45 d/6:9:17 (attached)	[illegible]
PLURENDON CAMP	13-9-17		Brigade Sports. [illegible] Jones to Hospital.	[illegible]
" "	14-9-17		Ceremonial Parade	[illegible]
" "	15-9-17		Training. [illegible] Strength B.213 – 18 Officers. Total Strength – 30 Officers	[illegible]
" "	16-9-17		Church Parades. Draft arrival [illegible] 511 O.R. 630 O.R.	[illegible]
" "	17-9-17		Training. [illegible] joined the Battalion. Draft – arrival 2 N.C.O's + 30 men	[illegible]
" "	18-9-17		Ceremonial Parade – Presentation of medals [illegible]. Band Competition – 1st – The [illegible] Regt 2nd – The 1st R. Inniskilling Fus. [illegible] A.J.C. [illegible] rejoined from [illegible] Corps Depôt.	[illegible]
" "	19-9-17		Training. Divisional Boxing Contests. Draft arrival – 2 N.C.O's + 7[illegible] men. Draft arrival – 5 N.C.O's 56 men	[illegible]
" "	20-9-17		Leave for CARIBU – vide B.O. No. 49 d/17:9:17 (attached.)	[illegible]
CARIBU	21-9-17		Training	[illegible]
"	22-9-17		Training. Strength B.213 20 Officers 7[illegible]9 O.R	[illegible]

2449 Wt. W14957/M90 750,000 1/16 J.B.C. & A. Forms/C.2118/12.

Army Form C. 2118.

Instructions regarding War Diaries and Intelligence Summaries are contained in F. S. Regs., Part II. and the Staff Manual respectively. Title Pages will be prepared in manuscript.

WAR DIARY
or
INTELLIGENCE SUMMARY

(Erase heading not required.)

Place	Date	Hour	Summary of Events and Information	Remarks and references to Appendices
CARIBU	23-9-17		Training	[illegible]
"	24-9-17		Training	[illegible]
"	25-9-17		Training	[illegible]
"	26-9-17		Training	[illegible]
	27-9-17		Training	[illegible]
	28/9/17		Bn moves up and relieves 1st Essex Regt in Dulwich Camp	[illegible]
	29/9/17		Strength 29.O 955 OR Ration Strength 20.O. 700 OR. Bn moves up and relieves the 2nd Hants A & D Cos in the front line B & C in support and reserve. A very successful relief all companies having reported relief complete at 9.25 pm. 2Lt Taylor wounded during operations.	
	30/9/17		Rather quiet day in the line. A few enemy snipers reported active from [illegible] the other side of the BROEMBEEK. Support Company sustained a few casualties as a result of a [illegible] accurate [illegible]. Bn Hdqrs was shelled intermittently all day. The Adjutant (Capt [illegible]) Capt [illegible] and the Regimental Sgt-Major were wounded. Lt E.E.J. Moore [illegible] on with the adjutant's duties. Casualties 5 O.R.	[illegible]

[illegible] Lieut Colonel,
Comdg: 1st Rl Inniskilling Fusiliers

4/10/17

2449 Wt. W14957/M90 750,000 1/16 J.B.C. & A. Forms/C.2118/12.

Secret.

Copy no.

1st Bn. The Royal Inniskilling Fusiliers. Order No. 39.

7 Sept 1917.

1. The Battalion will march to HERZEELE tomorrow.
2. Brigade Starting Point – Brigade H.Qrs.
3. Dress – Marching Order. Caps. Water bottles will be carried filled.
4. Hour of parade – 2 pm. An interval of 200 yards will be observed between Cos. and between Battalion and Transport.
5. All Kits, mess stores, medical stores, Lewis Guns and equipment will be packed on Transport by 1 pm.
6. The Camp will be ready for inspection by Commanding Officer by 1.30 pm.

Copies 1. Staff
2 & 3. War Diary
4.5.6.7. Cos.
8. M.O.
9. T.O.
10. Qm.
11.

[signature]
Capt. & Adjt.
1st Royal Innis Fusiliers.

Copy No.

SECRET.

1st Bn The Royal Inniskilling Fusiliers. Order No. 41.

Ref. Map. 1/20,000
27 N.E.
28 N.W.
20 S.W.

1. The Battalion will move to CARIBU. A11. d. 8 7. tomorrow in relief of 1/Irish Guards.

2 Route
27/E 16 b 85.20 – 27/F 1 c. 20 05 – BELGIAN CHEMIN MILITAIRE Road Junction 28/A 2 b. 95 30 – Road Junction 20/S 27 a 2 0 Road Junction 20/S 28 d. 9.2. DE WIPPE CABS.

3. Dress.
Marching Order. Steel helmets will be worn, water bottles will be filled.

4. Hour of parade
The Battalion will be formed up in mass in the field opposite the camp at 9.30 am

5 Starting Point
Brigade H Qrs at 9 45 am

6 Order of march
Drums D. A. B. C. H Qrs. An interval of 200 yards will be observed between companies and between the battalion and transport.
Sgt McBrien and 15 police will march in rear of transport to collect stragglers.

7. Kits
All Officers' kits, mess stores, &c to be stacked at Q.M. stores by 8 am.
Lewis Guns and equipment, signalling stores will be packed on transport tonight.

8 Advance Party.
An advance party under 2/Lt G O'Brien will leave at an hour to be notified later.

9 Camp to be thoroughly clean and ready for inspection by 8 30 am

Copies 1. Staff.
2 & 3. War Diary.
4 5 6 7 Cos
8. M.O.
9. T.O.
10. Q.M.

[signature]
Capt & Adjt.
1st Royal Inniskilling Fusiliers

SECRET.

87TH INFANTRY BRIGADE ORDER NO. 45.

Reference Map 1/20,000
Sheets 27.N.E.
19.S.E.
20.S.W.
28.N.W.

6th SEPTEMBER, 1917.

1. The Brigade will move to the HERZEELE Training Area on 8th SEPTEMBER, 1917, returning to this Area on 12th SEPTEMBER, 1917.

2. Units will march on 8th and 12th SEPTEMBER, 1917, in accordance with March Tables attached.

3. A C K N O W L E D G E.

[signature]

CAPTAIN,
BRIGADE MAJOR, 87TH INFANTRY BRIGADE.

Issued at 2230

Copied to:-
Staff
War Diary.
File.
S.W.B.
K.O.S.B.
R.Innis.Fus.
1st Bord Regt.
87th M.G.C.
87th T.M.B.
87th Fd.Ambce.
87th Bde.Sigs.
86th Inf.Bde.
88th Inf.Bde.
29th Div. "G".

ADDENDA TO 87th BRIGADE ORDER No. 45.

1. Units will take their Reserve of Tools with them.

2. Units will take Tents to the new Area from their present camps as follows :-

   T.M.Bty. - 8. (2 from their present camp and 6 from Rl. Inniskilling Fusrs Camp.)

   M.Gun Coy. - 11. (9 from their present camp and 2 from Rl. Inniskilling Fusrs Camp).

   2/S. W.Bords. - 18. From present Camp.

   1/K.O.S.B. - 29. From present Camp.

   1/R. Innis. Fus. Nil.

   1/Border Regt. - 12. From present Camp.

   The Officer Commanding 1st Royal Inniskilling Fusiliers will hand over 6 tents to the Trench Mortar Battery, and 2 tents to the Machine Gun Company on demand.
   Instructions as to whether the tents are to be left in the Training Area or brought back, will be issued later.

3. No extra transport will be allotted to units to take the tents to the new camp, with the exception of the Trench Mortar Battery.

4. Units will not take their Regimental Reserve of Bombs, S.A.A., with them.

5. Rations will be delivered direct to units by lorry. Units must have a guide at the present Refilling Point, daily, in order to guide the lorry to their new Quartermaster's Store.

6. Rations for transport, and other personnel left behind in present camps, will be delivered to the present Refilling Point.

7. The Brigade Post Office will be at the Brigade Headquarters in HERZEELE, and Units will draw mails from there.

Captain,

7th September, 1917. Brigade Major, 87th Infantry Brigade.

S E C R E T.

87TH INFANTRY BRIGADE ORDER NO.46. (TRAINING.)

Reference Map,
Training Area 1/10,000

8th SEPTEMBER, 1917.

1. A General Attack will take place against the enemy's positions on 11th SEPTEMBER, 1917, at Zero Hour.

2. The 87th Infantry Brigade will attack the RED and BLUE Lines.
The 88th Infantry Brigade on the Right and the 8th French Regiment on the Left will co-operate.

OBJECTIVES:- The Brigade Objectives are:-
RED Line - D.5.d.90.65. - D.5.d.60.00 - D.11.b.50.90.
D.11.b.15.30.
BLUE Line- D.5.a.50.20. - D.5.c.75.55.
LASALLE Farm.

3. The 2nd South Wales Borderers on the Right and 1st Royal Inniskilling Fusiliers on the Left will take the RED Line.
The 1st King's Own Scottish Borderers on the Right and the 1st Bn. The Border Regiment on the Left will take the BLUE Line

4. BOUNDARIES of the Brigade are as follows:-
On the Right - D.6-d.35.00 - GRUYTERSZALE Farm (inclusive)
D.5.Central - D.5.a.50.20.

On the Left - D.12.c.30.55 - LASALLE Farm (inclusive)

Boundary between Battalions is D.12.a.90.10. - D.5.d.40.00. - D.5.c.70.45.

5. ACTION
(A.) Forming up :-
2nd South Wales Borderers and the 1st Royal Inniskilling Fusiliers will be formed up East of the BROEMBEEK, at one (1) hour before Zero.
1st King's Own Scottish Borderers and the 1st Bn. The Border Regiment, will be in position half an hour before Zero.
Battalions will report to Brigade Headquarters as soon as they are in position.

(B.) A Liaison Party consisting of half a Company 1st Bn. The Border Regiment, plus two (2) Machine Guns, acting as Flank Detachments, will move forward behind the Left of the 1st Royal Inniskilling Fusiliers. This party less two (2) Machine Guns will go forward with the 1st Bn. The Border Regiment when they pass through the 1st Royal Inniskilling Fusiliers. Half a Company of the 1st Royal Inniskilling Fusiliers plus two (2) Machine Guns will move forward behind the Left of the 1st Bn. The Border Regiment, to act as the Flank Detachment to their Advance.

(C.) BARRAGE. The advance will take place under cover of a Creeping Barrage, moving at the rate of 100 yards every 5 minutes. The Barrage will halt beyond the RED Line from Zero plus 35 to Zero plus 1-30, to enable the leading Battalions to consolidate. It will then move forward at the same rate and halt on the S.O.S.Line, 200 yards beyond the BLUE Line from Zero plus two (2) hours five (5) minutes to Zero plus 5 hours, when it will gradually die down.

(D.) CONSOLIDATION AND STRONG POINTS.
The Objectives, when gained, will at once be consolidated.
The following Strong Points will be made :-
RED Line:- Blockhouses at D.11.b.25.35., about D.11.b.50.80., at Farm at D.11.b.85.90., about D.5.d.90.70.
BLUE Line:- LASALLE Farm - Blockhouses about D.5.c.80.20. - Farm at D.5.d.80.60 and about D.5.a.60.00.

6. The Officer Commanding the 87th Machine Gun Company will allot guns to the Battalions as follows :-
2nd South Wales Borderers. - 2
1st King's Own Scottish Borderers. - 2.
1st Royal Inniskilling Fusiliers - 2.
1st Bn. The Border Regiment - 4.
These guns will report to the respective Units by 10-p.m. on the 10th SEPTEMBER, 1917.
The remaining 6 Guns will be in Brigade Reserve.

7. The Officer Commanding 87th Trench Mortar Battery will detail 1 Gun and Team to report to each Battalion by 10- p.m. on the 10th SEPTEMBER, 1917.

8. DRESS - FIGHTING ORDER - men will carry the following :-
50 % Picks and Shovels.
1 in 4 GREEN FLARES.
per Platoon - 2 S.O.S.Grenades.

9. Brigade Headquarters will be at the Road Junction D.7.d.0.5.
1st King's Own Scottish Borderers and 2nd South Wales Borderers Headquarters will be at Blockhouses at D.12.b.3.7.
1st Royal Inniskilling Fusiliers and 1st Bn. The Border Regiment Headquarters will be at the Blockhouses D.12.c.4.7.
On the BLUE Line being gained the 1st King's Own Scottish Borderers' Headquarters will move to GRUYTERSZALE Farm.
The 1st Bn. The Borderers' Headquarters to NEY Farm

10. GROUND FLARES will be lighted when called for by Aeroplanes (a) by sounding " A " on the Klaxon Horn (b) by White Very Lights.

11. A C K N O W L E D G E.

W K Innes
CAPTAIN,
a/BRIGADE MAJOR, 87TH INFANTRY BRIGADE.

Issued at 1045

Copies to:-
Staff.
War Diary.
File.
S.W.B. 87th Bde.Sigs.
K.O.S.B. 86th Inf.Bde.
R.Innis.Fus. 88th Inf.Bde.
1st Bord.Rgt. 29th Div. "G".
87th M.G.C.
87th T.M.B.

S E C R E T.

87TH INFANTRY BRIGADE INSTRUCTION NO.1.

(vide 87th Brigade Order No.46.)

9th SEPTEMBER, 1917.

1. BLOCKHOUSES.
(a) Canvas Squares have been erected on the Training Area to represent Concrete Blockhouses.
(b) LOUVOIS Farm is represented by another Canvas erection.
(c) A Canvas Square has been erected East of the BROENBEEK for purposes of demonstration, in the shape and defences of Enemy "Pill-Boxes".

2. FLAGS.
(i) Blue Flags left behind when the Barrage moves forward will represent positions where our troops are held up by the enemy.
(ii) Red Flags advancing will represent an Enemy Counter-Attack. Before an Enemy- Counter-Attack is launched a concentration of Red Flags will probably be noticed.

3. DINNERS.
Battalion Cookers will accompany Units and dinners will be issued during the consolidation of the BLUE Line. There will be no cessation of operations. Ration Parties will be sent back and dinners issued to reliefs of the consolidating parties.

4. S.O.S.
The S.O.S. Signal will be a succession of White Very Lights. All Battalions Very Pistols will be carried.

5. FLARES.
Contact Planes will probably be available and ground flares will be used when called for.

6. CONSOLIDATION.
Each Company will consolidate a Strong Point. Strong Points will not be made in grass fields but the nearest stubble or ploughed field to the co-ordinate mentioned will be used.

7. FILLING IN.
If these Strong Points cannot be filled in on the 11th, parties will be detailed to fill them in on the 12th. These parties will return to PROVEN 4 Area after their Battalions.

8. MESSAGE CARRYING ROCKETS.
Three (3) Message Carrying Rockets will be issued per Battalion. Two (2) of these will be issued to Companies.

9. BARRAGE PARTY.
Lieut.-Col. A.J.ELLIS, 1st Bn. The Border Regiment will be in charge of the Barrage arrangements. One (1) Officer and twenty (20) other ranks per Battalion with 20 Signalling Flags, and three (3) Brigade Orderlies with 20 Red and 10 Blue Flags will report to Colonel ELLIS, after the demonstration on Monday, and again at 8-a.m. on 11th SEPTEMBER, 1917.

10. FORMING UP
The troops will actually be formed up at the hours stated in Brigade Order No.46.

11. ZERO HOUR.
Zero Hour will be 9-a.m.

Issued at__________ a/
CAPTAIN,
BRIGADE MAJOR, 87TH INFANTRY BRIGADE.

Copies to:-
Staff.
War Diary.
File.
S.W.B.
K.O.S.B.
R.In.Fus.
Bord.Rgt.
M.G.C.
T.M.B.
Bde.Sigs.

S E C R E T.

87TH INFANTRY BRIGADE INSTRUCTION NO.1.

(vide 87th Brigade Order No.46.)

9th SEPTEMBER, 1917.

1. BLOCKHOUSES.

(a) ~~Canvas Squares have been erected on the Training Area to represent Concrete Blockhouses.~~

(b) LOUVOIS Farm is represented by another Canvas erection.

(c) A Canvas Square has been erected East of the BROENBEEK for purposes of demonstration, in the shape and defences of Enemy "Pill-Boxes".

No flags will mark objectives

2. FLAGS.

(i) Blue Flags left behind when the Barrage moves forward will represent positions where our troops are held up by the enemy. A Red flag will represent the point holding them up.

(ii) Red Flags advancing will represent an Enemy Counter-Attack. Before an Enemy- Counter-Attack is launched a concentration of Red Flags will probably be noticed.

3. DINNERS.

Battalion Cookers will accompany Units and dinners will be issued during the consolidation of the BLUE Line. There will be no cessation of operations. Ration Parties will be sent back and dinners issued to reliefs of the consolidating parties.

4. S.O.S.

~~The S.O.S. Signal will be a succession of White Very Lights. All Battalions~~ Very Pistols will be carried.

5. FLARES.

Contact Planes will probably be available and ground flares will be used when called for.

6. CONSOLIDATION.

Each Company will consolidate a Strong Point. Strong Points will not be made in grass fields but the nearest stubble or ploughed field to the co-ordinate mentioned will be used.

7. FILLING IN.

If these Strong Points cannot be filled in on the 11th, parties will be detailed to fill them in on the 12th. Those parties will return to PROVEN 4 Area after their Battalions.

8. MESSAGE CARRYING ROCKETS.

Three (3) Message Carrying Rockets will be issued per Battalion. Two (2) of these will be issued to Companies.

9. BARRAGE PARTY.

Lieut.-Col. A.J.ELLIS, 1st Bn. The Border Regiment will be in charge of the Barrage arrangements. One (1) Officer and twenty (20) other ranks per Battalion with 20 Signalling Flags, and three (3) Brigade Orderlies with 20 Red and 10 Blue Flags will report to Colonel ELLIS, after the demonstration on Monday, and again at 8-a.m. on 11th SEPTEMBER, 1917.

-1-

10. FORMING UP

The troops will actually be formed up at the hours stated in Brigade Order No.46.

11. ZERO HOUR.

Zero Hour will be 9 a.m.

Issued at __________ a/ CAPTAIN,
BRIGADE MAJOR, 87TH INFANTRY BRIGADE.

Copies to:-

Staff.
War Diary.
File.
S.W.B.
K.O.S.B.
R.In.Fus.
Bord.Rgt.
M.G.C.
T.M.B.
Bde.Sigs.

The Bn will parade in fighting order, Capes. Waterbottles will be carried filled. Flares [illegible] & flares will be carried.

Coys will proceed to the area independently & be in position by 8 a.m.

~~Zero Hour will be 9 a.m.~~

SECRET

1st. Royal Inniskilling Fusiliers Order No 1 ~ Training
9.9.17.

Reference Map – Training Area 1/10,000.

1. A general attack will take place against the enemy's positions on the 11th Sept. 1917. Zero hour will be 9 a.m.
The 87th Infantry Brigade will attack the RED and BLUE lines as marked on the map. The 8th French Regiment will co operate on the left.

2. The 1st Royal Inniskilling Fusiliers, in conjunction with the 2nd. S.W.B. on the right will take the RED line.
'A' on the right 'B' on the left will form the first wave.
'C' " " 'D' " " " will form the second wave, and remain in support on the capture of the RED line.
Distance between waves – 100 yards.
Companies will march on a compass bearing of 322°

3. Boundaries.
The boundaries of the Battalion are as follows:–
Right D12 a 9.1 to D.11. b 60.85.
Left D12 c. 30 55 to D 11. b 20.40.

4. The Battalion will be formed up east of the BROEMBEEK one hour before Zero.

5. Creeping barrage
The advance will take place under a creeping barrage moving at the rate of 100 yards every 5 minutes. The barrage will halt beyond the RED line from ZERO + 35 to Zero + 1.30 to enable the Battalion to consolidate.

6. Consolidation
The RED line when gained will at once be consolidated and the following strong points will be made:–
Blockhouse D11 b 25.35 'B' Co.
D11 b 5 8. 'A' Co.
'C' & 'D' Cos will dig in on a line D12 a. 00 55 to D11 b 7.1 and will make the following strong points at D11 b 9.5 – 'C' Co and D11 b 8 2 – 'D' Co.

7. Two machine guns from the 87th M.G.C will be attached to the Battn and will be sent forward to the strong points in the RED line as soon as consolidated. One gun & team from 87th T.M.B will be attached to the Bn and follow 'C' Co. as far as NEY FARM.

8. Ground flares will be lighted when called for by aeroplanes (a) by sounding A on the KLAXON horn (b) by WHITE Very lights.
The S.O.S signal will be a succession of WHITE Very lights.

9. The capture of the RED line will be reported to Battn H.Q by means of message carrying rockets – one each will be issued to 'A' 'B' Cos.

10. Battalion H Qrs. will be on the BROEMBEEK D12 c 50.85 Lone TREE ~~at blockhouse D12 C 4.4 and will move forward to NEY FARM as soon as the RED line has been captured~~

Lieut Col

Comdg 1st Royal Inniskilling Fusiliers

SECRET

1st Royal Inniskilling Fusiliers Order No. 1 — 19/9/17

1. Blockhouses.

(a) LOUVOIS FARM is represented by another canvas [illegible]

(b) A canvas square has been erected East of the BROEMBEEK for purposes of demonstration on the shape and defences of enemy "Pill boxes". No flags will mark objectives.

2. Flags.

(i) Blue flags left behind when the [illegible] forward will represent positions where our troops are held up by the enemy. The [illegible] flag will represent the [illegible] holding them up.

(ii) Red flags waving will represent an enemy counter attack. Before an enemy counter attack is launched, a [illegible] of Red flags [illegible] be noticed.

3. [illegible]

[illegible] will accompany [illegible] and changes will be assumed during the consolidation of the BLUE LINE. There will be no [illegible] of operations [illegible] parties will be sent back and [illegible] of the [illegible] consolidating parties. [illegible] their parties [illegible]

4. S.O.S.

Very Pistols will be carried.

5. Flares.

[illegible] flares will probably be available and ground flares will be [illegible] when called for. Flares will be [illegible]

6. Consolidation.

Each Company will consolidate [illegible] will be [illegible] in greater [illegible] than the [illegible] to indicate [illegible]

7. [illegible]

If [illegible] cannot be [illegible] to [illegible] FROYER [illegible]

8. The [illegible] will [illegible] a canvas [illegible] will [illegible]

[illegible]

[illegible]

Royal Innis Fusiliers

SECRET Appendix 3

1st Bn. The Royal Inniskilling Fusiliers [illegible]

Ref your Training Area Map 1/10,000 11.9.17

1. The Battalion will march to [illegible] Camp [illegible] via [illegible] ROAD JUNCTION E21 b 4.6 – E16 c 2.8. An interval of 200 yards will be observed between Cos. & 200 yards between battalion and transport.

2. The Battalion will be formed up with the head of the column at road junction near A be D10B35 by 10.15 am in the following order: [illegible] C, D, H.Qrs B, A

3. Dress – Marching Order – Caps.

4. All Officers' Kits will be stacked outside their billets by 9 am.

5. A limber for Lewis Guns & equipment, [illegible] will be at each Co. H.Qrs by 9 am.

6. Billets to be left scrupulously clean and all rubbish burnt.

7. Cookers & Water Carts will leave immediately after breakfast.

8. Particular attention is to be paid to the [illegible] of [illegible].

Copies 1 Staff
2 & 3 War Diary
4. 5. 6. 7. Cos.
8 M.O.
9 Q.M.
10. T.O.

[illegible] Capt & Adjt
1st Royal Inniskilling Fusiliers

M A R C H   T A B L E.

DATE	UNIT	FROM	TO	VIA	TIME	Starting Point.	REMARKS.
12th SEPT. 1917.	87th Brigade Headquarters.	HERZEELE	P.4. Area. (Present Camps.)	HOUTKERQUE Road Junction- E.21.b.4.6. - E.16.c.8.8.	9-30 a.m.	D.10.c.0.7.	200 yards interval will be maintained between Companies and between Units and their Transpor
"	2nd S.W.Borderers.	"	" "	" "	9-34 a.m.	"	
"	1st K.O.S.Borderers.	"	" "	" "	10-0 a.m.	"	
"	1st Border Regiment.	"	" "	" "	10-15 a.m.	"	
"	1st R.Innis.Fusiliers	"	" "	" "	10-30 a.m.	"	
"	87th M.G.Company.	"	" "	" "	10-45 a.m.	"	

M A R C H   T A B L E.

DATE	UNIT	FROM	TO	VIA	TIME	STARTING POINT	REMARKS.
th SEPT. 1917.	87th Brigade Headquarters.	Camp	HERZEELE	Cross Roads R.22.d.7.6.	2- p.m.	Brigade Headquarters	200 yards interval between Companies and 200 yards between Battalions and their Transport.
"	2nd S.W.Borderers.	"	"	"	2-4 p.m.	"	
"	1st R.Innis.Fusiliers	"	"	"	2-20 p.m.	"	
"	1st Bn.The Border Regt.	"	"	"	2-35 p.m.	"	
"	1st K.O.S.Borderers.	"	"	"	3- p.m.	"	
"	87th M.G.Company	"	"	"	3-15 p.m.	"	

S E C R E T.

87TH INFANTRY BRIGADE ORDER NO. 49.

Reference Map. 1/20,000
Sheets:- 19.S.E.,
27.N.E.,
20.S.W.,
28.N.W.,

17th SEPTEMBER, 1917.

1. (A.) The 29th Division will relieve the Guards Division in the Left Sector, XIVth Corps, commencing on the 20th SEPTEMBER, 1917.

(B.) The 87th Infantry Brigade will relieve the 1st Guards Brigade in the FOREST Area on the 20th SEPTEMBER, 1917.

2. The relief will be carried out in accordance with March Table attached.

3. Completion of reliefs will be notified to these Headquarters in "B.A.B." Code

4. Instructions with regard to Advanced Parties will be issued later.

5. ACKNOWLEDGE.

[signature]

CAPTAIN,
BRIGADE MAJOR, 87TH INFANTRY BRIGADE.

Issued at 1030

Copies to:-
Staff.
War Diary.
File.
2/S.W.B.
1/K.O.S.B.
1/R.In.Fus.
1/Bord.Rgt.
87th M.G.C.
87th T.M.B.
87th Fd.Amb.
87th Bde.Sigs.
No.3.Coy.Train.
455th W.R.FdaCo.
86th Inf.Bde.
88th Inf.Bde.
Div. " G ".

MOVEMENT TABLE.

Date.	Unit.	From.	To.	In relief of.	Route.	Time.	Starting Point.	Remarks.
20th.	2/S.W.B.	PLUMSTEAD.	DE WIPPE. (A.11.b.5.4).	2/Gren.Gds.	27/E.16.b.55.20-27/F.1.c.	9-30. a.m.	Bde.H.Q.	An interval of 200 yards will be maintained between Companies and between Units and their transport.
"	1/R.Inn.F.	PLURENDON.	CARIBU.A.11.d.8.7.	1/Irish Gds.	20.05.-BANGIAN CHEMIN	9.45.a.m.	"	
"	1/Border.	POLL HILL.	HAMLEY.A.4.d.8.2.	3/Cold.Gds.	MILITAIRE-Road Junc. 28/A.2.b.95.	10.a.m.	"	
"	1/K.O.S.B.	PADDOCK WOOD.	DUBLIN.A.11.c.4.5.	2/Cold.Gds.	30.-Road Junc. [struck-out line] 20/S.27.a.2.0.-Road Junc.20/ S.25.d.9.2.-DE WIPPE CABR.	10.15. a.m.	"	
"	87th M.G.Co.	PESWELL.	FOREST A[illegible]A.	1/Gds.M.G.C.		10.30.a.m.	"	
"	87th Bde.H.Q. Signals. 87th T.M.B.	Present Camps.	FOREST A[illegible] (A.5.a.).	1/Gds.Bde. etc.		10.35.a.m.		

SECRET.

87th INFANTRY BRIGADE ORDER No.50.

Sept. 26th. 1917.

1. The 87th Infantry Brigade will relieve the 88th Infantry Brigade in the line commencing on the night of 29th/30th. September.

2. Movements and reliefs will be in accordance with the Relief Table attached. Details of relief will be arranged mutually between Officers Commanding Units concerned.

3. All Defence Schemes, Trench Maps, Aeroplane Photos and Trench Stores will be taken over.

4. During the process of relief the Units in RUGBY and DULWICH CAMPS will come under the Orders of the Brigadier General Commanding Brigade/~~in~~ holding the line.

5. The Brigadier General Commanding 87th Infantry Brigade will assume command of the Divisional Front on the night of the 29/30th September.

6. ACKNOWLEDGE.

[signature]
CAPTAIN.
BRIGADE MAJOR, 87th INFANTRY BRIGADE.

Issued at ......

Copies to:- Staff.
War Diary.
File.
2/S.W.B.
1/K.O.S.B.
1/R.Innis.Fus.
1/Border Regt.
87th M.G.Co.
87th T.M.B.
Signals.
Int.Officer.
Supply Officer.
88th Brigade.
86th Brigade.
29th Division. 'G'.

Secret

AMENDMENT TO 87TH INFANTRY BRIGADE ORDER NO.50.

27th SEPTEMBER, 1917.

1. ADD to para. 6. :-

During the Relief the Newfoundland Regiment and 2nd South Wales Borderers will use BRIDGE Street and the 2nd Hants Regiment and 1st Royal Inniskilling Fusiliers will use HUNTER Street.

In the event of HUNTER Street being heavily shelled the 2nd Hants Regiment and 1st Royal Inniskilling Fusiliers will use CLARGES Street.

2. MARCH TABLE.

For 30th " 1st King's Own Scottish Borderers from DUBLIN Camp to RUGBY Camp."

substitute :-
DUBLIN Camp to WHITE MILL (B.14.d.8.8.)

and delete :-
" 2nd Hants Regiment. "

[signature]

CAPTAIN,
BRIGADE MAJOR, 87TH INFANTRY BRIGADE.

Copies to :-
All Recipient of
87th Brigade Order
No. 50.

RELIEF TABLE.

Date.	Unit.	From.	To.	Take over from.	Remarks.
29th.	2/S.W.Bordrs.	De WIPPE.	RUGBY CAMP. (B.9.a.8.6).	4th Worcester Regt.	To leave Camp at 2.p.m.via Track 11.
" "	1/R.Innis.Fus.	CARIBOU.	DULWICH CAMP. (B.8.c.6.9).	1st Essex Regt.	To leave Camp at 2-30.p.m. via Track 11.
" 29/30th.	2/S.W.Bordrs.	RUGBY CAMP.	Left front line.	1st N.F.L.D.	To be arranged mutually between Officers Commanding Units concerned.
" "	1/R.Innis.Fus.	DULWICH CAMP.	Centre front line.	2/Hants Regt.	
" "	87th Bde.H.Q.	FOREST AREA.	Line.	Similiar Units of 88th Inf.Bde.	
" "	87th M.G.Co.	FOREST AREA.	Line.	Similiar Units of 88th Inf.Bde.	
" "	87th T.M.B.	FOREST AREA.	Line.	Similiar Units of 88th Inf.Bde.	
" 30th.	1/K.O.S.Bordrs.	DUBLIN CAMP.	~~RUGBY CAMP.~~ White Mill (B.9.a.8.6).	~~2/Hants.~~	To leave Camp at 2.p.m.via Track 11.
" 30th.	1/Border Regt.	HENLEY CAMP.	CHARTERHOUSE. (B.9.c.8.5).	1/N.F.L.D.	To leave Camp at 2-30.p.m. via Track 11.

SECRET. Order No. "2"

1st BATTALION THE ROYAL INNISKILLING FUSILIERS. No 42.

1. The Battalion will relieve the 1st ESSEX REGIMENT in DULWICH CAMP on the afternoon of the 28th inst.
The Transport Lines will be situated near MICHAL FARM.

2. The Battalion will be ready to march off at 2-30.p.m.via Track 11 in the following order:-Drums, Hd. Qr, A.B & D Coys. An interval will be observed of 200 yds between Companies & between Battalion & Transport.
Particular attention will be paid to march discipline.

3. DRESS:-Marching Order. Steel Helmets will be worn and Water Bottles will be carried filled.

4. All Officers Kits, Mess Stores and Medical Stores will be stacked outside the Officers Mess at 1-30.p.m.
All Lewis Guns and Equipment and Signalling Equipment will be loaded on Transport during the morning. Limbers will be sent to Company Area for this purpose.
All picks, Shovels and Mauls to be stacked outside the Guard Room by 9-0.a.m.

5. Camp to be thoroughly clean and ready for inspection by 2-0.p.m.

Copies to:-

1. Staff.
2 & 3 War Diary.
4, 5, 6 & 7 Coys.
8. M.O.
9. T.O.
10. Q.M.

Captn & Adjt,
27/9/17. 1st Bn. The Royal Inniskilling Fusiliers.

SECRET.

Copy No. "3"

1st. BATTALION THE ROYAL INNISKILLING FUSILIERS ORDER No. 43.

I. FOOT will relieve FLANK in the centre Front Sector tomorrow evening.
DRESS:- Fighting Order Gas Helmets in the Alert position.

2. ORDER of Relief.
Right Front "D"Coy. Left Front "A"Co. Support "B"Co. Reserve "C"Co.
Route:- CLARGES STREET.
Companies will move off in the above order.

3. The leading Platoon will leave Camp at 5.30.p.m. and an interval of 100 yards will be observed between succeeding platoons.

4. Guides, one per platoon will meet Coys at SAULES FARM, advanced Brigade Headquarters at 7.15.p.m.

5. PACKS with the exception of the Details will be stacked by Cos. adjacent to No.12.Track by 10.0.a.m.
Officers Kits at 3.0.p.m.

6. WATER will be drawn by Coys as they pass Battalion Hd.Qrs.near MARTINE MILL.

7. Completion of Relief will be reported to Bn.Hd.Qrs, Coys.sending two runners one to remain the other to return.

8. Receipts for all Tremch Stores and S.O.S.Signals will be forwarded to Bn.Hd.Qrs.

9. During the period the Battalions is in the Line the Following Reports and Returns will be rendered by the Hour specified:-

Work Report Intelligence Report. Casualty Report. Variation in Strength. Effective Strength. Captured Martieral.	8-0.a.m. Daily.
Situation Report	2-30.a.m.& 2-30.p.m. Daily.

At the bottom of the Work Report a List of articles salved during the previous 24 Hours should be added.
a minimuim of movement is to be observed during the day.
Coy Commanders will make their rounds at Dusk and Dawn.

Copies to:-
1 STAFF.
2 & 3 WAR DIARY.
4,5,6 & 7 Coys.
8.M.O.
9.Q.M.
10.T.O.

28/9/17.

Captn & Adjt,
1st Rl Inniskilling Fusiliers.

REFERENCE
TO BAMBECQUE
NEY FARM
TIENTIR.
STATION.
D
16
17
18
15

Confidential

War Diary

of

1st Battalion The Royal Inniskilling Fusiliers

From 1st October 1917 To 31st October 1917

Volume 31.

Army Form C. 2118.

WAR DIARY
or
INTELLIGENCE SUMMARY
(Erase heading not required.)

Instructions regarding War Diaries and Intelligence Summaries are contained in F. S. Regs., Part II. and the Staff Manual respectively. Title Pages will be prepared in manuscript.

Volume 31 — 1st Royal Inniskilling Fus

Place	Date	Hour	Summary of Events and Information	Remarks and references to Appendices
	October 1		Position: D Co on the right with right flank resting on Langemarck Railway and left 100 yds right of Langemarck-Kockuit-road. A Co on the left with left flank 220 yds left of Langemarck-Kockuit-road. A patrol went out from D Co under 2/Lt O'Brien to reconnoitre ground South side of the Broembeek and succeeded in getting into touch with enemy strong point alongside the Langemarck Railway. After obtaining important information his patrol fired on a working party [illegible] strong point and dispersed them. Bn Hdqrs was again shelled consistently all day. No casualties	
	2		Bn relieved by the 1st K.O.S.B's and moved into White Mill Camp. No casualties.	
	3		Improving camp and fatigue party went up the line to Snoek's Farm (carrying party)	
	4		Improving White Mill Camp	
	5		Bn relieved moved up to the Canal Bank. B Company sent forward as support to the 2nd S.W.B's and took up their position at Martin's Mill with their Hdqrs on the Langemarck Railway	
	6		1 NCO + 30 men from A Coy sent on fatigue party carrying bombs. 1 OR killed. C Company went up to reinforce the 2nd S.W.B's and were kept in reserve with Hdqrs at 2nd S.W.B's Headqtrs. A fatigue party of 1 officer 2/Lt O'Brien and 88 men sent up as a carrying party. No casualties	
	7		2 fatigue parties of 25 OR and 1 O + 40 OR sent on fatigue to Norman Junction and 173 Tunnelling Co Boesinghe. The Bn was relieved on the	

2449 Wt. W14957/M90 750,000 1/16 J.B.C. & A. Forms/C.2118/12.

Army Form C. 2118.

Instructions regarding War Diaries and Intelligence Summaries are contained in F. S. Regs., Part II. and the Staff Manual respectively. Title Pages will be prepared in manuscript.

WAR DIARY
or
INTELLIGENCE SUMMARY

(Erase heading not required.)

Place	Date	Hour	Summary of Events and Information	Remarks and references to Appendices
	7		night of the 7th vide B.O. No 54 and moved back to Cardoen Camp. Strength Return. Ration Strength 15 O 696 OR Effective S. 26 O 942 OR Casualties during 5th & 6th inst 6 OR wounded 2 OR Killed.	
	8.		Reorganization.	
	9.		The Battalion moves to Prattle Camp near Proven vide Bn. O. No 47. attached.	
	10–13		Improving the Camp and training. Ration Strength 13/10/17 21 O 871 OR Effective Strength 13/10/17 21 O 940 OR	
	[illegible]		The following officers reported for duty on the 13th inst Lt. B. Bucknall T/2/Lt Mahoney T/2/Lt Elvery T/2/Lt G Washington T/2/Lt B.L. Griggs	
	14th		Training 2/Lt S.S. Hunter reported for duty	
	15th		The Battalion moves to the Third Army Area by rail vide Bn. O. No 48 attached	
	16th		Battalion arrives and billets Bailleulval	
	17th		Training 2/Lt W.M.M. Elvery went to Hospital.	
	18th			
	19		Lt. W.R. Webster rejoined from Hospital	
	20th		Ration Strength 27 O 861 OR Effective Stgth. 33 O 928 OR. The Commanding Officer interviewed the French farmers and agreed to assist them as far as possible in their agricultural work by detailing men to work in the field and carriage of produce in our limbers.	

2449 Wt. W14957/M90 750,000 1/16 J.B.C. & A. Forms/C.2118/12.

Instructions regarding War Diaries and Intelligence Summaries are contained in F. S. Regs., Part II. and the Staff Manual respectively. Title Pages will be prepared in manuscript.

WAR DIARY
or
INTELLIGENCE SUMMARY
(Erase heading not required.)

Army Form C. 2118.

Place	Date	Hour	Summary of Events and Information	Remarks and references to Appendices
[illegible]	21-28		Training: Ration Strength 27/10/17 29 Offrs 866 OR Effective Strgth. 33 Offrs 933 OR	
	29		Training: Military funeral of Col Sgt Price	
	30		Training	
	31		Training	

[signature] Lieut. Col.
Comdg 1st R. Inniskilling Fusiliers

2449 Wt. W14957/M90 750,000 1/16 J.B.C. & A. Forms/C.2118/12.

S E C R E T.

87TH INFANTRY BRIGADE ORDER NO.51.

1st OCTOBER, 1917.

1. The 1st Bn. The Border Regiment will relieve the 2nd South Wales Borderers in the Left Sector, and the 1st King's Own Scottish Borderers will relieve the 1st Royal Inniskilling Fusiliers in the Centre Sector of the Line on the night of the 2nd/3rd OCTOBER, 1917. Details of the relief will be arranged mutually between Officers Commanding Units concerned.

2. After relief the 1st Royal Inniskilling Fusiliers will go to WHITE MILL Camp (B.14.d.8.8.) vacated by the 1st King's Own Scottish Borderers, and the 2nd South Wales Borderers into CHARTER HOUSE Camp (B.9.c.8.5.) vacated by the 1st Bn. The Border Regiment.

3. All defence schemes, aeroplane photographs, trench maps and stores will be handed over.

4. During the relief the 2nd South Wales Borderers and the 1st Bn. The Border Regiment will use BRIDGE Street. The 1st Royal Inniskilling Fusiliers and 1st King's Own Scottish Borderers may use either HUNTER Street or CLARGES Street.

5. A C K N O W L E D G E.

Issued at 1300

[signature]

CAPTAIN,
BRIGADE MAJOR, 87TH INFANTRY BRIGADE.

Copies to:-
- Staff.
- War Diary.
- File.
- 2/S.W.B.
- 1/K.O.S.B.
- 1/R.In.F.
- 1/Bord.Rgt.
- 87th M.G.Coy.
- 87th T.M.Batty.
- 87th Bde.Sigs.
- Intelligence Off.
- Staff Captain.
- 86th Inf.Bde.
- 88th Inf.Bde.
- 29th Division "G".

S E C R E T.

87TH INFANTRY BRIGADE ORDER NO. 52.

1st OCTOBER, 1917.

Reference 1/10,000.
BROENBEEK.

1. The attack of the enemy's positions will be resumed at a time (Zero Hour), and on a date to be notified later.

2. The 4th Division on our Right will be co-operating.
The attack will be carried out by the 1st Royal Dublin Fusiliers on the Right, their Objective being:-
U.17.d.00.00. - U.18.c.00.45. -
U.18.c.80.80.to- U.18.d.30.80.
The 1st King's Own Scottish Borderers will send two (2) Platoons, exploit BEAR Trench SUPPORT Trench and will establish Posts at U.17.d.40.50., U.17.d.00.45., U.17.c.65.60.
The 1st Bn. The Border Regiment and the 2nd South Wales Borderers will remain in Brigade Reserve, ready to move after Zero Hour, on receipt of orders.

3. The Boundary between the 29th Division and the 4th Division will be from :-
U.23.b.70.50. - through - U.18.d.25.80.

4. The attack will be carried out under cover of a Creeping Artillery Barrage, and at Zero the attacking troops will be drawn up on the RED Line, (line of departure) and no troops will be forward of this before Zero Hour.
This RED Line runs :-
U.16.c.00.80 - U.16.c.35.65. - U.16.d.00.50. -
U.17.c.00.20. - U.17.c.30.30. - U.17.c.90.00. -
U.23.b.70.50.
At Zero the Barrage will fall 150 yards in front of the RED Line, when the attacking troops will leave the RED Line and get close under the Barrage as possible.
The Barrage will commence to 'creep' at Zero plus three (3) minutes.
Lifts will be for 50 yards at a time.
From the first lift, for 200 yards, the Barrage will advance at the rate of 50 yards in two (2) minutes, thence to the first Objective at 50 yards in three (3) minutes.
Barrage Maps attached.

5. Objectives gained, the following lines will be consolidated :-
(A) The GREEN Line.
(B) KANGAROO Trench to 't GOED DER VESTEN Farm.
In addition a Central Support Line will be consolidated from :-
U.18.c.40.00. - U.17.d.90.00.
An Out-Post Line will be established in front of all Lines during the consolidation.

6. The S.O.S. Signal will be a succession of S.O.S. Riflo Rockets, each bursting into 4 RED Lights. No other light Signal will be employed, except the RED FLARES which will be used to show the position of the Infantry to Contact Aeroplane Patrols.

7. Contact Patrol will fly over the Front at Zero plus one (1) hour and thirty (30) minutes - Zero plus three (3) hours - Zero plus 5 hours, and subsequently as ordered by Corps Headquarters.

Battalion Headquarters will mark their Headquarters by ground sheets of authorised shapes with the Code letters of the Unit laid out with white strips alongside. These letters should be 9 feet in depth. Signalling to Aeroplanes will be carried on with Panels.

8. There will be a Prisoners of War Collecting Post at the ADELPHI (C.3.central.) and the Divisional Prisoners Cage will be at the CACTUS PONTOON.

9. A Battle Aid Post will be established in EAGLE Trench from Zero Hour onwards.

There will be a Bearer Relay Post of the 87th Field Ambulance at REITRES Farm.

A Combined Regimental Aid Post of the 4th Division will be at the PIG and WHISTLE (U.28.b.4.3.)

10. A C K N O W L E D G E.

Brodie[signature]

Issued at 2100

CAPTAIN,
BRIGADE MAJOR, 87TH INFANTRY BRIGADE.

Copied to :-

Staff.
War Diary.
File.
2/S.W.B.
1/K.O.S.B.
1/R.In.Fus.
1/Bord.Rgt.
87th M.G.Coy.
87th T.M.Bty.
87th Fd.Ambce.
87th Bde.Sigs.
86th Inf. Bde.
88th Inf.Bde.
11th Inf.Bde.
Intelligence Off.
Staff Captain.
29th Division " G ".

S E C R E T.

87TH INFANTRY BRIGADE ORDER NO.53.

4th OCTOBER, 1917.

1. The following reliefs and movements of Units will take place on the night of the 5th/6th OCTOBER, 1917.

The 2nd SCOTS GUARDS will relieve the 1st Bn. The BORDER REGT. (less twp (2) Platoons).

The 4th GRENADIER GUARDS will relieve the 1st KING'S OWN SCOTTISH BORDERERS (less four (4) Platoons) and two (2) Platoons of the 1st Bn. The BORDER REGIMENT.

The 2nd SOUTH WALES BORDERERS will relieve the Right Compy. of the 1st KING'S OWN SCOTTISH BORDERERS and the Left Company of the 1st ROYAL DUBLIN FUSILIERS in the FRONT LINE. The Third (3rd) Company of the 2nd SOUTH WALES BORDERERS will be in support across the Railway about U.17.c.55.00. The Fourth (4th) Company will be in reserve relieving 1½ platoons of the 1st KING'S OWN SCOTTISH BORDERERS at MARTIN'S MILL. Battalion Headquarters of the 2nd S.W.Borderers will be at SPRING Fm.

The 1st ROYAL INNISKILLING FUSILIERS will relieve a Battalion of the 4th Division in CANAL BANK from C.13.c.0.4. to C.7.c.0.6. This relief may take place any time after 6-p.m.

2. Details of reliefs etc., will be arranged mutually between Commanding Officers concerned.

3. On relief the 1st Bn. The BORDER REGIMENT will move to CHARTERHOUSE Camp and the 1st KING'S OWN SCOTTISH BORDERERS to WHITE MILL Camp.

4. The 87th INFANTRY BRIGADE HEADQUARTERS will move to VULCAN CROSSING.

5. Further details as to the relief of the remainder of the 1st ROYAL DUBLIN FUSILIERS will be issued later.

6. DIVISIONAL BOUNDARY. The new Divisional Boundaries will be lines drawn parallel to the main LANGEMARCK Railway and roughly 250 yards from it on each side.

7. The Officers Commanding, MACHINE GUN COMPANIES will arrange reliefs mutually.

8. ACKNOWLEDGE.

W.K. Innes
~~CAPTAIN,~~

Issued at 8.50 a/

BRIGADE MAJOR, 87TH INFANTRY BRIGADE.

Copies:- Staff.
War Diary.
File.
2/S.W.B. 3rd Guards Bde.
1/K.O.S.B. 1st R.Dub.Fus.
1/R.In.Fus. 86th Inf.Bde.
1/Bord.Regt. 88th Inf.Bde.
87th M.G.C. Right.Bde. (10th)
87th T.M.B. Left.Bde.
29th Divn. "G" 2nd Scots Gds.
4th Divn. "G" 4th Gren. Gds.
81th M.G.C.

SECRET.

INSTRUCTION TO BE ATTACHED TO 87th INFANTRY BRIGADE ORDER No.52.

1. With reference to sentence No.3, para 2 of 87th Infantry Brigade Order No.52.
The two platoons of the 1st KING'S OWN SCOTTISH BORDERERS to take part in the attack, will form up on the RED before Zero. At Zero they will go forward, getting close under the barrage and advancing with it to their Objective.

2. One (1) platoon will advance to and establish a Post at ~~U.17.d.63.45.~~ U.17.c.65.60.

The second platoon will advance to and establish a Post at U.17.d.00.45., sending two sections forward to capture the enemy machine guns at U.17.d.40.50. and to establish a Post there.

3. As soon as the objectives have been taken, consolidation will commence, and platoon commanders will leave two (2) sections. The left platoon commander withdrawing two (2) sections to his original line.
The right platoon commander will pay particular attention to and arrange moppers-Up for any dug-outs which may be in the Railway Embankment.

4. At dark the Officer Commanding will detail parties to go forward to wire and complete the posts.

5. At Zero, as soon as the two (2) platoons move forward, a third platoon should be detailed to occupy their places inthe original front line, to help, if necessary, to destroy counter attacks.

6. The Left Company of the 1st Royal Dublin Fusiliers are sending a party to meet the Section of the 1st King's Own Scottish Borderers at U.17.d.40.50.

7. The following will be carried :-
Each man 4 Sandbags.
" " 170 rounds S.A.A. (Except Lewis Gunners and Bombers who will carry 50 rounds only)
50 % will carry Picks and Shovels.
The unexpended portion of the day's Rations, plus Iron Rations to be carried.
The Officer Commanding, 87th Trench Mortar Battery will detail one (1) man to go with the Right Platoon. This man should carry three (3) shells to deal with dug-outs.
Each Platoon will carry 4 S.O.S.Grenades Signals and Wire Cutters.
50 % will carry Ground Flares for signalling to Aircraft.

Issued at 1900 ACKNOWLEDGE. W.T.K. Innes
CAPTAIN,
BRIGADE MAJOR, 87TH INFANTRY BRIGADE.

Copied to:-
All Recipients
Brigade Order No.52.

SECRET.

ADMINISTRATIVE ORDER NO. 18.

Reference 29th Division Order No. 158 of 3rd September 1917, as amended.

1. TRANSPORT.

The following will be the position of Brigades and Machine Gun Companies Transport Lines on moving into the new Area.

Brigade in the Line (87th Brigade)

Transport of Brigade Group, less Field Company and Field Ambulance, will be at A.18.b.9.3., near DROMORE CORNER. This site is now unoccupied.

The present lines near MICHEL FARM will be cleared by 2 p.m. 5th instant.

Brigade in Support (88th Brigade) less M.G.Company, Field Company and Field Ambulance, on the DE WIPPE - DROMORE CORNER Road.

Bde. H.Q......... CARIBOO CAMP, A.11.d.9.7.
One Battalion.................. A.18.b.1.2.
Two Battalions .... A.18.a.8.9.
One Battalion .... A.11.d.9.7.

These Lines will be empty at 12 noon on 6th instant, - Present Lines to be cleared by that time.
Machine Gun Company Lines will be at COPPERNOLLE, A.16.b.6.9., on the east of POPERINGHE CANAL, which is now unoccupied.

Brigade in Reserve (86th Brigade)

Transport of Brigade Group, less Machine Gun Company, Field Company and Field Ambulance will be opposite "G" Camp at, A.16.a.5.3.

These Lines will be clear by 10 a.m. on the 7th inst. present lines to be vacated by 12 noon on that date.

The Machine Gun Company Lines will be at COPPERNOLLE, A.16.b.5.9., on the west of POPERINGHE CANAL. These Lines are now unoccupied.

The Transport of No. 227 Machine Gun Company will be in the stabling West of CORNISH CROSS - A.1[illegible].d.0 5.95. These Lines will be clear by 2 p.m. on the 6th inst., by which time the present lines will be vacated.

Companies of Divisional Train will be located as follows:-

No. 1 Company........... present Camp A.2.d.9.9.
No. 2 Company........... present Camp BARNES FARM
H.Qrs & No. 3 Company... PATERS FARM A.9.a.7.4.
No. 4 Company........... BALDWIN FARM A.3.a.0.1.

The Mobile Veterinary Section will move to INTERNATIONAL CORNER on the 6th instant, to the stabling at A.9.a.2.2.

P.T.O.

A.D.M.S., A.D.V.S., D.A.D.O.S. and Divisional Ordnance Store, D.B.O., the Employment Company, and Transport of Signal Company and Divisional Headquarters will be located at DRAGON CAMP.

Details of all three Infantry Brigades will be in BEDFORD CAMP.

HOUNSLOW CAMP will be vacated by 12 noon on 5th inst.

Captain DOWLING with Headquarters at ELVERDINGHE CHATEAU, has been appointed Area Commandant Left and Centre Division Areas.

Tentage required to establish all Camps will be drawn from Area Tent Store, ELVERDINGHE CHATEAU; amount of tentage to be drawn and date of drawing will be notified to Brigades and Units from Divisional Headquarters by wire.

2. HUTTING SECTIONS will be transferred from Left Division to Centre Division Area as follows:-

86th Brigade Section on 7th instant to Camp in DRAGON WOOD for work on Brigade Transport Lines of Reserve Brigade.

87th Brigade Section to Camp, ELVERDINGHE CHATEAU, on 6th instant, for work on Forward Brigade Transport Lines, etc.

88th Brigade Section to Details Camp, BEDFORD, on 6th instant, for work on Intermediate Brigade Transport Lines.

Progress Reports on work done in Left Division Area to be rendered to the C.R.E., 29th Division.

3. DIVISIONAL GRENADE DUMP will remain at GOUVY FARM, B.11.a.7.5. and will be shared with Guards Division.

Brigade Dumps are at REITRES FARM. U.22.d.1.1., and LANGEMARCK, U.22.d.9.1. The latter Dump will require augmentation as a considerable amount has been lost by shell fire. Three hundred boxes of S.A.A. have been dumped at SPRING FARM, U.22.c.3.3., and will be taken over by the Brigade in the Line.

4. TOOLS, AMMUNITION & GRENADES on Battalion and Brigade Establishment will be taken with Units on transfer and will not be handed over.

5. DIVISIONAL R.E. BATTLE DUMP, will be at VULCAN CROSSING.

6. MEDICAL.

Field Ambulance Headquarters at BLEUET FARM, and Advanced Dressing Stations at BOESINGHE CHATEAU and GREEN MILL, and the Regimental Aid Post at ROUSSEAU FARM will be shared with Guards Division. A new Regimental Aid Post will be established at REITRES FARM, and that at the "PIG & WHISTLE" will be shared with 4th Division.

7. BATHS.

The Bath at BOX CAMP will be handed over to the Guards Division.

8. DIVISIONAL THEATRE will remain at ONDANK, where Divisional Baths and Divisional Canteen Officer will be quartered.

9. SALVAGE.

The Divisional Salvage Company will work from the WIDJENDRIFT ROAD back to the CANAL; but all Units in this Area, including Artillery, will assist in getting the ground clean as rapidly as possible. For this purpose a Divisional Dump will be established at VULCAN CROSSING, U.27.c.4.6., and marked with a sign-board. The clearing of this Dump to the Corps Dumps at RUGBY and ELVERDINGHE will be done by the Divisional Salvage Officer as far as possible by tram line.

Forward of the WIDJENDRIFT - LANGEMARCK Road the Brigade in the Line will be responsible for salvage, and Brigade Dumps will be established at the points where pack transport is met by the ration parties. The 87th Brigade will report places selected for these Brigade Dumps, and mark them with notice boards to be obtained from Divisional Salvage Officer. Salvage from the Forward Area will be taken by empty returning pack transport to the Forward Brigade Transport Lines near DROMORE CORNER and collected from there by the Divisional Salvage Officer.

L H A Goodwin

4-10-17.

Lieut. Colonel,
A.A. & Q.M.G., 29th Division.

NOTICE (published with XIV C.R.O. dated 5/10/17).

Change from summer to winter time will take place on night 6/7th October 1917. At 1 a.m. watches will be put back to midnight.

SECRET. Copy No "2"

IST BATTALION THE ROY'L INNISKILLING FUSILIERS ORDER No.45.

5th.October 1917.

Ref.Map. 1/10.000.
28.N.W.

I. The Battalion will relieve a Battalion of the Fourth Division in the CAN'L BANK from C.13.c.0.4. to C.7.c.0.6.

Battalion Headquarters will be at C.13.c.2.8.

2. DRESS Marching Order.

3. Companies will parade at 5.45.p.m. and will leave Camp at 6.0.p.m. sharp with an interval of 50 yards between Platoons in the following order A,B.C. D. & Hd.Qr.Coy.

4. All Officers Kits & Mess Stores,Lewis Guns etc to be stacked inside the Orderly Room by 4.0.p.m.
BLANKETS.
Blankets will be rolled in bundles of 10 properly labelled showing Regt.No.Rank Name and Coy.and stacked inside Orderly Room by 4.0.p.m.

(Sd) E.E.J.Moore. Captn.
Adjt.Ist.Royal Inniskilling Fusiliers.

Copies to
I.Staff.
2 & 3 War Diary.
4.5.6 & 7 Coys.
8 Qr.Mr.
9. T.O.
10.M.O.

SECRET

87th INFANTRY BRIGADE ORDER No 54.

Reference Map 1/10,000
Sheet - BROEMBEEK
1/20000
Sheet - 28 N.W.

HEADQUARTERS, 87th INFANTRY BDE.

6th October 1917.

1. On the night of the 7th/8th ~~October~~ 1917. the Divisional Front will be divided into 2 Brigade Sectors the 1/LANARKSHIRE FUSILIERS (86th BRIGADE) taking over the Right Sector from the 2/SOUTH WALES BORDERERS and the 4th WORCESTER REGIMENT taking over the left Sector from the 2nd SOUTH WALES BORDERERS.
The 1st ROYAL INNISKILLING FUSILIERS will be relieved by the NEWFOUNDLAND REGIMENT on the CANAL BANK.

2. Moves will take place in accordance with March table attached.

3. The new Divisional Boundaries and Boundarys between Brigades are as follows -

Divisional Boundaries

RIGHT U.18.D.35.45 - U.18.B.75.00 - U.24.A.00.30 -
U.23.D.00.50 - U.23.C.40.00 - U.28.B.30.00 -

LEFT U.17.C.40.50 - U.22.B.70.80 - U.22.D.00.50 -
U.27.C.15.80.

Inter Brigade Boundary

U.17.D.80.60 - U.17.D.50.20 - U.23.A.10.65 -
U.22.D.50.20 - U.28.A.40.30 - U.27.D.40.20 -

4. The G.O.C. 88th Infantry Brigade will relieve the G.O.C. 87th Infantry Brigade on the night of the 7th/8th October 1917 at VULCAN CROSSING

5. Details of relief will be arranged between Commanding Officers concerned.

6. Four (4) teams of the 88th TRENCH MORTAR BATTERY will relieve 4 teams of the 87th TRENCH MORTAR BATTERY on the night of the 7th/8th October 1917. Officer Commanding 88th Trench Mortar Battery will meet the Officer Commanding 87th Trench Mortar Battery at VULCAN CROSSING at 2 p.m. on the 7th October 1917.

7. The 88th Infantry Brigade will move by RAILWAY ST, the 86th Infantry Brigade by the PILCKEM - AU BON GITE Road.

8. ACKNOWLEDGE

W. K. Innes[?]
Captain
a/Brigade Major 87th Infantry Brigade

Copied to Units concerned -
88th Inf. Bde
86th Inf. Bde
[illegible] Inf. Bde
29th [illegible]

S E C R E T.

1st BATTALION THE ROYAL INNISKILLING FUSILIERS ORDER NO46.

1. The Battalion will be relieved on the 7th October 1917 and will proceed to CORDOUEN Camp A.18.b.2.7.

2. Order of Relief. D,& Hd.Qr.Coys on CANAL BANK will be relieved by the NEWFOUNDLAND REGIMENT.
B & C Coys will be relieved in conjunction with 2ns South Wales Borderers to whom they are at present attached.
200 yards will be observed between Coys.

3. ROUTE- via BOESINGHE,WHITE HOPE CORNER,ELVERDINGHE Rd - POPERINGHE Rd DROMORE CORNER to Camp.

4. Transport will be at BARD DUMP,at 2-30p.m. for conveying Kits,Mess Stores etc for D,A,& Hd.Qr.Coys and will be at WHITE HOPE CORNER to meet B & C Coys.

(sd)E.E.J.Moore Captn,
Adjt 1st Royal Inniskilling Fusiliers.

MARCH TABLE

DATE	UNIT	FROM	TO	RELIEVED BY	TIME of STARTING	REMARKS.
7th/8th October 17.	57th Infantry Brigade Headquarters.	Vulcan Crossing	~~Dragon Camp~~ Caribou A.11 D.6.8. (Bgde. Tel: J.C.083)	58th Infantry Brigade	As arranged	Intervals of 200 yards will be maintained between companies and between Battalions and their Transport.
— " —	2nd South Wales Borderers	Front Line	White Mill	4th Worcester Regiment	As arranged.	
— " —	1st Kings Own Scottish Borderers	White Mill	Dragon Wood	2nd South Wales Borderers.	Camp to be cleared by 1-p.m.	
— " —	1st Royal Inniskilling Fusiliers	Canal Bank	Cardoen Camp	1st Newfoundland Regt.	As arranged.	
6th/7th October 1917	1st Border Regiment	Charterhouse	Dublin	Advanced Parties 3rd Guards Brigade	Camp to be clear by 2-p.m.	
7th/8th October 1917	57th Machine Gun Company	Front Line	Copperknole Camp CA.16.B.1.99	Ditto —	As arranged	
"	57th Trench Mortar Batty	Front Line	Dragon Camp	— —	As arranged	

SECRET.

87TH INFANTRY BRIGADE ORDER NO.55.

Reference Map 1/20,000
Sheet 27.N.W.

8th OCTOBER,1917.

1. The 87th Infantry Brigade will move to PROVEN NO.1. Area, tomorrow, 9th OCTOBER,1917, and will take over Camps from the 50th BRIGADE.

2. Units will proceed by train in accordance with attached table.

3. Transport will move by road and will leave this Area in time to reach their Camps before dark.

4. Units of the 50th Infantry Brigade will not be leaving their Camps until 4 to 5 hours after the arrival of the 87th Infantry Brigade Units.
This double-banking is unavoidable and every consideration ought to be given to the fact that the 50th Brigade are moving into the Line.

5. Acknowledge

W.K. Innes
CAPTAIN,
A/BRIGADE MAJOR, 87TH INFANTRY BRIGADE.

Copied to:-
STAFF.
War Diary.
File.
2/S.W.B.
1/K.O.S.B.
1/R.In.Fus.
1/Bord.Rgt.
87th M.G.Coy.
87th T.M.Batty.
87th Fd.Ambce.
87th Bde.Sigs.
No.3. Coy. Train.
455th West Rdg.Fd.Coy.
Staff Capt.
86th Inf.Bde.
88th Inf.Bde.
29th Divn. "G".

SECRET. Copy No. " "

IST BATTALION THE ROYAL INNISKILLING FUSILIERS ORDER No.47.

9th.OCTOBER 1917.

Map Ref.
27.N.E.

I. The Battalion will move to PRATTLE CAMP (F.16.d.1.4.) PROVEN No.I AREA today entraining at ELVERDINGHE at 12.0.noon and will take over Camps from the 59 Brigade.

2. The Battalion will parade at 10.50.a.m. and will move off at 11.0.a.m. in the following order:- A.B.C.D. & Hd.Qr.Coy. 200 Yards will be observed betweenxCompanies.

3. Officers Kits, Mess Stores Lewis Guns etc will be stacked by 10.30.a.m. in "C"Coys Hut.

4. Camp and Huts will be left clean and ready for inspection by 10.30.a.m.

5. DRESS Marching Order, Caps will be worn Blankets will be Carried on the man.

(Sd) E.F.J.Moore. Captn.
Adjt.Ist.Royal Inniskilling Fusiliers

Copies to:-
I.Staff.
2 & 3 War Diary.
4.5.6 & 7 Coys.
8.Qr.Mr.
9 T.O.
10.M.O.

SECRET.

The Officer Commanding,
2nd South Wales Borderers.
1st K.O.S.Borderers.
1st R.Innis.Fus.
1st Border Regiment.
87th M.G.Company.
87th T.M.Battery.

All Units will send on advanced parties, to take over Camps and Transport Lines allotted to them in the P.1.Area., as early as possible tomorrow morning.

Each battalion will be allotted One lorry. They must send most of their surplus stores by train, using the lorry to take them to the station. The lorry can then go to the new area with one load, dump it in the new camp and pick up the rest of the stores.

One lorry will be shared by the 87th Trench Mortar Battery and 87th Machine Gun Company.

It will go to the Trench Mortar Battery first and will take one load to P.1.area. It will then return and [move] the 87th Machine Gun Company's Stores.

All Units will have a guide at these Headquarters CARIBOU Camp (Sh.28./ A.11.d.9.7) at 6-30.a.m.tomorrow. The Machine Gun Company will take the lorry back after the Trench Mortar Battery have finished with it.

Units must leave representatives behind to hand over their present camps and transport lines. Copies of receipts for Camp stores, tents etc.handed over will be forwarded to these Headquarters by 6.p.m.on the 10th.inst.

Baggage wagons have been ordered to report as follows:-

Brigade Headquarters.	10.a.m.
S.W.Borderers.	7.a.m.
K.O.S.B.Borderers.	9.a.m.
R.Innis.Fus.	9.a.m.
Border Regiment.	9.a.m.

Will units notify the Officer Commanding, No.3.Company Train direct if these times are not suitable.

Supplies for the 10th.inst.will be delivered to the New Area tomorrow.

Location lists will be forwarded as soon as possible.

T. Fairfax Ross
CAPTAIN.
STAFF CAPTAIN.87th INFANTRY BRIGADE.

Oct.8th.1917.

S.E.C.R.E.T.

87th INFANTRY BRIGADE ORDER NO. 56.

(WARNING ORDER.)

11th OCTOBER,1917.

1. It is expected that orders will be received tomorrow, 12th instant, for despatch of Advanced Parties to the new Area by train.

All parties should take their bicycles with them.

2. The size of parties will probably be restricted to 1 Officer and 6 Other Ranks per Battalion and a corresponding number for the smaller Units.

At least 3 days rations will be required.

3. Please arrange for your advance parties to be ready to move at short notice.

4. ACKNOWLEDGE.

CAPTAIN,
STAFF CAPTAIN, 87TH INFANTRY BRIGADE.

Copies to:-
Staff.
File.
2/S.W.B.
1/K.O.S.B.
1/R.In.Fus.
1/Bord.Rgt.
87th M.G.Coy.
87th T.M.Batty.
87th Fd.Ambce.
87th Bde.Sigs.
455th W.Rdg.Fd.Co.R.E.
No.3.Coy.Train.
Staff Captain.

A Co Sgt Horngold
B Co " Robinson
C Co " Nickall
D Co " McCormick
Hdqtrs Hitcher
" ~~[illegible]~~ Windebank

29th Division No. 2014/2.

1. The following orders and instructions are issued regarding the move of by rail of the 29th Division (less artillery).

2. Time table and order of entrainment attached. Approximate length of journey seven hours.

3. The A.P.M. will make the necessary arrangements to control traffic on the road approaches to the entraining Stations, and no troops or transport should be allowed to enter the Station Yards until the R.T.O. is ready.

4. (a) All trains consist of 1 Officers carriage: 17 flat trucks: 30 covered trucks.
   (b) (i) Each flat truck will take an average of 4 axles.
   (ii) Each covered truck will take 6 H.D.Horses, or 8 L.D. Horses or Mules., or 40 men.
   (c) No personnel or stores will be allowed in the brake vans at each end of the train, or on the roofs of the trucks. No covered trucks should be used for baggage as it restricts space available for personnel.

5. The transport of Infantry Battalions will arrive at entraining stations 3 hours and personnel 1½ hours before the departure of the train.
   Other Units will arrive complete 3 hours before the departure of the train.

6. (a) The following fatigue parties are required at entraining stations:-

At PESELHOEK

87th Brigade will detail 1 Company from 1st Border Regiment to load Nos. 1, 2, 3, and 4 Trains.

88th Brigade will detail 1 Company from 1st Newfoundland Regiment to load trains from No. 5 to 11 inclusive.

The Royal Guernsey Light Infantry will be responsible for the loading of their own train.

At HOUPOUTRE.

87th Brigade will detail 1 Company, Royal Inniskilling Fusiliers, to load trains Nos. 1, 2, and 3, and the Company of Royal Inniskilling Fusiliers travelling by No. 7 train will be detailed to load trains from No. 4 to No. 7 inclusive.
The 86th Brigade will detail 1 Company Royal Dublin Fusiliers, to load trains Nos. 8 to 11 inclusive.
The Monmouth Regiment will be responsible for the loading of their own train.
These parties will report to the R.T.O. at entraining stations three hours before the departure of the first train they have to load.

(b) The following fatigue parties will be required at detraining stations.

AT SAULTY.

The 87th Brigade will detail 1 Company 1st K.O.S.B. to unload trains Nos. 1, 2, 3, and 4.

The 88th Brigade 1 Company, 4th Worcester Regiment, to unload Trains Nos. 5 to 11 inclusive.

The Royal Guernsey Light Infantry will be responsible for unloading train No. 12.

AT BEAUMETZ.

The 87th Brigade will detail 1 Company South Wales Borderers to unload trains Nos. 1, 2, 3, and 4.

The 86th Brigade will detail 1 Company 2nd. Royal Fusiliers to unload trains Nos. 5, 6, and 7, and 1 Company of 16th Bn. Middlesex Regiment to unload trains Nos. 8 to 11.

The Monmouth Regiment will be responsible for unloading train No. 12.

7. Brigades will detail an Officer to remain at the entraining station until the last train of the Brigade Group is ready to be despatched. He will report to the R.T.O. three hours prior to the departure of the first train and render all necessary assistance.

An Officer will also be detailed to remain at the station until the detraining of the Brigade Group is complete. He will also report to R.T.O. at Detraining Station immediately on arrival.

8. A complete marching out state showing the numbers of men, horses, G.S., limbered G.S., and 2 wheeled wagons and bicycles should be sent down with the transport of every unit, so that accommodation in the train can be checked by the R.T.O. at the beginning of the entrainment.

9. Supply and baggage wagons will accompany their own Units in every case.

10. The entrainment of all units must be completed half an hour before the time of departure of train.

11. Breast ropes for horse trucks must be provided by the Units themselves: ropes for lashing vehicles on the flat trucks will be provided by the railway.

12. Pickets must be provided at all stops for each end of the train to prevent troops leaving.

13. All doors of covered trucks and carriages on the right-hand side of the train, when on the main line, should be kept closed.

H M Cook

Lieut. Colonel,
A.A. & Q.M.G., 29th Division.

16.10.1.7

SECRET.

ADMINISTRATIVE ORDER NO. 20.

Reference 29th Division Order No. 163 dated 14.10.17.

1. ENTRAINMENT ORDERS are issued separately herewith.

2. TRANSPORT.

Lorries will be detailed as follows, to convey baggage etc. to entraining stations:-

15th instant. One to report at Clothing Store, PROVEN, at 7 a.m.
Two to report London Field Company at 7 a.m. to convey party to ONDANK to dismantle the "theatre" and convey it to PROVEN Railhead.
Four to report 87th Brigade Headquarters at 7 a.m.
Three to report Divisional Headquarters at 7 p.m.
Two to report 86th Brigade Headquarters at 11 p.m.

16th instant. Two to report 88th Brigade Headquarters at 1 a.m.
Two to report to Clothing Store, PROVEN, at 9 a.m.

17th instant. One to report to Royal Guernsey Light Infantry at 5 a.m.
One to report to Monmouth Regiment at 3 a.m.

As it will be necessary to use the same lorries throughout, Brigades and Units etc. will release their lorries at the earliest possible moment, in order that they may be passed on to the next Brigade or Unit requiring them.

The lorry drivers will receive their orders direct from the Officer Commanding Divisional Sub-Park as to where to report on release by the Brigade or Unit under which they are working.

3. DIVISIONAL SUPPLY COLUMN.

The Divisional Supply Column, S.A.A. Lorries of Ammunition Sub-Park and Motor Ambulance Cars will accompany the Division and will move by road in such detachments as may be necessary via HAZEBROUCK - LILLERS - ST POL - ARRAS to BEAUMETZ, reporting on arrival at BEAUMETZ to "F" Corps Supply Column.

Column to be clear of HAZEBROUCK by 12 noon.

4. SUPPLIES.

Troops will entrain with Rations for the day following the day of detrainment.

5. RAILHEAD.

Railhead for 87th Brigade will be at BEAUMETZ RIVIERE on 16th instant, and for 86th and 88th Brigades at PROVEN.

Railhead for whole Division will be at BOISLEUX on 17th inst.

P.T.O.

6. <u>DETRAINMENT</u>.

Units will be billeted in the North Division Reserve Area of the VI Corps, south west of ARRAS, as per location table attached.

Captain QUILL, D.A.A.G., with Captain GROOME, G.S.O. 3, and Captain BROWNE, Attache "Q", will superintend detrainment. Officer Commanding Signals will detail two D.R's., for duty under Captain QUILL, to report at Divisional Headquarters, BASSEUX, by 4 p.m. on 15th instant.

Six lorries will be detailed by VI Corps for carriage of blankets etc from each detraining station to billets.

The 1st Bn. Royal Dublin Fusiliers will probably be billeted for one night in BEAUMETZ, prior to joining the 16th Division, and will be provided by VI Corps with 2 lorries for baggage for the move.

7. <u>AREA COMMANDANT</u>.

The Area Commandant is Colonel TAYLOR, with Headquarters at BASSEUX. Sub-Area Officers are Major MURPHY at HENDECOURT, Lieut. Colonel MACLEOD at BAILLEULVAL and Major STEWART at BERLES.

Area Officers have a reserve of Tents to supplement existing accommodation if required.

8. <u>CANTEENS</u>

Canteens will be established by the Divisional Canteen Officer as follows:-

BASSEUX	(Billet No. 18)
BERLES	(Billet No. 93)
HENDECOURT	Hut "D", "A" Camp.

9. <u>DIAMOND TROUPE</u>

Diamond Troupe will re-open in the Divisional Theatre at HENDECOURT. The C.R.E. will detail personnel to re-erect the Theatre. Adrian Huts suitable for entertainments also exist at BAILLEULVAL and BAILLEULMONT.

10. <u>BATHS</u>.

Baths exist at the following places:-

HENDECOURT	-	12 sprays.
BLAIREVILLE	-	12 sprays.
BAILLEULVAL	-	10 sprays.
BAILLEULMONT	-	8 sprays.
BELLACOURT	-	6 sprays.
BERLES AU BOIS	-	12 sprays.
BIENVILLERS	-	12 sprays.

The Divisional Baths Officer will supply two men to look after each Bath, Brigade Groups making arrangements for remaining personnel required.

The Divisional Baths Officer will arrange for one change of clothing per week from Corps Clothing Exchange, BOISLEUX, to be drawn under Brigade arrangements from Divl Clothing Store, BAILLEULVAL, Billet No. 23, where Foden [illegible] will be placed.

Lieut. Colonel,
A.A. & Q.M.G., 29th Division.

14.10.17.

S E C R E T.

87th INFANTRY BRIGADE ORDER No. 56.

14th OCTOBER, 1917.

1. The 87th Infantry Brigade Group will move to the THIRD ARMY Area by RAIL tomorrow, 15th OCTOBER, 1917.

2. Movements will be in accordance with 29th Divisional Instruction and Train Table attached.

3. Units entraining at PESELHOEK (A.23.b.) will march via :-

PROVEN,
NORTHERN CHEMIN MILITAIRE,
INTERNATIONAL CORNER, and
ROAD JUNCTION - A.27.d.

Units entraining at HOPOUTRE will march via the

PROVEN - POPERINGHE Road.

4. The 1st Bn. THE BORDER REGIMENT will detail one (1) Company to load trains No. 1, 2, 3, and 4 at PESELHOEK.
The 1st ROYAL INNISKILLING FUSILIERS will detail one (1) Company to load trains No. 1, 2, and 3 at HOPOUTRE.
The Company of the 1st ROYAL INNISKILLING FUSILIERS travelling on Train No.7 will be required to load trains Nos. 4 - 7 inclusive.
1st KING'S OWN SCOTTISH BORDERERS will detail one (1) Company to unload trains 1, 2, 3 and 4 at SAULTY.
2nd SOUTH WALES BORDERERS will detail one (1) Company to unload trains Nos. 1, 2, 3 and 4 at BEAUMETZ.
Officers in charge of Loading Parties should report to their respective R.T.Os. three (3) hours before departure of No. 1 train, in each case.

5. Lieutenant OLIPHANT will superintend the entraining of all the Brigade GROUP at HOPOUTRE, and Captain INNES at PESELHOEK.

6. Attention is drawn to 29th Divisional Letter No. 2014/G, attached.

7. ACKNOWLEDGE.

Issued at 1620

CAPTAIN,
BRIGADE MAJOR, 87TH INFANTRY BRIGADE.

Copied to:- Staff.
War Diary.
File.
2/S.W.B.
1/K.O.S.B.
1/R.In.Fus.
1/Bord.Rgt.
87th M.G.Coy.
87th T.M.Btty.
87th Bde.Sigs.
87th Fd.Ambce.
455th W.Rdg.Fd.Coy.R.E.
No.3.Coy.Train. A.S.C.
29th Divn. " G ".

S E C R E T. COPY No. " "

IST BATTALION THE ROY'L INNISKILLING FUSILIERS.

1048

14th.OCTOBER 1917.

I. The Battalion will move to the Third Army 'rea by Rail tomorrow 15th.October 1917.

2. B.C.D.& Hd.Qr.Coys will parade at 2.20.p.m. and will move off in the following order at 2.30.p.m.
B.C.D.& Hd.Qr.Coy.

3. "A"Coy.is detailed to procced to HOUPOUTRE to load trains Nos 1.2.& 3.
"A"Coy will move off at 8.10.a.m. and will entrain on No.3. Train leaving at 8.35.p.m.
2 Pipers and I Drummer will parade with this party.

4. "D"Coy is detailed to load trains No.4&5&6&7 and will entrain on No.7 Train leaving at 12.25.p.m. 16th.inst.

5. Officer Commanding "A" & "D"Coys will report to their respective R .T.O's on arrival at HOUPOUTRE Station.

6. DRESS. Marching Order.Blankets and Waterproof Sheets will be carried.

7. TRANSPORT. The Transport will move off at 2.30.p.m. tomorrow and will proceed to HOUPOUTRE to be loaded on to No.3 Train.
The O.C.transport will report to R,T.O.No.3 Train on arrival.

8. ROUTE. PROVEN - POPERINGHE ROAD.

9. OFFICERS KITS,ORDERLY ROOM and SIGNALLING STORES are to be stacked outside the Qr.Mr's Stores by 12.0.noon.
Lewis Guns to be stacked at the Trasport Lines by 12.0.noon.
Officers Mess Stores to be stacked outside the Qr.Mr's Stores by 12.0.noon.

10. I Cooker will proceed with "A"Coy.
I Cooker will proceed with "B" & "C"Coys.
I Cooker will proceed with "D"Coy.

11. RATIONS. Two days rations will be carried.

(Sd) E.E.J.Moore. Captn.
Adjt.Ist.Royal Inniskilling Fusiliers.

Copies to:-
I. Staff.
2 & 3 War Diary.
4.5.6.& 7 Coys
8. Qr.Mr.
9. T.O.
10. M.O.

Entrain PESELHOEK.
Detrain

No. of Train.	Unit.	Date.	Time of Departure.
1.	1st K.O.S.B. less 1 Coy., 1 Cooker & team	15th	14-30
2.	87th Bde. H.Q. 87th M.G.Co. 87th T.M.B. 87th Bde. Signals. 1 Coy., 1 Cooker and team, 1st K.O.S.B.	15th.	18-20.
3.	No. 227 M.G.Co. 87th Field Ambulance.	15th	22-30
4.	1st Border Regt., less 1 Co., 1 Cooker and team.	16th	2-30
5.	4th Bn. Worcester Regt.	16th	6-30
6.	2nd Bn. Hampshire Regt.		10-20
7.	88th Brigade H.Q. 88th M.G.Co. 88th T.M.B. 88th Brigade Signals. 1 Coy. 1st Border Regt, 1 Cooker and team.	16th	14-30
8.	1st Bn. Essex Regt.	16th	18-20

Entrain LOUPOUTRE.
Detrain

No. of Train.	Unit.	Date.	Time of departure.
1.	2nd Bn. S.W.Bords.	15th	12-25.
2.	H.Q., Div. R.E. No. 455th (W.Riding) Field Co. No. 3 Co. Div. Train.	15th	16-45
3.	1st Bn. R.Inn. Fus., less 1 Co., 1 Cooker & team.	15th	20-35
4.	29th Div. H.Q. H.Q. and No. 1 Sect. Div. Signals. 1 Employment Co.	16th	0-45
5.	2nd Bn. Royal Fusiliers	16th	4-45
6.	1st Bn. Lancashire Fusrs.	16th	8-35
7.	86th Brigade H.Q. 86th M.G.Co. 86th T.M.B. 86th Brigade Signal Co. 1 Coy. Royal Innis. Fus., 1 Cooker and team.	16th	12-25
8.	16th Bn. Middlesex Regt.	16th	16-45

PTO

Entrain PESELHOEK.
Detrain

No. of Train.	Unit.	Date	Time of departure.
9.	H.Q. Div. Train. No. 4 Co. Div. Train. No. 510th . (London) Field Coy.	16th	22-30
10.	88th Field Ambulance. 18th Mobile Veterinary Sect. 1 Coy. Royal Guernsey Light Infantry, 1 Cooker, 1 team. ½ Employment Co.	17th	2-30
11.	1st Newfoundland Regt.	17th	6-30
12.	Royal Guernsey Light Infantry less 1 Coy., 1 Cooker and team.	17th	10-20

Entrain HOUPOUTRE.
Detrain

No. of Train.	Unit.	Date	Time of departure.
9.	No. 497 (Kent) Field Co. No. 2 Coy. Div. Train.	16th	20-35
10.	89th Field Ambulance. 1 Coy. Monmouth Regt, 1 Cooker and team.	17th	0-45
11.	1st Royal D.Fus.	17th	4-45
12.	1/2nd Monmouth Regt., less 1 Coy. 1 Cooker and team.	17th	8-35

A 135

23rd December 1917

87/29

Headquarters
15th Infantry Brigade

Herewith War Diary Volume 32 for the period 1st to 30th November 1917.

Kindly acknowledge.

[illegible] Capt & Adjt
1/1st R.I.F.
Comdg 1st Bn Inniskilling Fusiliers

87/59

Army Form C. 2118.

WAR DIARY
or
INTELLIGENCE SUMMARY
(Erase heading not required.)

Instructions regarding War Diaries and Intelligence Summaries are contained in F. S. Regs., Part II. and the Staff Manual respectively. Title pages will be prepared in manuscript.

Hour, Date, Place	Summary of Events and Information	Remarks and references to Appendices
November		Vol 21
[illegible] 1–5	Training and Sports. Major [illegible] takes over command of the Battalion during the absence on leave of Colonel [illegible] [illegible] [illegible] [illegible] [illegible] [illegible] [illegible] [illegible] [illegible] [illegible]	[illegible] Collins [illegible] Marchant
6	[illegible] [illegible] [illegible] [illegible] the following officers [illegible] [illegible] [illegible] [illegible] Malony. [illegible] Outposts and Advanced Guards Scheme.	
12–14	" " "	
15th	Practice manoeuvres in the [illegible] with Advanced Guards [illegible] Division. Field Marshall Sir [illegible] [illegible] was present at the manoeuvres. The Battalion commenced to return [illegible] to [illegible]	[illegible]

X 31

1247 W 3299 200,000 (E) 8/14 J.B.C. & A. Forms C. 2118/11.

Instructions regarding War Diaries and Intelligence Summaries are contained in F. S. Regs., Part II. and the Staff Manual respectively. Title pages will be prepared in manuscript.

WAR DIARY

or

INTELLIGENCE SUMMARY

(Erase heading not required.)

Army Form C. 2118.

Hour, Date, Place	Summary of Events and Information	Remarks and references to Appendices
[illegible] 17th November 1917	The Battalion moved by train to the III Corps Area [PERONNE] (see attached Bgde Order No. 57 & B.O. No. 49 d/16-11-17)	
HAUT-ALLAINES 18th November 1917	The Battalion marched to FINS vide Bgde Order No.	
FINS 19th November 1917 20th November	The Battalion moved to the assembly area vide B.O. No. 51 d/19-11-17. Zero hour was at 6.20 a.m. on the 20th. The Battn moved off in accordance with Instruction No. 1 (attached) d/19-11-17, & was concentrated in GULLIES at R 8 c 9. Lieut J. O'BRIEN, Commanding "D" Coy, & 11 O.R. were wounded while the Battn was passing through VILLERS PLOUICH. At 10.20 a.m. orders were received for the Battn to move forward in accordance with Instruction No. 1 para 5 ACTION, & with the exception of 2/Lieut NELSON being wounded, suffered no casualties [illegible] reached the Canal bank MARCOING. At 2.30 p.m. the Battn crossed the Canal & formed up in attack formation on the North bank with the left flank resting at a point L 23 d 1.5 & right at L 24 c [illegible]. The Commanding Officer then went forward to reconnoitre the immediate front & decided to assault at once. The Battn. immediately advanced in open formation A & B Coys in the front line & C & D Coys in the 2nd line.	

Instructions regarding War Diaries and Intelligence Summaries are contained in F. S. Regs., Part II. and the Staff Manual respectively. Title pages will be prepared in manuscript.

WAR DIARY
or
INTELLIGENCE SUMMARY

(Erase heading not required.)

Army Form C. 2118.

Hour, Date, Place	Summary of Events and Information	Remarks and references to Appendices
MARCOING 20th November 1917	On debouching from the cover of the bank, the Battn. proceeded until it came under heavy machine gun fire & rifle fire. The Battn. then [illegible] & advanced by platoon rushes, under its own covering fire, for a distance of 500 yards when the Commanding Officer came forward & led the charge against the nearest gunpits. Before reaching the gunpits it was necessary to get through 30 yds of barbed wire. While the wire cutters were going forward the remainder of the Battn. covered them with rifle fire standing. One officer placed a lewis gun on the shoulder of a man & used it in that way. When the Battn. charged the first line of pits, the majority of the enemy [illegible] to pits in rear, and those remaining were either killed or captured. On reaching this point the two centre Companies kept up a heavy fire while the right & left Companies worked round their respective flanks. When this movement was completed the Battn. again charged & converged on the pits from three sides. The majority of the enemy retired on to the MARCOING - RUMILLY RD. Two strong points at [illegible] held out stubbornly - one was manned with [illegible] & the other with three machine guns. These were soon captured, & 3 dead German officers were found. The possession for each pit was stubbornly contested. No time was lost in pushing	

1247 W 3299 200,000 (E) 8/14 J.B.C. & A. Forms/C. 2118/11.

Instructions regarding War Diaries and Intelligence Summaries are contained in F. S. Regs., Part II. and the Staff Manual respectively. Title pages will be prepared in manuscript.

WAR DIARY
or
INTELLIGENCE SUMMARY

(Erase heading not required.)

Army Form C. 2118.

Hour, Date, Place	Summary of Events and Information	Remarks and references to Appendices
MARCOING 20th November 1917	& beyond these pits. The Battn advanced right up to the wire in the Battalion area & came under heavy flank fire from houses on the MASNIERES - CAMBRAI ROAD, and were also fired upon by a machine gun at G.14.c.5.5. The Battalion was therefore withdrawn about 100 yds as it was impossible to get through the wire. On seeing that there were no troops up on our right the Commanding Officer decided to form a defensive flank & for that purpose [illegible] the right Company and placed them facing the MASNIERES - CAMBRAI ROAD. The right centre was withdrawn into support. The Battalion then commenced to dig themselves in. The undermentioned officers were wounded during the action: Lieut. H. LEE (Died of Wounds) 2/Lieut. E.A. MAHONEY " J. O'BRIEN " W.H. GOOD " M. [illegible] " J.E. NELSON Casualties [illegible] Other Ranks 141 { Killed 20, wounded 116, missing 5 } During the operations the Battalion captured the following: 54 prisoners, including 5 officers. 5 Machine Guns. Number of dead actually counted 46.	

1247 W 3299 200,000 (E) 8/14 J.B.C. & A. Forms/C. 2118/11.

Army Form C. 2118.

WAR DIARY
or
INTELLIGENCE SUMMARY
(Erase heading not required.)

Instructions regarding War Diaries and Intelligence Summaries are contained in F. S. Regs., Part II. and the Staff Manual respectively. Title Pages will be prepared in manuscript.

Place	Date	Hour	Summary of Events and Information	Remarks and references to Appendices
[illegible]	21st November 1917		The Battalion was engaged in digging in, and during the night 21st/22nd November carried up and placed in front of the trenches, over [illegible] yards of wired [illegible]. During the day the enemy snipers were very active. The enemy had not brought up any artillery. Casualties. wounded 15.	
	22nd November 1917		Enemy snipers active. A strong point was [illegible] in front of C Companies trenches.	
	23rd November 1917		Enemy [illegible] [illegible] slightly with field guns. [illegible] of strong point continued. Casualties wounded 2.	
	[illegible] November 1917		[illegible] and support trenches were shelled by the enemy. Trenches were improved, but the [illegible] [illegible] of the men in the battalion was by this time sorely tried.	
	[illegible] November 1917		The Battalion was relieved by the 1st ESSEX Regt. ([illegible] [illegible] [illegible] to be attacked) Casualties - wounded 13	

Army Form C. 2118.

Instructions regarding War Diaries and Intelligence Summaries are contained in F. S. Regs., Part II. and the Staff Manual respectively. Title Pages will be prepared in manuscript.

WAR DIARY
or
INTELLIGENCE SUMMARY
(Erase heading not required.)

Place	Date	Hour	Summary of Events and Information	Remarks and references to Appendices
	November			
MARCOING	26th		The Battalion [illegible] in billets	
	27th		"	
	28th		The Battalion relieved the 1st [illegible] Regt & the 1st HAMPSHIRE Regt, taking over the right sub sector from the MARNIERES–CAMBRAI ROAD to the communication trench in the front line at [illegible] (Vide Brigade Order No. 64 attached)	
	29th		The enemy shelled the canal bank during the day. There were no casualties	
	30th		About 7.0 a.m. the Germans attacked the Division on our right; the Germans [illegible] were seen advancing towards MARCOING COPSE, but were driven back by a counter attack about 9 a.m. About 8.0 a.m. a [illegible] attack was [illegible] by the enemy on the [illegible] point held by a platoon of "B" Coy but it was driven off with loss to the enemy. The [illegible] [illegible] the Canal bank [illegible] Headquarters and [illegible] [illegible] [illegible] the enemy who had advanced [illegible] MARCOING COPSE. The [illegible] front was shelled with high explosive [illegible] during the day. Casualties killed 7 wounded 12 missing 8	
			[illegible] Major, Commanding 1st Inniskilling Fus. 2/12/17.	

2449 Wt. W14957/M90 750,000 1/16 J.B.C. & A. Forms/C.2118/12.

SECRET. 1st Bn The Royal Inniskilling Fus.rs Order No 49

1. The 87th Brigade Group will move by train to the VI Corps Area on the 17th inst (See Bde Order No 57)

2. The Battalion will leave present billets at 1.30 pm, and march to entraining point (BOISLEUX-AU-MONT) thence RANSART (by train from BAILLEULVAL) to ADINFER - HENDECOURT.

3. 1st & 2nd Line Transport will go by road on 16th November (See Bde Order No 58)

4. DRESS :- Marching Order, one blanket to be carried, caps to be worn. Lewis Guns will be carried

5. The extra blankets will be rolled in bundles of ten, labelled & stored in the Quarter Master's Stores by 9.30 am 17th November

6. Officers valises (1 per Co) & mess boxes will be stored outside [illegible] Officers Mess by 12.30 pm 17th November

16/11/17

Sd. E. G. [illegible] Capt & Adjt,
1st Royal Inniskilling Fusiliers

Copy No 1 Staff
2, 3 War Diary
4, 5, 6, 7 Companies
8 T.O.
9 M.O.
10 Qr Master

Copy No. 2

SECRET. 1st Royal Inniskilling Fus.

Order No 50 18/11/17

1. The Brigade will march to FINS tonight.

2. The Battalion will parade at 8-20 pm on the road immediately in front of their present billets.

3 DRESS :- Marching Order, caps to be worn. Lewis Guns to be carried.

4 Transport, less Cookers, Mess cart and Watercarts will be brigaded under the Staff Captain.

5. The following intervals will be observed between Battalions and between Companies 100 yards. Between Units' Transports 100 yards.

6 The remainder of the Transport will start from [illegible] by Brigade Headquarters at 9.15 pm.

7 ROUTE :- MOISLANS Cross Roads C.18.c.5.7 road junction D.20.d.0.5.

Copy 1 Staff
2 & 3 War Diary
4 5 6 & 7 Companies
8 T.O.
9 M.O.
10 Sh. mtr

(Sd) C. E. J. Moore Capt.
Adjt 1st R. Inniskilling Fus.

19/11/17.

S E C R E T.

IST BATTALION THE ROYAL INNISKILLING FUSILIERS ORDER No. 51.

Ref. Map. 57.C.S.E.

I. The Battalion will move to the assembly area Q.30.b & c. tonight 19/20th. inst.

2. ROUTE. FINS - GOUZEAUCOURT.

3. ORDER of March. "A"Co. Hd.Qrs., "B".,"C". & "D"Cos.

4. The Battalion will parade ready to march off at 1.0.a.m. outside their billets.
Movement will be in file.
DRESS. Marching order Steel helmets will be worn.

5. Absolute silence will be observed and no Smoking or lights permitted.

6. 100 yards interval will be observed between Companies.

7. Pack animals will march in rear of the Battalion, under Battalion Transport Officer.

Copy No. I. Staff.
2 & 3. War Diary.
4. 5. 6 & 7. Cos.
8. M.O.
9. T.O.
10. Qr.Mr.

C. [signature]
Capt & Adjt.
Ist. Bn. The R. Inniskilling Fusiliers.

SECRET.

87th. INFANTRY BRIGADE ORDER No. 57.

Ref Map.
Sheets 5.18 & 5.10.
1/40,000.

I. The 87th. INFANTRY BRIGADE GROUP will move to the III Corps Area by rail on the 17th. inst.

2. Movement will be in accordance with the attached movement table.

3. Lieut. J. Oliphant will be in charge of the entraining of the Group and will report to the R.T.O. BOISLEUX-AU-MONT at 5.0 p.m. on the 17th. inst., and will entrain on the train carrying the last Unit of the Brigade. Units will be at the entraining station ONE hour before the departure of the train.

4. Transport will move by road on the night of the 16/17th. November. Details will be issued later.

5. On the march to the entraining station 200 yards will be observed between Companies.

6. ACKNOWLEDGE.

(Sd) E. Forbes-Robertson.
Captain.
Brigade Major, 87th. Infantry Brigade.

November 15th. 1917.
Issued 2100.

SECRET.

87TH INFANTRY BRIGADE ORDER No. 60.

November 19th. 1917.

Ref. Map 57. C. 1/40,000.

I. The 87th. INFANTRY BRIGADE GROUP will march to the assembly Area in Q.36.b & c tonight the 19/20th. inst.

2. Movement will be in accordance with TABLE attached.

3. Pack animals will march in rear of their Units under Battalion Transport Officers.

4. Starting Point for all Units will be marked with a RED LAMP.

5. The following intervals will be observed between Battalions and Companies - 100 yards.

6 BRIGADE HEADQUARTERS will be at Q.29.b.3.1.

7. Absolute silence will be observed and no lights or smoking permitted.

8. Strict punctuality must be adhered to.

9. ACKNOWLEDGE.

(Sd) Brodiemair.
Captain.
Brigade Major 87th. Infantry Brigade.

S E C R E T.

Officer Commanding.
2nd. S. W. Borderers.
Ist. K. O. S. Borderers.
Ist. R. Innis. Fusiliers.
Ist. Border Regiment.
87 th. M. G. Company.

I. Each Transport will be loaded this afternoon and move to Units Camps between 4.0.p.m. and 6.0.p.m., to arrive not later than 6.0.p.m.

Transport animals will move in rear of their respective Units tonight to the assembly position.

2. When the troops move forward from the Assembly Area Pack Transport will be Brigaded withing the assembly area and as circumstances will permit to VILLERS PLOUICH.

3. The Brigaded Transport will be under the Command of Lieut. Aitcheson he will be assisted by Lieut. Williams 2nd South Wales Borderers, the senior Transport Officer.

4. Pack Transport will be moved forward from VILLERS PLOUICH when possible after Zero Hour and form a forward dump at a place to be selected and return to transport lines to refil, under orders of Lieut Aitcheson.

5. Forward Transport Lines will be formed at Railhead as 60cm track is advanced.

Only sufficient animals will be sent forward carrying necessary supplies, the remainder stopping in the present Transport Lines.

6. Copy of 29 th. Division Instructions No. 13. with reference to Pack Transport will be issued to Transport Officers direct.

19 th. November 1917. (Sd) J. R. Wharton. Captain.
Staff Captain 87 th. Infantry Brigade.

Officer Commanding
2nd. S. W. Borderers
Ist. K. O. S. Borderers.
Ist. R. Innis. Fusiliers.
Ist. Border Regiment.

87th. M. G. Company.
87th. T. M. Battery.

Reference verbal instructions issued today in connection with Annexe to Brigade Orders No.59.,

	Dump.	Quantity and Remarks.
S. A. A.	At FINS DUMP and DESSART WOOD.	To be drawn on before establishment in Transport Lines is touched.
Rifles Grenades No. 23 and Hales.	"	To be drawn as necessary to complete establishment.
P. W. A.	"	Up to 500 rds. per Unit (2/S. W. B. 700 rds.)
Hedging Gloves.	"	50 per Battalion in addition to those allotted to Transport.
Sandbags.	"	Sufficient for 2 per man to be drawn. These will form part of Dress Equipment and are an addendum to Annexe to Bde. Order No. 59.
Tracer Ammunition.	"	666 rds. may be drawn by 87th. M. G. Company.
Water Crates.	Brigade Transport Lines	to complete to establishment. (W. 13. b.)
Petrol Tins.	"	"
Pack Saddles.	D. A. D. O. S. at SOREL (D. A. D. O. S. office is situated in Barn at cross Roads in centre of SOREL and has the name SOREL written large on the East Wall.)	To make establishment up to 24 will be drawn.
Rope.	On application to Brigade Headquarters.	Tarred Rope up to abou 600 feet per Unit is available.
Tracing Tapes.	" "	Extra Tracing Tapes are available on application
Socks.	Billet No. 45. SOREL.	To bring up to 3 per man can be drawn today 19th. instant.

(Sd) J. R. Wharton.
Captain.
Staff Captain. 87th. Infantry Brigade.

19th. November 1917.

SECRET

[illegible] Batt. The Royal Inniskilling Fusiliers

Administrative Order [illegible]

With reference to [illegible] [illegible]

1/ Following battle stores will be [illegible]

1 Bandolier [illegible] per man

2 [illegible] [illegible] [illegible] per [illegible]

1 [illegible] [illegible] per [illegible]

75% [illegible] [illegible] [illegible]

4 [illegible] [illegible] per section

12 S.O.S. [illegible] per [illegible]

3 [illegible] [illegible] per [illegible]

1 [illegible] [illegible] per [illegible]

2 [illegible] per [illegible].

2/ Packs will be [illegible] [illegible] [illegible] [illegible]

4 days [illegible] [illegible] [illegible]

3/ Blankets and [illegible] [illegible] [illegible] [illegible]

10 [illegible] and [illegible] will be [illegible] [illegible]

[illegible] [illegible] Q.M.S. [illegible] [illegible] [illegible]

4/ [illegible] [illegible] [illegible] by the [illegible]

[illegible] [illegible] [illegible] [illegible] [illegible] [illegible]

at [illegible] [illegible]

19/4/17

Issued at 4.30 p.m.

Copies to [illegible] Staff

[illegible] [illegible]

4 [illegible] [illegible]

8 [illegible]

[illegible]

[illegible] [illegible]

[illegible] Inniskilling Fusiliers

S E C R E T.

87th. INFANTRY BRIGADE ORDER No.62.

November 25th. 1917.

I. The following reliefs will take place tonight the 25/26th. November.

The IST ESSEX REGIMENT will take over the line held by the IST ROYAL INNISKILLING FUSILIERS plus 200 yards of the IST BORDER REGIMENT.

The NEWFOUNDLAND REGIMENT will relieve the IST BORDER REGIMENT taking over the left sub-sector less the first 200 yards of their right front line.

2. Details of relief will be arranged mutually between Officer's Commanding Units concerned.

3. The IST ESSEX REGIMENT and NEWFOUNDLAND REGIMENT will come under the orders of B.G.C.87th.Infantry Brigade from midday today.

4. After the relief the IST BORDER REGIMENT and IST ROYAL INNISKILLING FUSILIERS will go into billets in MARCOING.

5. Units will bring back with them their Battalion allotment of picks and shovels. Remaining trench stores, S.O.S. flares will be handed over to relieving Units.

6. Completion of relief will be reported to these Headquarters.

7. ACKNOWLEDGE.

Issued at 11.30. (Sd) F. Brodiemair. Captain.
Brigade Major 87th. Infantry Brigade.

SECRET. Copy No 1

1st Bn Royal Inniskilling Fusiliers Order No 53

1. 87th Infantry Brigade will relieve 88th Infantry Bde in the left Bde Sector on the night of the 28th/29th Nov 1917
2. Battalion will take over the right sub sector from the MASNIERES – CAMBRAI Road to the communication trench in the front line at G.13.a.90.15.
3. "B" Co will take over left "C" Co will take over centre "D" Co " " " right "A" Co will be in support
4. Guides will meet companies at the bridge over the canal at L.23.d.95.25. at
5. Companies will move up from the present billets at 5.30pm. 100 yards will be observed between "B" & "A" Cos
6. All picks & shovels, S.O.S. Signals, flares etc and maps will be taken over.
7. Completion of relief will be reported to Bn H.Q.

(Sd) E. C. J. Moore Capt
Adjt 1st R. Inniskilling Fus

SECRET.

87th. INFANTRY BRIGADE ORDER No. 64

Ref. Map 1/10.000.
Sheets MARCOING and RUMILLY.

November 28th. 1917.

1. The 87th. Infantry Brigade will relieve the 88th. Infantry Brigade in the left Brigade sector tonight 28/29th. November 1917.

2. The Ist Royal Inniskilling Fusiliers will take over the right sub sector from the MASNIERES-CAMBRAI Road to the communication trench in the front line at G.13.d.70.15.
The Ist Border Regiment will take over the left sub-sector from G.13.d.70.15. to the river ESCAULT. Bridge.
The 2nd South Wales Borderers. will take over the Bridge Head Defences.
The Ist. King's Own Scottish Borderers. will remain in MARCOING in Brigade reserve.
Details of relief wil be arranged mutuall between Officers Commanding Units concerned.

3. The 87th. Machine Gun Company and 87th. Trench Morter Battery will relieve similes Units of the 88th. Infantry Brigade.

4 Units will take over all picks and shovels, S.O.S. Signals, flares etc., also those maps handed over by them.

5. Completion of relief will be reported to Brigade Headquarters.

6. On completion of relief the Command of the Left Brigade sector will pass from the G.O.C. 88th. Infantry Brigade to the G.O.C. 87th. Infantry Brigade.

7. ACKNOWLEDGE.

(Sd) F. Brodiemair.
Captain.
Brigade Major 87th. Infantry Brigade.

SECRET 1ST. ROYAL INNISKILLING FUSILIERS. Instruction No.1.

1. On a date and an hour (Zero) to be notified later, an attack is to be carried out by the III Corps.
The attack on the 1st. Objective (BLUE LINE) and 2nd. Objective (BROWN LINE) by the 12th. Division (Right), 20th. Division (Centre) and 6th. Division (Left).
The 29th. Division will be in Corps reserve and will be used for the capture of the 3rd. Objective (RED LINE) after the BROWN Line has been taken.
The [illegible] Brigade with the [illegible] Brigade on right and the 88th. on Left will attack MARCOING and seize bridges over the CANAL at L.[illegible], L.[illegible] and L.[illegible] and will push forward and capture the RED LINE from the CAMBRAI road at [illegible] (inclusive) to [illegible].

2. The Battalion with the first Regt. on left will capture 3rd. Objective from [illegible] to [illegible]. Objectives and boundaries are marked on map.

3. There will be no preliminary bombardment, but the attack on the BLUE and BROWN LINES will be made under the protection of Tanks with the assistance of Standing Artillery and Smoke Barrages which will lift from Objective to Objective as the attack progresses.
Four Tanks have been allotted to the 87th. Infantry Brigade which will be used as a screen behind which the troops will move. Twenty (20) other tanks, working independently of the Brigade will assist in the capture of MARCOING and the RED LINE. These twenty (20) tanks will move forward on to MARCOING directly that BROWN Line has been taken.
The Tanks allotted to the Brigade will be marked with the Divisional Badge and a Green Patch.

4. On Z/Y night the Battalion will be concentrated in [illegible].
As soon as troops assaulting BLUE and BROWN Line are clear of our old Front Line trenches the Battalion will move up to trenches in R.[illegible] and R.14.[illegible].

5. ACTION.
As soon as the BROWN LINE has been captured the Battalion will move forward in [illegible] formation, [illegible] leading, [illegible] "C" left and "D" rear, in support to [illegible] at 200 yards distance. [illegible]
The signal for Advance will be a [illegible] from Battalion Head Quarters.
The Objectives of the [illegible] are [illegible] over the Canal at L.[illegible] when they will form a bridgehead.
Directly the crossing has been effected [illegible] across the CANAL, companies will cross the Canal in the order of "A", "B", "C" and "D" and will [illegible] the RED LINE "A" Co. left, [illegible] will form front line. "C" Co. on Left and "D" Co. on Right will form support line.
Boundaries between Companies [illegible] to L.[illegible].
Should crossing at L.[illegible] be [illegible] cross by bridge at L.[illegible].
Should all crossings [illegible] Companies will [illegible] cover of MARCOING COPSE [illegible].
The attack on Red Line will take place [illegible] cross Canal at [illegible].

6. CONSOLIDATION

On capture of RED LINE consolidation will commence at once. C/S.W.Bs will then be in support to Battalion N. Side of Canal. and will hold themselves in readiness to take over and consolidate RED LINE. from G.14.c.[illegible] to G.14.[illegible]

7. PATROLS

"A" Company will push forward a platoon to high ground about G.[illegible] to establish outpost line with 1st. Border Regt..

"B" Company will push forward one platoon to reconnoitre RUMILLY

8. MACHINE GUNS.

One Section M.G. Company will be at the disposal of the Battalion after the capture of RED LINE.

9. HEADQUARTERS

During the advance to Canal Battalion Headquarters will be with "B" Company. During crossing of CANAL Battalion H.Q. will be established at L.[illegible] and on Capture of RED Line will move forward to L.[illegible]

10 HOSTILE GUNS.

In the event of capture of hostile guns information will be at once sent to Battalion H.Q. giving exact location of gun, nature of gun and whether ammunition is at hand.

11 COUNTER ATTACKS.

Throughout the day an aeroplane with [illegible] mission will be to detect the approach of enemy counter attacks. It will signal [illegible] counter attack by dropping [illegible] over that portion of the front at which the enemy is [illegible] This [illegible] trail of [illegible] behind it.

12 CONTACT PLANE

Contact Planes will fly over the front [illegible] of Patrols.

Battalion Headquarters will be marked by [illegible] code letters of Units' [illegible]

Leading troops will light flares [illegible] Contact Planes.

(a) [illegible]

(b) [illegible] of [illegible]

13. [illegible]

[illegible]

[illegible] and the [illegible]

14. [illegible]

[illegible]

15. PRISONERS.

[illegible]

prisoners [illegible]

[illegible]

16. COMMUNICATION

[illegible]

L.[illegible]

17. MEDICAL.

[illegible]

Issued [illegible]

Copy No.1 [illegible]

[illegible]

[illegible]

SECRET Copy No.

1st Bn Royal Inniskilling Fus. Order No. [illegible]

1. Battalion will be relieved on the night of the 25/26th inst by 1st Essex Regt and will move to billets in MARCOING

2. Four Battalion Runners will conduct relief to the line, and bring companies down to Battalion Head Quarters where they will be met by guides

3. A Co will be relieved by W Co
B Co — " — X Co
C Co — " — Y Co
D Co — " — Z Co

4 Companies will bring down their company allotment of picks & shovels, [illegible] the remainder, also bombs, grenades etc will be handed over in Trench Stores & receipts obtained for same

5 Completion of relief will be reported to Bn HQrs

(Sd) [illegible] Moore Capt

Comdg 1st R. Inniskilling Fus.

SECRET.

87th. INFANTRY BRIGADE INSTRUCTION No. I.

Ref maps.
1/20/000.
NIERGNIES and
GOUZEAUCOURT sheets.

I. On a date and at an hour (ZERO) to be notified later an attack is to be carried out by the III Corps.
The attack on the Ist objective (BLUE LINE) and 2nd. objective (BROWN LINE) by the 12 Division (right), 20th. Division (centre), and 6th. Division (left).
The 29th. Division will be in Corps Reserve and will be used for the capture of the 3rd objective (RED LINE) after the BROWN LINE has been taken.

2. The attack by the 29th. Division will be carried out
(a) by the 88th. INFANTRY BRIGADE on the right with MASNIERES as their objective. Pushing forward to establish themselves in the RED LINE to the North and east of that village.
(b) By the 86th. Infantry Brigade on the left who will capture NINE WOOD and the RED Line from the Wood to the river ESCAULT.
(c) The 87th Infantry Brigade will attack MARCONING and seize the bridges over the CANAL at L.23.b.1.8., L.23.a.7.0. and L.23.c.9.3. and will push forward and capture the RED Line from the CAMBRAI Road G.14.d.h.0. (inclusive.) to G.7.c.1.3.

The boundaries between Brigades have already been issued.

3. There will be no preliminary bombardment but the attack on the BLUE and BROWN lines will be made under the protection of tanks with the assistance of standing artillery and smoke barrages which will lift from objective to objective as the attack progresses.
Four tanks have been attached to the 87th. Infantry Brigade, which will be used as the screen behind which the troops will move. Twenty (20) other tanks, working independently of the Brigade will assist in the capture of MARCONING and the RED LINE. These twenty (20) tanks will move forward on to MARCONING directly the BROWN LINE has been taken.

4. On Y Z night the Brigade Group will be concentrated in Q.30.a. with Brigade headquarters at Q.29.d.2.9. The positions to be taken up will be shown to Officers Commanding Units "X" day.
As soon as the troops assaulting the BLUE line and BROWN lines are clear of our old front line the Brigade will move up to the old front line as follows:-
The 2nd South Wales Borderers our front and support lines from the sunken road in R.8.d. (inclusive) to COPS Road in R.8.c. with the Ist. ROYAL INNISKILLING FUSILIERS in gullies under cover just behind.
The Ist KING's OWN SCOTTISH BORDERERS in our front and Support lines from COPS ROAD in R.8.c. (exclusive) to R.7.b.9.0. with the Ist BORDER REGIMENT in gullies behind.
These positions will be pointed out to Officers Commanding Units together with the routes from the assembling area by the Brigade Major on "Y" Day.
Brigade Headquarters will be at R.8.c.9.0.

5. **ACTION.** As soon as the BROWN LINE has been captured the Brigade will be ordered to move forward from our old front line. The general line of advance is 40° true. The signal for the advance will be a "G" sounded on a bugle from Brigade Headquarters. This signal will be repeated by buglers as Battalion Headquarters.
The Officer Commanding 2nd SOUTH WALES BORDERERS will detail a bugler to report to Brigade Headquarters on Y/Z night.
Units will move on to there objectives as follows:-
(a) On the right the 2nd SOUTH WALES BORDERERS followed at 800 yards distance by the Ist. ROYAL INNISKILLING FUSILIERS in support. The objectives of the 2nd SOUTH WALES BORDERERS will be MARCONING COPS and the crossing over CANAL at L.24.d.8.4.
(b) On the left the Ist KING'S OWN SCOTTISH BORDERERS followed at a distance of 600 yards by the Ist BORDER REGIMENT will capture MARCONING and the crossings at L.23.c.6.9. and L.23.b.1.8. both the 2nd SOUTH WALES BORDERERS and the Ist. KING'S OWN SCOTTISH BORDERERS on moving out from our old front line on to their objectives will throw out advance guards and each will detail one Company as a Liaision Company on its outer flank.
Two Vickers guns should be sent with each of these liaision Companies. One section WEST RIDING FIELD COMPANY will be attached to the Ist KING'S OWN SCOTTISH BORDERERS on Y/Z night and will proceed with their advance guard to assist them in clearing obstacles and preparing bridges.
The two leading Battalions on gaining their objectives will if the crossings are in-tact, each send two companies across the CANAL to form a bridge head from the east of the loch in L.24.c. to the lock in L.17.d. and will at once send forward to reconitre the MASNIERES - BEAUREVOIR line.
If the crossings over the CANAL are found to be destroyed the 2nd. SOUTH WALES BORDERERS and the Ist. KING'S OWN SCOTTISH BORDERERS will form an outpost line along the west bank of the CANAL to cover the construction of bridges by the R.E and will send Officers to reconitre any possible crossings.
Directly the crossings have been captured and the Tanks are across the CANAL the Ist. ROYAL INNISKILLING FUSILIERS and the Ist. BORDER REGIMENT will cross the CANAL and, following the Tanks, assault the RED LINE, the Ist. ROYAL INNISKILLING FUSILIERS from the CAMBRAI ROAD (exclusive) at G.14.d.8.0. to G.14.c.2.9. and the Ist. BORDER REGIMENT from G.14.c.2.9. to the CANAL at G.12.c.9.3.
If the Tanks cross the Canal and move forward on to this RED LINE the before the Ist. ROYal INNISKILLING FUSILIERS and Ist. BORDER REGIMENT are across and ready to attack one company each from the 2nd SOUTH WALES BORDERS and the Ist. KING'S OWN SCOTTISH BORDERERS already across the CANAL will follow the tanks rejoin their other Companies as soon as they are relieved by the Ist ROYAL INNISKILLING FUSILIERS and Ist. BORDER RGT. respectively.
The attack of the RED LINE will take place where the tanks cross the CANAL or not.
On the capture of the RED LINE Consolidation will commence at once by the Ist BORDER REGIMENT and the Ist ROYAL INNISKILLING FUSILIERS the remaining two companies of the 2nd SOUTH WALES BORDERERS will cross the CANAL and form behind their bridge head and await orders.

5cgd

5ctd Patrols will be pusd forward and an outpost line established on the HIGH GROUND in G.2. and 3 by the Ist ROYAL INNISKILLING FUSILIERS and Ist BORDER REGIMENT.
The 2nd SOUTH WALES BORDERERS should hold themselves in readiness on receipt of orders from brigade to take over and consolidate the CENTRE of the RED LINE from G.14.c.8.8. to the BANK at G.14.a.o.2. from the Ist ROYAL INNISKILLING FUSILEERS and Ist BORDER REGIMENT who will be that section.

6. MACHINE GUNS

THE OFFICER COMMANDING 87th MACHINE GUN COMPANY will detail one section to the 2nd SOUTH WALES BORDERERS and one section to the Ist KINGS OWN SCOTTISH BORDERERS.
The officers commanding these two Battalions will each send two of these guns with there flank companies.
The other two guns with each Battalion will each afterwards on the formation on the bridge head move forward to the bridge head defence.
These sections should join their Battalion on "Y" day prior to the march to the assembly area.
The Officer Commanding 87th. MACHINE GUN COMPANY will send his remaining two sections to the HIGH GROUND in L.34.s. of MARCONING to the assist the attack of MARCONING by covering fire. After the Red Line has been captured these twosections on receipt of orders from the Brigade will move forward to the RED LINE one section reporting to to Officer Commanding Ist. ROYAL INNISKILLING FUSILIERS and one section to the Officer Commanding Ist. BORDER REGIMENT.

7. TRENCH MORTAR BATTERY.

The Officer Commanding 87th. TRENCH MORTAR BATTERY will send up FOUR guns behind the supporting Battalions and place them in position to cover the bridge head defences.
The remaining FOUR guns will remain in the transport lines.

8. HEADQUARTERS

Brigade Headquarters will be established at R.8.c.8.0. to which place each Unit will send one Officer to report asxson as their Unit is in position and ready to move. On the capture of MARCONING Brigade Headquarters will move to L.34.central.
On the capture of the RED LINE Brigade Headquarters will move to MARCONING.
Units will always inform Brigade Headquarters when they are moving and to where.

9. HOSTILE GUNS.

In the event of capture of Hostile guns information will at once sent to Brigade Headquarters giving exact location of guns, nature of guns, and whether ammunition is at hand.

10. COUNTER ATTACKS.

Throughout the day an aeroplane will be up whose sole mission will be to protect the approach of enemy counter-attacks. It will signal an enemy counter-attack by dropping a smoke bomb over that portion of the front at which the enemy is advancing.
This smoke bomb will burst into a white parachute flare leaving a trail of brown smoke behind it.

II. CONTACT PLANE.
Contact planes will fly over the front during the operations. Battalion Headquarters will be marked by ground sheets with code letters of unit laid out. Leading troops will light flares when demanded by contact planes i.e.
(a) Sounding its KLAXON HORN.
(b) By a series of white lights.

12. S.O.S. SIGNALS.
S.O.S. Signals will be a rifle granade bursting into two green and two white lights.

13. CODE.
BAB Code books will NOT be taken into action.

14. COMMUNICATION.
There will be a Divisional Visual signal station at L.34.d.5.7.nand R.7.b.and L.16.c. These stations will send forward as well as receive.

Each Battalion will be allotted two pairs of pigeons on "Y" day.
The Brigade will establish a permanent visual station at D.34.d.5.7.after the Brigade Headquarters have moved to MARCONING.

15. PRISONERS.
Units should send prisoners to the Divisional cage at W.5.b.1.?. and a receipt being obtained from the A.P.M. All Officer prisoners should be searched at once and there papers taken from them and snet with their escort to the cage. N.C.O's and men will be searched atthe cage.
Refugees should be sent to VILLERS PLOUTCH where there will be a psot of gendarmes.

16. There will be a forward advanced dressing station on the road in R.5.b. also at GOUZEAUCOURT Q.36.d.4.9.
Regimental aid posts will have already been established at i.e. R.20.d.7.4.
R.20.0.2.9.
as soon after zero as circumstances permit. RELAY POSTS will be established at i.e.
L.28.b.central.
L.34.b.8.5.
L.36.a.5.0.
Units will increase their stretcher bearers from 16 to 32 per battalion.

17. ACKNOWLEDGE.

(Sd) G. Brodie-mair.
Captain.
Brigade Major 87th. Infantry Brigade.

S E C R E T

ACCOMMODATION in NEW AREA.

****

UNIT	LOCATION	ACCOMMODATION. (Huts numbered)
2nd S.W.Borderers.	300 yards North of "Z" in AIZECOURT.	50 Tents. 3 Huts.
1st K.O.S.Borderers.	East Side of Main Road, North end of HAUT ALLAINES.	55 56 57 58 59 61 62 63 64
1st R.Innis.Fus.	West of Main Road, North end of HAUT ALLAINES.	38 39 40 41 42 43 44 45 46 47 48
1st Border Regiment.	East of Main Road South end of HAUT ALLAINES.	72 73 74 75 76 77 78 79 80 81 82 83 84
Machine Gun Coy.	East of Main Road in HAUT ALLAINES.	60 65 66
Trench Mortar Bty.	With R. Innis. Fus. West of Main Road North end of HAUT ALLAINES.	49 50
87th Field Ambulance.	North end of Main Road - HAUT ALLAINES.	37 52 53 54
No.3 Coy. Train and 1st Line Transport.	ALLAINES.	

Copies to:-
2nd S.W.B.
1st K.O.S.B.
1st R.Innis.
1st Border Rgt.
Machine Gun Cy.
T.M.Bty.
87th Field Amb.
No.3 Coy. Train.

CAPTAIN,

STAFF CAPTAIN, 87TH INFANTRY BRI

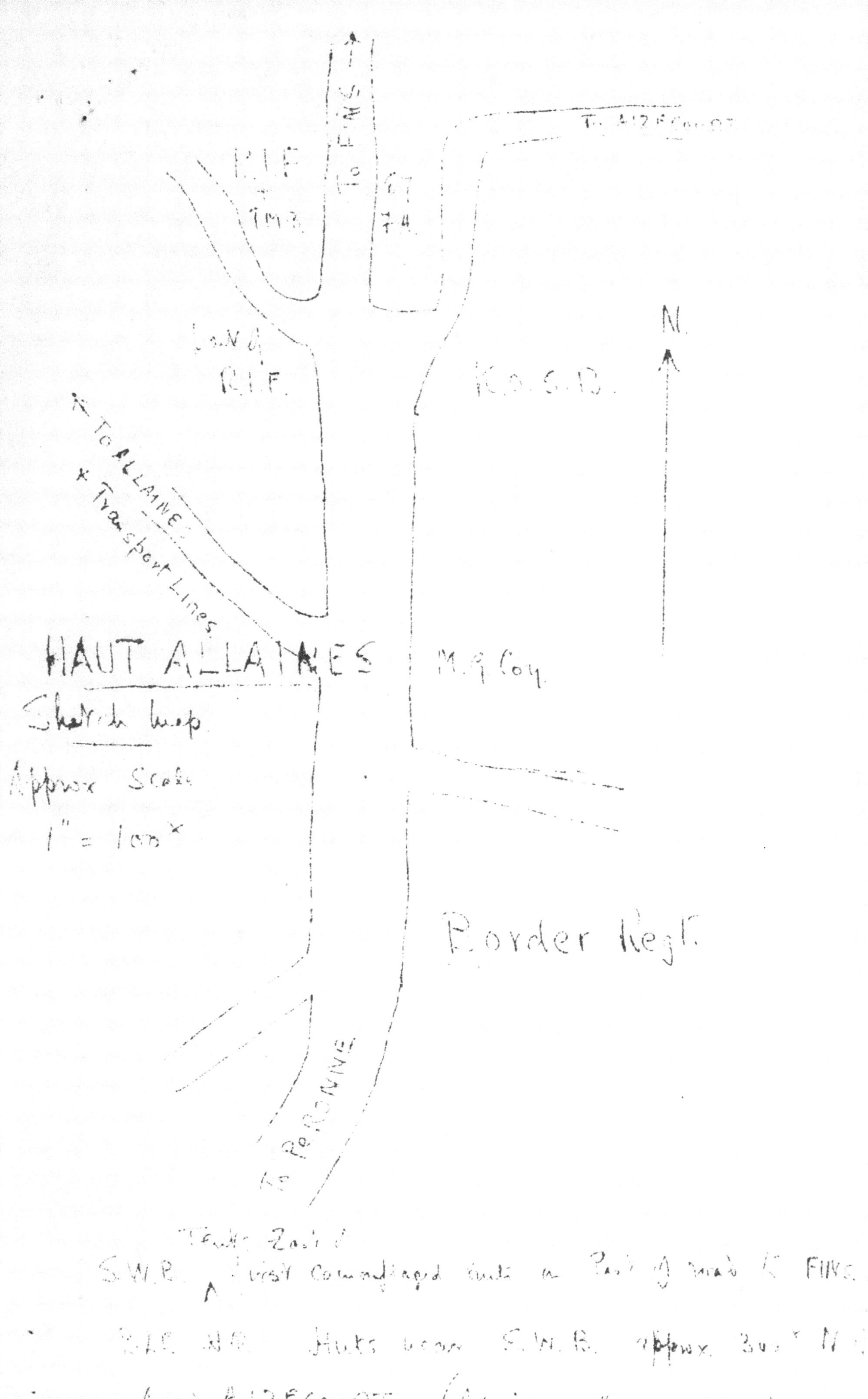
To FINS
To AIZECOURT
R.I.F.
T.M.B.
N.
R.I.F.
K.O.S.B.
To ALLAINES
Transport Lines
HAUT ALLAINES
Sketch Map
Approx Scale
1" = 100x
M.G. Coy.
Border Regt.
To PERONNE
S.W.B.
FINS
Huts
AIZECOURT
(Amiens Sheet)

Instructions regarding War Diaries and Intelligence Summaries are contained in F. S. Regs., Part II. and the Staff Manual respectively. Title pages will be prepared in manuscript.

Volume 33

WAR DIARY
or
INTELLIGENCE SUMMARY.
(Erase heading not required.)

Army Form C. 2118.

Vol 21

1st R. Inniskilling Fus.

Place	Date	Hour	Summary of Events and Information	Remarks and references to Appendices
[illegible] – [illegible]	Dec. 1		[illegible] bombarded MASNIERES heavily all day and a party of the enemy seen approaching D Co was heavily fired on and retired hurriedly leaving several casualties behind. Several counterattacks were beaten off from MASNIERES by the 86th Brigade. Owing to the exhausted condition of the 86th Brigade it was decided that they should evacuate MASNIERES and that we should throw back and extend our right flank to cover the ground left open by this manoeuvre. Our line was then to run [illegible] from the right of B Co at G.20.a.50.95 down the communication trench [illegible] from there to the Canal at a point G.19.c.2.6. It had been [illegible] intended to take up our position from the right of B Co [illegible] the line of communication pit running down from G.20.a.5.6 to G.20.a.1.1 [illegible] this plan was abandoned owing to the fact that (1) this position [illegible] the Canal Bank and [illegible] which was the key of the whole position (2) that there was an enemy barrage line and (3) no line had been any line previously, and the men were too worn and fatigued to dig in by morning.	
			The two [illegible] Companies (D & A) started their retirement at [illegible] 12.30 a.m. [illegible] successfully withdrew to their new positions [illegible] parties. In the meantime 3 Companies of Monmouths Regt [illegible] were sent to reinforce us and were put in the line [illegible] guarding the Canal and their left [illegible] the road at [illegible]. D Company took over from the road to the [illegible] trench at L.24.a.6.3 – C Co manned the communication trench [illegible] the right of B Co. B Company withdrew the garrison of their	

X.32

1577 Wt. W10791/1773 500,000 1/15 D. D. & L. A.D.S.S./Forms/C. 2118.

Instructions regarding War Diaries and Intelligence Summaries are contained in F. S. Regs., Part II. and the Staff Manual respectively. Title pages will be prepared in manuscript.

WAR DIARY
or
INTELLIGENCE SUMMARY

(Erase heading not required.)

Army Form C. 2118.

Hour, Date, Place	Summary of Events and Information	Remarks and references to Appendices

1247 W 3299 200,000 (E) 8/14 J.B.C. & A. Forms/C. 2118/11.

WAR DIARY

or

INTELLIGENCE SUMMARY.

(Erase heading not required.)

Army Form C. 2118.

Instructions regarding War Diaries and Intelligence Summaries are contained in F. S. Regs., Part II. and the Staff Manual respectively. Title pages will be prepared in manuscript.

Volume 33

1st R. Inniskilling Fus.

Place	Date	Hour	Summary of Events and Information	Remarks and references to Appendices
[illegible]	Dec 3		to MARCOING. The 1st & 2nd patrol both returned and reported that the situation was well in hand and that there was no cause for uneasiness.	
	4		Bn [illegible] Major Dent arrived to take command of the Bn [illegible] Lt Col Sherwood-Kelly. The Bn moved to billets at [illegible] vide Bn O. 55. Capt Framingham M.C. rejoined.	
[illegible]	5		The Bn moved to BEAUFORT vide Bn order No 56.	
[illegible]	6		Reorganisation	
	7/8		Training. Inspection of the Battalion Billets by Commanding Officer.	
	[illegible]		[illegible] General [illegible] D.S.O. and congratulated [illegible] in the Cambrai Battle. He [illegible] on the [illegible] the men [illegible] marched [illegible].	
	11		[illegible] on 13/12/17 [illegible] officers [illegible] C F Robinson 2/Lt Hadley 2/Lt Bamford [illegible] Holland 2/Lt J Robinson 2/Lt McLean	
[illegible]	[illegible]		[illegible] to [illegible] Brigade Order No 67 [illegible] arrived at BOURBERS-SUR-CANCHE	
LE PARC	15		[illegible] vide Bn O. 58 Arrived at LE PARC	
COUPELLE VIEILLE	16		[illegible] vide Bn O. [illegible] Arrived at COUPELLE-VIEILLE [illegible] slippery condition of the road [illegible] unable to proceed	GoG

1577 Wt. W10791/1773 500,000 1/15 D. D. & L. A.D.S.S./Forms/C. 2118.

Army Form C. 2118.

Instructions regarding War Diaries and Intelligence Summaries are contained in F. S. Regs., Part II. and the Staff Manual respectively. Title pages will be prepared in manuscript.

WAR DIARY
or
INTELLIGENCE SUMMARY
(Erase heading not required.)

1st R Innis Killing Fus.

Hour, Date, Place		Summary of Events and Information	Remarks and references to Appendices
	Dec		
COUPELLE VIEILLE	20	Training Parades Improvement of billets Transport repairs	
	21-24	Training Preparations for Christmas	
	25	Christmas Festivities General Hunter Weston visits us and welcomes us back to the 8th Corps	
	31.	The Bn proceeds by march route to NAVRANS XIX Corps	vide Bn O No 63 Bde Order No 68

[signature]
Lieut-Colonel
Comdg 1st R Inniskilling Fus

1247 W 3299 200,000 (E) 8/14 J.B.C. & A. Forms/C. 2118/11.

S E C R E T.

IST BATTALION THE ROYAL INNISKILLING FUSILIERS ORDER No. 54

I. The Battalion will be relieved tonight by the 14th. BATTALION DURHAM LIGHT INFANTRY.

2. "A" Company will provide 2 guides to lead "A" Coy., of the relieving Battalion into the position at present held by the MONMOUTHSHIRE REGIMENT.
The guides will then lead the MONMOUTHS to the SUPPORT Line at present held by "A" Company.
"B" Company will be relieved by "B" Company of 14th. DURHAM LIGHT INFANTRY.
"D" COMPANY will be relieved by "D" Company of 14th. DURHAM LIGHT INFANTRY.
"C" Company will leave the trenches immediately "C" Company of 14th. DURHAM LIGHT INFANTRY have gone into the Support line.

3. All Companies will pass these H. Qrs., & will pick up guides to lead them to their billets near RIBECOURT at Bn. Hd. Qrs.

4. 2 guides per Company will report at Bn. Hd. Qrs., by 7.0 p.m. "C" Company will provide 2 guides to lead "C" Coy. 14th DURHAM LIGHT INFANTRY into position on left of "A" Company. These guides will then proceed to "C" Company & "C" Coy will then leave their trenches.

2:12:17.

Capt & Adjt.
Ist. Bn. The Royal Inniskilling Fusiliers.

S E C R E T.

IST ROYAL INNISKILLING FUSILIERS ORDER No. 56. 4/12/17

I. The Battalion will move to LE CAUROY area by rail tomorrow December 5th, entraining at ETRICOURT.

2. The Battalion will parade ready to move off at 8.30.a.m.

3. One Blanket per man will be carried, remainder to be stacked outside Bn.Hd.Qrs., in bundles of 10 by 5.30.a.m.

4. Transport will move by road halting at BAPAUME for the night except those vehicles to entrain at BAPAUME. Transport will move leaving 27th. Brigade Transport Lines at 6.30.a.m.

[signature]

Capt & Adjt.
Ist Royal Inniskilling Fusiliers.

S E C R E T.

87th. INFANTRY BRIGADE ORDER No. 56.

1. The Brigade personnel will move to LE COMUROY area by rail tomorrow 5th. December. Units will entrain at ETRICOURT and will be at the entraining point at 11.0.a.m.

2. Transport will move by road under Command of Lieut. F.R. Williams of 2/S.W.B. halting at BAPAUME for the night, except those vehicles to entrain at BAPAUME. Transport will move leaving 87th. Bde. Transport Lines (W.13.b.) at 6.30.a.m. in the following order.
    Brigade Headquarters.
    Machine Gun Company.
    South Wales Borderers.
    K.O.S.Borderers.
    R.Innis.Fus.
    Border Regiment.
    87th. Field Ambulance.
    W.Riding Field Coy.R.E.
    No. Company Train.

3. Lorries are allotted to Units for conveyance of blankets etc., to the entraining point as follows. R.Innis.Fus. 5.0.a.m.

(Sd) F. Brodiemair.
Captain.
Brigade Major, 87th. Infantry Brigade.

S E C R E T.

[illegible] BATTALION THE ROYAL INNISKILLING FUSILIERS [illegible]

INSTRUCTIONS TO ACCOMPANY BATTN. ORDER No. [illegible]

I. 2/Lieut. Stephenson, the C.Q.M. Sergeants [illegible] Fletcher will proceed in advance as Billeting Party.
They will leave [illegible] at [illegible] and will report [illegible]
to Area Commandant, [illegible]

2. Lewis Guns will be loaded on the limbers in the transport lines by [illegible] today.
Officers Kits and Mess [illegible] will be [illegible]
Q.M's by [illegible]
BLANKETS. Blankets will be stacked in [illegible] in bundles of [illegible] by [illegible] tomorrow.
PACKS. Packs will be stacked in [illegible] by [illegible] tomorrow. [illegible] to the [illegible] of the packs.

Orderly Room, [illegible] Stores to be stacked [illegible] by [illegible] tomorrow.

E.C. J. Moore

[illegible] Capt. [illegible]
[illegible] Royal Inniskilling Fusiliers.

S E C R E T.

IST BATTALION THE ROYAL INNISKILLING FUSILIERS ORDER No. 57.

Reference Map. LENS II. 1/100.000.

I. The Battalion will move to BOUBERS-SUR-CANCHE tomorrow 17th. Decemebr 1917.

2. The Battalion will parade ready to march off at 10.0.a.m. The head of the column will be on the main road outside Hd. Qrs. Mess. Order of March. Drums. A.B.C.D.& Headquarters Company. Transport.

3. ROUTE. LIENCOURT - FREVENT - BOUBERS-SUR-CANCHE.

4. DRESS. Fighting Order. Caps will be worn.

5. Strict march discipline will be maintained throughout the march.

6. There will be no interval between Companies.

Copies No. I. Staff.
2 & 3 War Diary.
4 5 6 & 7. Cos.
8. M.O.
9. T.O.
10. Qr. Mr.

16/12/17.

[signature] Capt & Adjt.
Ist. Bn. The R. Inniskilling Fusiliers.

17/12/17.

S E C R E T.

IST BATTALION THE ROYAL INNISKILLING FUSILIERS ORDER No.58.

Reference Map. LENS II. 1/100.000

I. The Battalion will move to LE PARQ tomorrow 18th.December 1917.

2. The Battalion will parade ready to march off at 9.20.a.m.
The head of the column will be on the main ~~road~~ FREVENT - HESDIN road outside No.16.Billet.
Order of march. Drums. Hd.Qr.Coy.B.C.D.A Coy. Transport.

3. ROUTE. Main road to VIEL-HESDIN - LE PARCQ.

4. DRESS. Fighting order. Steel helmets will be worn.

5. Strict march discipline will be maintained throughout the march.

6. There will be no interval between Companies.

(Sd) E.F.J.Moore. Capt & Adjt.
Ist.Bn.The Royal Inniskilling Fusiliers.

S E C R E T.

Administrative Instructions to accompany Bn.Order No.58.

I. 2/Lt.Stephenson and Sgt.Fletcher will proceed in advance on bicycles tomorrow to billet at COUPELLE-VIEILLE.in the FRUGES area. The area Commandant is located in billet No.33 at CREQUY.

2. The C.Q.M.S's and Copl.Logue will proceed in advance tomorrow to billet at LE-PARCQ.taking over from the Guernsey Light Ifty. They will leave Bn.Hd.Qrs.at 7.0.a.m. and report to Cpl.Mercer on arrival.

4. Each Coy.will make a dump by 8.15.a.m. of the following in there own Coy.area. All dumps should be as near the road as possible.
Blankets Officers Kits and Mess stores.
2 men per Coy. will be left with each dump for loading.
Hd.Qr.Coy. will make a dump with "D"Company.

(Sd) E.F.J.Moore.Capt & Adjt.
Ist.Bn.The Royal Inniskilling Fusiliers.

S E C R E T.

IST BATTALION. THE ROYAL INNISKILLING FUSILIERS ORDER No.59.

I. The Battalion will move to COUPELLE - VIEILLE tomorrow 19th. ins

2. Coys will parade oytside their own Coy. areas by 9.55.a.m.
Order of march. Drums. C.D.A.B. Hd.Qr.Coy.

3. Route. WAMIN - FRUGES.

4. Strict march discipline will be observed.

5. DRESS. Fighting order. Steel helmets will be worn.

6. Billets will be ready for inspection by 9.15.a.m, alltemporary latrines will be filled in.

(Sd) E.F.J.Moore. Capt & Adjt.
18/12/17. Ist.Bn.The Royal Inniskilling Fusiliers.

S E C R E T.

ADMINISTRATIVE INSTRUCTIONS TO ACCOMPANY BN.ORDER No.59.

I. The C.Q.M.S's will proceed on bicycles tomorrow to COUPELLE-VIEILLE where they will report to 2/Lt.Stephenson.
They will leave Bn.Hd.Qrs. at 8.0.a.m.

2. Coys will make dumps of the following by 8.45.a.m.
Hd.Qrs. will make a dump with "D" Company.
Blankets and Packs.
Officers Kits and Mess stores will be stacked outside the Qr.Mr.Stores by 8.45.a.m.

3. Lorries etc. will be loaded under Coy. arrangements.
I man per Company will accompany the lorries.

(Sd) E.F.J.Moore. Capt & Adjt.
Ist.Bn.The Royal Inniskilling Fusiliers.

SECRET

IST BATTALION THE ROYAL INNISKILLING FUSILIERS ORDER NO60.

---

29 th DECEMBER 1917

Reference
Map HAZEBROUCK. 5A.

I. The Battalion will move by march Route to XIX CORPS AREA. for work under XIX CORPS, leaving this area on December 31st.

2 The Battalion will move to WAVRINS on the 31st December & will parade ready to march off at 9.25.a.m.
Order of march:- D. A. B. C. Hd. Qr. Coy.
The head of the column will be at the road junction where the WAILLY - COUPELLE-VIELLE Road meets the FRUGES - COUPELLE-VIEILLI Road.
First Line Transport will accompany Battalion.

3 DRESS: Fighting Order
1 Blanket per man will be carried.

4 ROUTE:- VERCHOCQ
FAUQUEMBERGUCES
OUVE-WIRQUIN
REMILLY.

5 Strict march dicipline will be maintained.

6 Intervals will be observed as laid down in Infantry Training.

(SD) E. E. J. Moore. Capt & Adjt.
1ST Bn 5he Royal Inniskilling Fusiliers.

S E C R E T

IST BATTALION THE ROYAL INNISKILLING FUSILIERS ORDER NO 60.

S E C R E T.

ADMINISTRATIVE ORDER TO ACCOMPANY BATTALION
ORDER No.60.

29 th. DECEMBER 1917.

A.B.D.Hd,Qr.Coy.

I. The following will be stacked at the Qr.Mr's Stores by 8.30.a.m. tomorrow.

Remaining Blankets in bundles of 10 and labelled.

Packs each one must have name of owner on it.

Officers Kits.

Officers Mess Stores.

2. "C"Company will make a dump of the above near the road in their Company area by 8.0.a.m.

3. The following personnel will accompany the Transport.
Company Cooks.
Watercart men.
By O.C."A"Co. 2 Brakesmen to be detailed to report to T.O.at 9.15.a.m.
"B"Co. 2 " " " " " " " " " "
"D"Co. I " " " " " " " " " "

4. Latrines - other than Box Latrines - will be filled in. Screens of theses latrines will be returned to the Qr.Mr's stores.

5. Billets will be scrupulously clean and ready for inspection by 9.0.a.m.

6. Mufflers if worn during the march,will not be allowed to show above the collar.

7. I Officers Mess Cook per Coy.with Officers Mess Boxes can proceed on lorries.

8. Lewis Guns will be oiled and placed on the limbers by 5.0.p.m. tonight.

[signature] Capt & Adjt.
Ist.Battalion The Royal Inniskilling Fus

S E C R E T.

1ST BATTALION THE ROYAL INNISKILLING FUSILIERS ORDER NO.61.

31st. DECEMBER 1917.

Reference Map HAZEBROUCK. 5.A.

1. The march will be continued tomorrow to EBBINGHEM Area 4.

2. The Battalion will parade ready to move off at 10.5.a.m.

3. Order of march A.B.C.D.HdQrs.

Head of column will be on the main road outside "A"Compy billet.Head of "C" Company will be where road where "C" Company is billited joins main WAVRANS-LUMBRES road.

4. Route. LUMBRES.
WIZERNES.
ARQUES.
FORT-ROUGE.

5. Dress. Fighting Order one blanket will be carried.

6. There will be a halt tomorrow from12.50.pm. to 1.30.p.m. for mid-day meal.Officers will take haversack rations.

7. strict march discipline will be maintained.

8. Intervals between Companies will be observed as laid down in Infantry Training.

/ (Sd) E.E.J.Moore. Capt &Adjt.
1stBn Royal Inniskilling Fusiliers.

S E C R E T.

1ST BORDER REGIMENT.
1ST ROYAL INNISKILLING FUSILIERS.

---

1. The Brigade will move to billets at SOREL tonight entraining for another area tomorrow.

2. Units will proceed independently via TRESCAULT - METZ abd FINS. Strict attention must be paid to march discipline and movements E.of a line joining METZ - FINS will be carried out in bodies not larger than 1.Coy.at 200 yards distance

3. Transport will report to Units at 4.0.p.m.

4. The 1st.R.Innis.Fus.will move at 4.30.p.m. and the 1/Border Regt.at 5.0.p.m.

5. Billets have been arranged in SOREL and Units will be met on arrival.

6. Bde.Hd.Qrs. will move at 4.30.p.m. and will reopen at SOREL.

7. ACKNOWLEDGE.

(Sd) E.Brodiemair.
Captain.
Brigade Major. 87th.Infantry Brigade.

87th. INFANTRY BRIGADE ADMINISTRATIVE INSTRUCTIONS
TO ACCOMPANY BRIGADE ORDER No.63.

16th. December 1917.

I. Billetting areas for the nights 17/18th. and 18/19th. December are allotted in accordance with tables attached.

2. Units will send billetting parties in advance as follows:-

Battalions.	I Officer and 5 N.C.O's.
87th. M.G.Company.)	
227th. M.G.Company.)	I Officer and I N.C.O.
455. F.R.Coy.R.E.)	
Div. Hd.Qrs.personnel.)	
87th. Brigade Headquarters.)	2.O.R.
87th. Field Ambulance.)	
87th. T.M.Battery.)	
No.3 Coy.Train.)	I.N.C.O.
Div.Depot Bn.Details.)	

3. When taking billets previously occupied, parties will report to the Units of the 86th. Infantry Brigade in their respective areas on the evening previous to the day on which they will occupy them.
They will be billetted by these Units, will obtain all information necessary with reference to billets from them and will act as guides for their Units marching in.

4. Parties taking over billets previously empty, will report on 17th. by 10.0.a.m. to Area Commandant No.2 billet [illegible], and on 18th. will proceed in advance to their new areas and obtain necessary information from Maires.
There no Town Majors or Billet Wardens in the staging areas but Maires of all villages have a list of billets.

5. Lorries are allotted as follows and will report to Units at 8.0.a.m. on the 17th. inst. and will remain under their orders during the move:-

2/South Wales Borderers.	3.	
I st.K.O.S.Borderers.	3.	
I/R. Innis. Fusiliers.	3.	
1/Border Regiment.	3.	
87th. Bde. Headquarters.	I.	
87th. T.M.Battery)		
87th. M.G.Company.)	I.	
1/2nd. Monmouth Regiment.	2.	
Div.Depot Battalion.	I.	
227. M.G.Company.	½.	To load at M.G.Coy.and report
Div.Hd.Qrs.personnel.	½	to Div.Hd.Qrs.by 9.30.a.m.

In addition to above 2 Lorries are allotted to the 4 Battalions of the Brigade, ½ to each, to carry stuff not required on the march direct to the new area and return at once to [illegible] any surplus left by Brigade Units. They will report at 8.0.a.m. 18th. inst. to Officer of 2nd.S.W.Borderers as detailed below.

6. 2/nd SOUTHWALES BORDERERS will detail I Officer and 2 men to remain at LIENCOURT until all stuff is cleared from the area. Communications for them to be sent to present Hd.Qrs., of 2nd.SW Borderers No.24. billet LIENCOURT.
Any Units leaving surplus which cannot be carried on 17th.inst. will form dumps, leaving necessary personnel in charge and information the above mentioned Officer of the quantity and location.

7. [illegible]

(Sd) T.P. Wharton. Capt.

IST BATTALION THE ROYAL INNISKILLING FUSILIERS.

OPERATION ORDER No. 55.

I. The Battalion will move to billets at SOREL tonight.

2. Companies will move off in the following order, starting at 4,30.p.m., at 5 minutes interval.
C.D.A.B.Coys and Bn.Hd.Qrs.
Companies will move in file, route RIBECOURT - TRESCAULT - METZ and FINS. 200 yards will be observed between Coys., during the march.

3. Limbers for Lewis Guns will be on the Sunken Road above Bde. Hd.Qrs.
Companies will leave their Lewis Guns on the limbers as they march past.

4. Picks and shovels will be collected in Coy. area ready to hand over to relieving Unit or placed on mules and taken with the Battalion.

5. Guides will meet Companies at SOREL to conduct them to billets.

C.E. [signature]
Capt. & Adjt.
Ist. Bn. The Royal Inniskilling Fus.

S E C R E T.

APPENDIX to 87th. INFANTRY BRIGADE ORDER No.67.

I. If Units are not in possession of Map Sheet 51/C. the starting point will be found on LENS II. sheet at X Roads S.W. of the first E. in ETREE WAMIN.

2. The following Units will now pass the starting point at the following times and not as stated in the above question order:-

WEST RIDING FIELD COMPANY.	12.5.P.M.
87th. FIELD AMBULANCE.	12.11.P.M.
No.3.Coy Train.A.S.C.	12.15.P.M.
87th. M.G. COMPANY.	12.19.P.M.

S E C R E T. December 16th. 1917.

87th. INFANTRY BRIGADE ORDER No. 67.

Reference Maps Sheets. 51/C. 1/40.000.
and LENS II. 1/100.000.

I. The 29th. Division (less artillery) is to be transferred from the IVth. Corps to the X Corps (Second Army.) commencing on 16th. inst. and will be accommodated in the FRUGES AREA.

2. Transfer will be carried out by march route in accordance with march tables attached for marches 17th. and 18th. inst.

3. Distances of 200 yards will be maintained between Battalions and between other Units.

4. Transport will accompany Units.

5. Strict march discipline will be maintained throughout.

6. ACKNOWLEDGE.

(Sd) H. F. Sutcliffe.
Captain.
Acting Brigade Major. 87th. Infantry Brigade.

S E C R E T.

87th. INFANTRY BRIGADE ORDER No.62.

December 16th.1917.

1. The 87th. Infantry Brigade Group will continue the march to the FRUGES area on the 18th.December.

2. Movement will be in accordance with March Table attached.

3. A distance of 200 yards will be maintained between Battalions and other Units.

4. Strict march discipline will be maintained.

5. Transport will accompany Units.

6. All ranks will wear steel helmets on the line of march.

7. ACKNOWLEDGE.

(Sd) W.F.Sutcliffe. Captain.
Acting Brigade Major 87th.Infantry Brigade.

S E C R E T.

87TH. INFANTRY BRIGADE ORDER No. 68.

28th. December 1917.

I. The 87th. Infantry Brigade Group (Less 87th. M.G. Coy.& 87th. T.M. Battery) and 455th. Coy. West Riding Coy. R.E. will proceed by march route to XIXth. Corps Area, for work under XIXth. Corps, leaving this area on December 31st. 1917.

2. Dress:- Fighting Order.
Ground sheets and one blanket per man will be carried.
Lorries will be provided for:-
(a) Blankets.
(b) Packs of dismounted troops.

3. 87th. T.M. Battery will move to ROLLEUX on December 29th. Officer Commanding 87th. T.M. Battery will report to Staff Captain by 9.30.a.m., for orders.

4. 87th. Machine Gun Company and 87th. Trench Mortar Battery will be administered by 86th. Brigade from December 30th. 86th. Infantry Brigade Headquarters are at VERCHOCQ.

5. ACKNOWLEDGE.

(Sd) W.K. Innes. Captain.
A/Brigade Major. 87th. Infantry Brigade.

Instructions regarding War Diaries and Intelligence Summaries are contained in F. S. Regs., Part II. and the Staff Manual respectively. Title pages will be prepared in manuscript.

WAR DIARY
or
INTELLIGENCE SUMMARY
(Erase heading not required.)

Army Form C. 2118.

Volume 34. 1st R. Inniskilling Fusiliers

Hour, Date, Place	Summary of Events and Information	Remarks and references to Appendices
June [illegible] 1	The Bn marched to Ebblinghem	Vide Bn Order 61.
Ebblinghem 2	The Bn continued the march and proceeded to WEMAERS-CAPELLE	" Bn Order 62.
Wemaers-Capelle 3	The Bn proceeded to HERZEELE	" Bn Order 63.
Herzeele 4	The Bn proceeded to PADDINGTON CAMP. Major J. R. [illegible] D.S.O. reported for duty	" Bn Order 64.
Paddington Camp 5	The Bn less C & D Coys marched to LOWER [illegible] CAMP. C & D Coys were sent on in advance by rail to [illegible] work under the supervision of the C.R.E. 18th Division [illegible]	" Bn Order 65.
Lower [illegible] Camp 6	Working parties under the CRE 18th Division. Remainder of the [illegible] employed in [illegible] our camp [illegible]	Bn Order 65.
7/9	Working parties employing 400 men [illegible] every day [illegible] under RE supervision [illegible] [illegible]	

X. 33

Instructions regarding War Diaries and Intelligence Summaries are contained in F. S. Regs., Part II. and the Staff Manual respectively. Title pages will be prepared in manuscript.

Volume 35

WAR DIARY
or
INTELLIGENCE SUMMARY.
(Erase heading not required.)

Army Form C. 2118.

Place	Date	Hour	Summary of Events and Information	Remarks and references to Appendices
LOWER BIBOON(?) Camp	Jan 11		Capt [illegible] evacuated to England 29.12.17 & relinquishes acting rank from 15.12.17.	
"	"	" 12	Working parties under R E supervision laying cables and tramway lines. Remainder of Bn [illegible] camp. Ration Str 28 Ofs 651 OR. Effective Str 37 Ofs 749 O.R.	
"	"	13/14	Working parties employed under C.R.E. & A D Signals – cable lines & tramways. Major (A/Lt Col) Sherwood Kelly CMG DSO [illegible] 1st Bn R Innis Fus awarded Victoria Cross for conspicuous gallantry in the Cambrai operations November 1917	
"		15/17	Working parties employed under C R E & A D Signals on cable & tramway lines. 2nd Lt Robinson & 2Lt McRonald(?) proceeded to VIII Corps school for course. Capt Hamilton appointed Area Comdt at St Jean. Capt Hodgson Jones proceeded on leave to England. Capt Marshall RAMC attached in his place. Capt Williams awarded Military Cross. 14801 Pte Williams, 12323 Sgt McGregor, 29207 Cpl Watson, 24493 Sgt Ford, 3893 Pte Brestand, 19231 Cpl Barron awarded Military Medals for distinguished services in the Cambrai battles November 1917. The following Officers & N C Os have been mentioned in dispatches for good work in the same operations — Capt Williams, 2nd Lt Flemingham MC, 10230 Sgt Bedford, 8886 Sgt Jenkins	
	18		The Battn moved to 8th Corps Area & marched to Warrington Camp, Brandhoek Area.	Vide Bde Order No 72 & Bn Order " 66
Warrington Camp	19		Cleaning up Camp & Training. Ration Str 24 Ofs 506 O R. Effective Str 35 Ofs 744 O R.	
	20/24		Training. Capt Willcock proceeded on leave to U.K.	

Army Form C. 2118.

Instructions regarding War Diaries and Intelligence Summaries are contained in F. S. Regs., Part II. and the Staff Manual respectively. Title pages will be prepared in manuscript.

Volume 36

WAR DIARY
or
INTELLIGENCE SUMMARY

(Erase heading not required.)

Hour, Date, Place	Summary of Events and Information	Remarks and references to Appendices
[illegible]	2/Lt Davidson proceeded to 87th Bde Staff course. Capt Marshall proceeded on leave to U.K. [illegible] Hollingworth [illegible] appointed for duty in his place. [illegible] promoted to Lieuts.	
20	[illegible] distribution of medals by Gen [illegible]	
[illegible]	[illegible]	[illegible] Bde Order [illegible]
[illegible]	[illegible] employing 150 men under R.E. supervision [illegible] Training of Specialists.	[illegible]

J. [illegible] Crawford Lt Col
Comdg 1/R Inniskilling Fus

Forms/C. 2118/11.

S E C R E T.

IST BATTALION THE ROYAL INNISKILLING FUSILIERS ORDER NO.63.

2nd.JANUARY 1918.

Reference Map.
HAZEBROUCK 1/100.000.

I. The Battalion will march to HERZEELE tomorrow 3rd.January 1918.

2. The Battalion will concentrate ready tomove off at 9.15.a.m. on the WEMAERS-CAPPEL - L'ANGE Road.
The head of the column will be at the cross roads at the E. of L'ANGE.

3. Order of March:- D. C. Hd.Qrs.,B.A.
Ist Line Transport will accompany the Battalion.
Cookers will accompany the Companies.

4. Route:- ODEZEELE.

5. Dress:- Fighting Order. I Blanket will be carried on the man.

6. Strict march discipline will be maintained.

7. 100 yards interval will be observed between Companies.
25 yards interval will be observed between each six vehicles

8. Companies will march in threes.

(Sd) F.F.J.Moore. Capt & Adjt.
Ist.Bn.The Royal Inniskilling Fusiliers.

S E C R E T.

ADMINISTRATIVE ORDER TO ACCOMPANY BATTALION ORDER NO.63.

I. Companies will make a dump of the following in their own areas,near the road by 8.0.a.m. Remaining Blankets. Packs. Officers Kits. Officers Mess Stores.

2. One Officers mess cook will proceed on the lorry with mess boxes as yesterday. One man will be detailed to remain with blankets and kits.

3. "A"Company will detail 5.five brakesmen to report to Transport Officer at cross roads by Church at WEMAERS CAPPEL at [illegible].a.m.

4. Hd.Qr.Company will make a dump at Qr.Mr's Stores.

(Sd) F.F.J.Moore. Capt & Adjt.
Ist.Bn.The Royal Inniskilling Fusiliers.

SECRET.

IST. BATTALION THE ROYAL INNISKILLING FUSILIERS ORDER NO. 64.

3rd. JANUARY 1918.

I. The Battalion will move to the PROOSDY AREA (PADDINGTON CAMP) tomorrow.

2. The Battalion will concentrate ready to march off at the cross roads where the HOFLANDE RUE d' YPRES road crosses the HERZEELE - HOUTKERQUE Road at 9.50.a.m.

3. Order of March. C. Hd.Qrs., A. D. B.
Ist.Line Transport will accompany the Battalion. Cookers will accompany Companies.

4. Strict march discipline will be observed.

5. 100 yards interval will be observed between Companies.
25 yards interval will be observed between each six vehicles.

6. Route. HOUTKERQUE.

(Sd) F. E. J. Moore. Capt & Adjt.
Ist. Bn. The Royal Inniskilling Fusiliers.

SECRET.

ADMINISTRATIVE ORDER TO ACCOMPANY BATTALION ORDER No. 64.

I. Companies will make a dump of the following in their own areas near the road by 8.30.a.m.
Hd.Qrs. will make a du,p at Hd.Qrs.
Remaining Blankets. Packs. Officers Kits and Mess Stores.

2. One Officers Mess Cook per Company will proceed on lorry with mess boxes as yesterday. One man per Company will be detailed to remain with blankets and kits.

3. "B" Company will detail (5) five brakesmen to report to Transport Officer at concentrating point at 9.50.a.m.

(Sd) F. E. J. Moore. Capt & Adjt.
Ist. Bn. The Royal Inniskilling Fusiliers.

To.

Officer Commanding
Ist.Royal Inniskilling Fusiliers.

Reference 87th.Brigade Order No.71.of today's date, The Transport Lines of No.3 Coy.Train,2nd South Wales Borderers and Ist.Royal Inniskilling Fusiliers will be in the 18th. Divisional Area,near WHITE HOPE CORNER.
An Officer from No.3.Coy.Train and the Transport Officer of the 2nd.South Wales Borderers and Ist.Royal Inniskilling Fusiliers will report to the Area Commandant at BOESINGHE (B.12.a.6.3.) at 11.0.a.m., who will show them the accommodation available and they will then agree as to allottments to Units.
Transport of Ist.King's Own Scottish Borderers will be accommodated in the Ist.Divisional Area at the location reconnoitred today.

The Area Commandant BOESINGHE will allot one Nissen Hut each to the 2nd.South Wales Borderers and Ist.Royal Inniskilling Fusiliers for temporary Quartermasters Store, until other accommodation is available.

Supply Wagons will march with Units Transport and remain at Quartermasters Stores until picked up by No.3. Coy.Train.

A Dump of fuel will be formed near WHITE HOPE CORNER (B.10.d.5.6.) where it may be drawn by Units tomorrow afternoon.

Supplies will be delivered to the Ist.Border Rgt. by wagons on the 5th.and lorry on the 6th.and following days, as long as they remain in the PROOSDY Area.

Four (4) lorries are allotted to each Battalion for the move, one being detailed for Ist.Royal Inniskilling Fusiliers from those now attached to Ist.Border Regiment which will rejoin that Battalion on completion of the journey.
All lorries except those attached to the Ist. Border Regiment will be returned to XIXth.Corps tomorrow night.

(Sd) J.R.Wharton. Captain.
Staff Captain,87th.Infantry Brigade.

4/1/18.

SECRET

ADMINISTRATIVE NOTE TO ACCOMPANY BATTALION ORDER No.65.

4th. JANUARY [illegible].

1. Companies will make a dump of the following at the Qr.Mrs. Stores by 9.[illegible] a.m. tomorrow. All Blankets, Packs, officers Kits and Mess Stores.
2. O.C. "A" Company will detail 5 brakesmen to report to Transport Sergeant at 9.55.a.m. tomorrow.
3. O.C. "B" Company will detail one N.C.O. and 10 men to report to Transport Officer at Transport Lines at [illegible] a.m. tomorrow to reload limbers.
4. One Officers mess cook per Company will accompany the mess boxes on the lorries.
One man per Company will be detailed to remain with the blankets.

(Sd) [illegible].E.J. Moore. Capt & Adjt.
1st.Bn. the Royal Inniskilling Fusiliers.

S E C R E T.

1ST BATTALION THE ROYAL INNISKILLING FUSILIERS ORDER NO.[illegible].

4th. JANUARY 19[illegible].

Reference Maps Sheet 27. 1/40.000.
" 28. " "

1. The Battalion will find a Working Party as under tomorrow 5th. January 19[illegible].
"A" Company. 2 Officers & 2 Platoons.
"B" Company. 2 Officers & 2 Platoons.
"C" Company. 2 Officers. & 150 Ranks Other Ranks.
"D" Company. 2 Officers & 100 Other Ranks.

2. These parties will parade ready to move off at 8.[illegible] a.m. on main road outside present billets, and will march to [illegible] where they will be conveyed by train to BOESINGHE, leaving [illegible] at [illegible] a.m.

3. (a) The parties detailed from "A" & "B" Companies will proceed from BOESINGHE to LOWER [illegible] CAMP where they will await remainder of Battalion.
(b) The parties detailed from "C" & "D" Companies will report to [illegible] Signals XIX Corps at BOESINGHE.

4. These parties will return on completion of days work to LOWER [illegible] CAMP.

5. The remainder of the Battalion will march to [illegible] CAMP tomorrow, and will parade ready in present camp to move off at 8.55 a.m.

6. [illegible] - [illegible].

7. Dress;- For Working parties and remainder of Battalion. Fighting Order.

8. The 1st. Line Transport will accompany the remainder of the Bn.

9. The following intervals will be observed during the march.
100 yards between Companies.
100 yards between rear Company and Transport.
25 yards between each section of [illegible] six vehicles or 6 pairs of horses.

(Sd) [illegible] Capt. & Adjt.
1st. [illegible] Royal Inniskilling Fusiliers.

S E C R E T.

IST BATTALION THE ROYAL INNISKILLING FUSILIERS ORDER NO.66.

15th. JANUARY 1918.

Map reference
1/20 000. Sheet 28. N. W.

I. The 87th. Infantry Brigade will become the Reserve Brigade 29th. Divisional, and will relieve 23rd. Infantry Brigade in the BRANDHOEK Area on the 18th. inst.

2. The Battalion will move to WARRINGTON CAMP (H. I. b. 5. 9.) on the 18th. inst.

3. The Battalion will parade ready to march off on the plank track S.E. of the Camp at 11.55.a.m.
Order of march A. B. C. D & Hd. Qr. Coy.
The Head of the column will be at the bridge this side of the BOESINGHE CANAL

4. The following distances will be observed on the line of march.

Between Companies.	100 yards.
Between Unit and Transport.	100 yards.
Between every 6 vehicles.	25 yards.

The Battalion will move in file East of ELVERDINGHE.

5. Route:- ELVERDINGHE.
DROMORE CORNER.
DIRTY BUCKET CORNER.

6. Dress. Marching Order.
Steel helmets will be worn.

(Sd) E. E. J. Moore. Capt & Adjt.
Ist. Bn. The Royal Inniskilling Fusiliers.

SECRET.

ADMINISTRATIVE ORDER TO ACCOMPANY BATTALION ORDER NO. 66.

15th. January 1918.

I. The advance party consisting of the Qr. Mr. C.Q.M.S., Sgt. Fletcher will assemble at the Qr. Mr's Stores at 8.0.a.m. on the 16th. inst., and will proceed to WARRINGTON CAMP so as to arrive there by 10.0.a.m.

2. Lewis Guns will be oiled and loaded on the limbers on the plank track S.W. of the Camp at 3.30.p.m. tomorrow.

3. The following will be loaded on the wagons and limbers on the plank track S.W. of the Camp at 9.0.a.m. on the 16th. inst.
Remaining blankets rolled in bundles of 10 and labelled.
Officers Kits and Officers Mess Stores. Orderly Room and Signalling Stores.

4. The camp will be left scrupulously clean and ready for C.O's. inspection by 11.0.a.m. the 16th. inst,

5. One Officers Mess Cook per Company will proceed with the mess cart on the 16th. inst.

6. The following personnel only will accompany the Transport.
Company Cooks and Water cart men.

(Sd) E.E.J. Moore. Capt & Adjt
1st. Bn. The Royal Inniskilling Fusiliers.

www.ingramcontent.com/pod-product-compliance
Lightning Source LLC
Chambersburg PA
CBHW080846010526
44114CB00017B/2381
9781474514897